From A to B
(Antrim to Bermuda)

Bishop Williams with Vice-President Nixon,
Washington D.C., 1960

From A to B
(Antrim to Bermuda)

ANTHONY L. E. WILLIAMS

Dorset Publishing Company

MILBORNE PORT

SHERBORNE DORSET

First published 1972 *by*
Dorset Publishing Company
Milborne Port
Sherborne Dorset

SBN 902129 13 9

Printed in Great Britain by
F & M Naish & Co Ltd
at Benfleet, Essex

Contents

Illustrations

Foreword

MY FAMILY and friends have often suggested to me in recent years that I should write some account of my forebears, and also notes on my own life as well as something of the many interesting and important personages whom I have had the privilege of meeting and in some cases knowing very well and have counted as friends. This could include such names as General Sir George White (of Ladysmith fame), Archbishops Crozier and Gregg of Armagh, Lord Carson, Sir Roger Casement, Dr. Spooner of New College, Oxford, Dr. T. B. Strong (Dean of Christchurch, Oxford, twice Vice-Chancellor of Oxford University, later Bishop of Ripon then of Oxford), the Bishop of Durham (Bishop Hensley Henson), Archbishop Lord Fisher, the Earl of Halifax (Edward Wood), Presidents Truman, Eisenhower, Kennedy and Nixon, Harold Macmillan, Lord Quickswood, Lady Mountbatten: not to mention many other Bishops, Archbishops and clerical dignitaries, novelists, colonial VIPs, also some much prized contacts with the Royal Family.

The Christian name by which I was called by my relations, being my second name, Lewis, and my surname, being Williams, I was constantly called upon throughout my clerical career by impecunious Welshmen, and when Vicar of Bournemouth I was also always being rung up for the venue and times of meeting of the local Welsh Society, often, to my confusion, in fluent Welsh. So in 1956 I became Anthony.

Like so many people these days I am a complete mongrel, a European. I have Irish blood (Northern and Southern), Scottish (Highland only), a little English (one great-grandmother from Cumberland) and French (Huguenot); Williams, McNeill, Murray, Moyers; four families curiously differing in their origin, characteristics and not least in their politics, and passing on stresses that pull perhaps in opposite directions at times.

For the above reasons and a lifelong interest in other people, I have ventured to record some of my impressions and observations of life and people. Everyone who tries to write an autobiography runs the risk of being dubbed as an egoist or an egotist. Benvenuto Cellini has been branded a braggart, Cardinal de Retz dismissed as a boaster and liar. Even the inimitable Pepys has been despised personally, so has Horace Walpole, not to mention St. Simon Greville or Creevy. So even the humblest autobiographers can hardly expect to escape—if indeed a critic condescends to notice their efforts at all.   ANTHONY L. E. WILLIAMS.

CHAPTER 1

Ancestors

MY WILLIAMS ancestors originated at Herringstone Manor near Dorchester, Dorset. A younger son joined the army of William of Orange (William III) and fought in Ireland on the winning side at the Battle of the Boyne (1690). The offer of a grant of land in Co. Armagh decided him to settle there. I have an old seal with the Williams crest and a delightful oil portrait (by W. Mott) of my great-grandfather, John Williams of Richhill, Co. Armagh (1795-1877). One of his three sons was my grandfather, Alexander, who lived from 1827-99, a great student of the Bible and of Shakespeare. My father, his eldest son, was George Robert Williams. He became a doctor and lived from 1862-93.

Politics also brought my father's mother's people to Ireland. My paternal grandmother was Annie McNeill, descended from a McNeill from Barra in the Scottish Hebrides, an Episcopalian and a Jacobite. After the Jacobite debacle at Culloden (April 1746) he fled to Northern Ireland. There he married and settled. He was a handsome giant of 6ft. 8ins. and had five fingers on each hand! His son George McNeill married an Annie Hill. Her father, George Hill, had come from Bellaghy Castle, Co. Londonderry and was a solicitor or lawyer in Larne, Co. Antrim. He became the agent of the Earls of Antrim, and had married a Miss Ann Hill (no relation). He built himself a house on the Antrim coast some two miles out of Larne: very appropriately he called the house Hillmount, and there it still is today. George Hill had three daughters but no sons and his son-in-law, George McNeill (who married his second daughter Annie, as noted above) succeeded him in his legal practice and as the agent of the Antrim family.

I have a fine portrait of George Hill (painted about 1790) by Thomas Gainsborough's nephew. Hill was a man of impressive appearance and character. A noted loyalist during the Irish Rebellion of 1798, he fearlessly rebuked a rowdy mob who stoned his town house windows in Larne. Confronting the crowd at his front door he enabled an alarmed gathering of guests to escape by boat from an interrupted dance to Garrickfergus Castle. He was a considerable benefactor of the ancient Parish Church of Larne and

Inver and a generous contributor to its restoration. He was said to have married at the age of seventeen, his wife being two years younger! He died in his late fifties from a chill caught out hunting. His wife, having produced three daughters before she was twenty, lived to be eighty-four looking more like the sister rather than the mother of her daughter Annie who had married George McNeill.

George and Annie McNeill had eight children of whom my grandmother (another Ann) was the fifth.

In 1858 at the age of twenty-six this second Annie McNeill married my grandfather Alexander Williams. The wedding had been twice postponed because of my grandmother's "delicacy". Nonetheless she lived until 1924 to the ripe age of ninety-two, retaining all her faculties to a remarkable degree. Their home was the 'Old Bank House' at Larne and my grandfather was the Manager of the Belfast Bank for some forty years, ending up as a Governor of this old established banking firm. My grandfather Williams was a stern Presbyterian and his only daughter Maimie (later Mrs. Matthew Blackwood) followed in his steps. My grandmother remained an Anglican and all three of her sons (George, John and William) became Anglicans as they grew up.

My mother's name was Murray and her ancestor, who came from Blair Atholl in Scotland, was also deeply implicated in the Jacobite rising of 1745-6. Indeed one of the family, Lord George Murray had proved to be the only considerable Jacobite general. Our particular young Murray fled to Dublin and ultimately took Holy Orders, apparently a good alibi in those days. He became in due course Dean of Killaloe. His great-grandson was my mother's father, John Walton Murray (1827-93), an only child whose father died young. John was a brilliant boy and entered Trinity College, Dublin, as Senior Classical Scholar of his year. His subsequent academic career was equally notable. A Senior Moderator, he won several University Prizes and gold medals, ultimately being elected Donellan Lecturer. At the time of the birth of my mother, Adelaide Frances (his third daughter), my grandfather Murray was Rector of the large and important Parish of Ballymena, Co. Antrim. Shortly after he became Archdeacon of Connor and Chaplain to the Lord Lieutenant of Ireland (Earl Spencer). Later on he was to become Dean of Connor. For many years he was a leader of the Church of Ireland not only in the county and in the large and growing city of Belfast but also in the Synod in Dublin. The eldest of his three sons John Oswald Murray had an almost identically brilliant career at Trinity College, Dublin.

Dean Murray married twice. His first wife was Margaret Moyers (my grandmother) daughter of William Moyers of Fortfield Co. Dublin. The Moyers were French Huguenots in origin and had fled from France after the Revocation of the Edict of Nantes, rather than give up their Protestant faith in the face of bitter religious persecution. My great-grandfather William Moyers was in his day a noted architect and built most of the fine old houses in Kingstown (now again called Dunleary). Many of these still survive in Vesey Place and Longford Terrace, etc. His elder son George, also an architect of some note, built the Dublin City Markets, became Lord Mayor of Dublin and received a knighthood from King Edward VII (when Prince of Wales). My grandmother died after an operation in 1886 at the comparatively early age of forty-four. Her two elder daughters had pre-deceased her and my mother, still in her teens, took over the management of the Rectory, became her father's hostess and mothered her two young brothers.

There are many good stories about my grandfather Dean Murray, who was a man of wit and humour.

For some obscure reason he was considered rather dangerously "High Church" (for those days in Ireland). One reason for this was that he had an 8.00 a.m. Communion every Sunday at his Parish Church. Another was that as one of the Revisors of the Irish Church Hymnal he was thought to be responsible for the introduction into the new edition of certain "High Church" hymns including "Ten thousand times ten thousand" apparently a bete-noir of all good Evangelical stalwarts!

He probably took the following occurrence with a better grace than some clerical dignitaries in the Victorian era would have done. He had just conducted a New Year Watch Night Service at St. Patrick's Church and retired quickly to the vestry, disrobed and stepped out into the darkness of the 1st of January of another Year. A tall gaunt female figure suddenly confronted him and, enveloping him in her arms, kissed him full on the mouth. In triumphant tones she then cried,

"Salute to my lord and master: a Happy and Blessed New Year!"

My grandfather, doing his best to extricate himself from her embrace and such an embarrassing situation, gasped out, "I think that there is some mistake, Madam!"

With a shriek of horror the female fled into the bushes; but not before my grandfather had recognised the rather elderly wife of their still quite young and personable organist, Dr. Cooney. He was still laughing when he got home ten minutes later and narrated this tender contretemps.

An amusing story was told by him of an enthusiastic young Belfast reporter to whom he lent a draft of the speech he was to make on a certain important occasion. Anxious (more than some) that his account of the proceedings should be quite accurate the reporter later showed his effort to my grandfather *before* the speech was actually made, as time pressed for the printing of the article. My grandfather handed the effusion back to the young reporter with the words,

"Yes, I think that you have got the gist of my argument very well; but don't you think it a little premature to conclude with the sentence 'The Dean sat down amidst a perfect hurricane of applause'?"

With all his other work his Parish was never neglected and he also found time to write some excellent manuals on Irish Church History and its leading figures. A lover of the theatre he built his own toy theatre, painted scenerey and figures, and evolved his own lighting effects. He wrote his own pantomimes, abridged well known plays and entertained many drawing-room audiences of adults and children.

In 1922 Dr. Henry Patton (Bishop of Killaloe 1924-1943) published his history of the Church of Ireland since the Disestablishment, calling it "Fifty Years of Disestablishment". It has become more or less a standard work of reference. On the death of my grandfather he says (p. 137);

> The death of the Very Rev. John Walton Murray LL.D., Dean of Connor and for 28 years Rector of Ballymena, deprived the great Northern Diocese [Down, Connor and Dromore, including Belfast] of an able Churchman who had been Donellan Lecturer in the University of Dublin, and whose gifts on platform and in the pulpit were widely known.

After my grandfather's death the new Rector of Ballymena was Dr. Darcy (later Archbishop of Dublin and then of Armagh). He had as his two curates Dr. John Gregg (also later Archbishop of Dublin and afterwards of Armagh) and Mr. Ross (who became Bishop of Tuam).

Speaking to me when staying in Bournemouth in the 1950's Archbishop Gregg said:

"I was never fortunate enough to know Dr. John Murray personally; but we all lived in his shadow, Dr. Darcy, Ross and myself. The people were never tired of telling us that we were not doing too badly; but the Golden Age of Ballymena was in the days of Dean Murray."

CHAPTER II

My Father And Mother (1886-93)

FROM THE time of her Mother's death in February 1886 my Mother (Adelaide) kept house for her father until she married in April 1889.

The Rectory remained a social centre for one of the largest and busiest Parishes in Northern Ireland. My Mother had to shoulder heavy responsibilities. There was a large circle of friends in the district and county. There were constant comings and goings of V.I.P.s. There were the two younger brothers: Ion, shortly to go to Trinity to repeat his father's brilliant academic career: and Willie, still just a child.

About a year after my Mother took over all the management of the Rectory she met at a dance a tall, fair-haired young doctor who had recently come to the district by name George Robert Williams of Larne. They had two waltzes together, one being the "supper dance". A new world opened up for them both that night. It was literally love at first sight. Although their short married life was to be ideally happy while it lasted, the course of true love did not at first run at all smoothly. My grandfather was inclined to think that a young doctor was hardly 'good enough' for his daughter. Other suitors had been men of more established position and higher social position: a Baronet, a Major in the regular Army, the younger son of a peer: any one of whom at least from a worldly point of view would have seemed a better match. Dean Murray acknowledged that he liked the young country doctor very much and that he heard nothing but praise of him both professionally and as a man.

The mutual love of George and Adelaide was too deep and strong for any difficulties or outside pressures to overcome it; but my Mother was quite ill for a time. Gradually Dean Murray thawed. George had so much to commend him. He was a splendid looking creature, athletic, well over six foot tall. He was first rate at his job, loved and trusted by his patients. He was courteous and kind. Added to all this he was a brilliant pianist and exceptionally well read. My Grandfather began to become very attached to him. They had much in common in their ideas about the world of books, in their reactions to current events, in their Church views. The Dean saw that nothing would make his daughter cease to care. Also he himself was for another reason more inclined personally to be favourable to their matrimonial aspirations.

After about three years of widowhood Dean Murray was engaged again. It was someone only about five years older than his daughter: a Miss Mildred Brownrigg, daughter of a Mr. Brownrigg (a Country Inspector of the R.I.C. and son of Sir Henry Brownrigg head of the Royal Irish Constabulary and a well known figure in Dublin). Mildred was a handsome and dignified woman and very suited to the position. The wedding took place after only a short engagement. It was followed by that of George and Adelaide, who were married in St. Patrick's Church, Ballymena on St. George's Day, 23rd April, 1889. The Dean officiated, assisted by Canon Patman, Rector of nearby Ahoghill, Co. Antrim. The Church, which seats 800, was full to overflowing and all the approaches to it were crowded with people.

There was, however, one incident at this wedding which cast a temporary cloud over the proceedings and which was recalled some years later by the more superstitious as having been an untoward omen. The bride should not traditionally arrive at the church before the groom. When my Mother arrived (as arranged) two minutes late there was no bridegroom present. She was taken round the side of the Church to the Vestry and there she waited for over a quarter of an hour which no doubt seemed like eternity. The explanation of this embarrassing occasion was characteristic of her future husband and his profession. George Williams was an exceptionally conscientious young doctor and just as he and his best man (his brother John) were leaving his house at Ahoghill there came an urgent notification of an accident to a man in the village — a case of severe haemorrhage. He went at once and saved a life; but the result was that he was twenty minutes late for his wedding.

The honeymoon was spent in London. Amongst its highlights was a visit to the Savoy Theatre, then enjoying the first triumphant season of the D'Oyley Carte Company's production of 'The Yeoman of the Guard'.

Back at Ahoghill as the wife of the local doctor in a large village Adelaide had a very busy and happy life. She took an active part in all that went on and became a pillar of the pretty little church and a close friend of Canon and Mrs. Patman and their two children. George also was a keen Churchman and his strong Christian faith made him even more effective as a doctor, according to the opinion of his patients. He was not only a Sidesman, but sang in the choir, since besides being so musical he was the possessor of a very pleasant tenor voice. Ion and Willie Murray were constantly at their sister's new home. The young couple were very much in demand socially and there was a great deal of entertaining in the county round about. George had his surgeries and two rounds a day — one of which he drove and the other, whenever possible, he walked. He also managed to keep up his piano music. Beethoven's piano Sonatas were his great interest. There were the leading books and more considerable novels of the day to be read and discussed. Both were great walkers and my Mother enjoyed nothing more than to accompany him when he walked his rounds. The lovely Co. Antrim countryside was all around them, utterly unspoilt with its rivers and woods, its high hawthorn hedges and elegant ash trees, whilst Slemish, St. Patrick's mountain, dominated the landscape from its isolated position in the Glens a few miles away.

When they had been married nearly a year they had their first sorrow. A baby daughter was born — dead. A slow and difficult birth proved fatal to her.

It was two years later (February 1892) that their second child, a boy (myself), was born. Spoilt from the first, I had more than the normal number of godparents — two godfathers and *two* godmothers. They were Canon Anthony Lewis Elliott, my father's old friend from Dublin days, Canon Patman, then Rector at Ahoghill, Florence Patrick (née Rutherfoord) of Dunminning and Mrs. Maria Collum (wife of Mr. Archie Collum, my Mother's godfather, one of the Collums of Bellevue, Co. Fermanagh).

My father was very happy in his country practice and he and my Mother had naturally a tremendous number of friends all around; but some of the older medical men who knew something of my Father's ability strongly advised him to move so as to get more experience. By the summer of 1892 my Father had bought a country practice in England, a little way outside the city of Norwich, with surgeries in Saxlingham and Hempnall and a link with the large hospitals in the city. He hoped before long to begin to specialise in ear, nose and throat complaints and he certaintly received great encouragement from more than one of the leading medicos in Norwich. My Father left for his new sphere of work in August 1892 and my Mother followed with me about the end of September. A Norfolk girl, Eliza Pollard, was engaged as my nurse, a very sweet and dependable woman she was. They had bought a charming Elizabethan house "The Hill House" at Saxlingham Nethergate. All through that autumn the young couple searched amongst the numerous antique shops of Tomblands and added many charming additions towards the beautification of their new home. An early winter followed and soon with the keen frost and the fall of heavy snow my Father was doing his rounds in a sleigh instead of his dog cart. From the first they met with amazing kindness and hospitality and there were many adventurous evening drives in the snow to dinners and dances. As usual my Father both worked and played hard. He was soon appointed Medical Officer of Health for the District. In January a severe epidemic of influenza followed by pneumonia swept across East Anglia and there was no rest by day or by night.

One day early in March my Father came in at lunch time, but could eat no lunch. He was hot and shivering. My Mother saw at once that he was ill and felt that he must go to bed immediately. He said that he had one or two things he must still do; but he would be back soon and go to bed. He returned about eight p.m. looking dreadful. As M.O.H. he had been called upon to inspect a cess pool to see if it was all right. It was not. Then he had called on two pneumonia cases and found both patients at their crises. He had stayed some hours with each and thought they would now pull through—which they did. Somehow or other my Mother got him into bed and telephoned to his young Doctor friend Charles Hyde-Cosins in Norwich. By the time Dr. Cosins arrived his temperature was verging on 105° and he was hardly conscious. For two days this good friend practically never left the house. On March 7th typhoid fever was suspected (shades of the cess pool). On the 8th he was dead. John Williams was telegraphed for and my Mother, reduced by shock to a semi-conscious state, together with me and my nurse Eliza, were taken to the Cosins' home in Norwich. John arrived and the sorry little cortege set off by train on the long journey to Ballymena. My father's funeral was conducted in St. Patrick's Church, Ballymena, by Dean Murray. It was less than four years since George and Adelaide had been married there. Again the Church was crowded. Mother this time in the deep crepe mourning of the period, sat in the Vestry with the door open and was helped into the Church by her former bridesmaid, so as to lay a cross made entirely of violets upon the coffin just before the procession left the Church.

My Grandfather Murray insisted that my Mother and I (thirteen months old) should come to live at the Rectory at any rate for a time. So my Mother had a new home and was surrounded by love. Alas, it did not last long. The influenza-pneumonia epidemic having spread all over Great Britain reached Northern Ireland and began to take its toll there also. In less than two months my Grandfather followed my Father to the grave, and my Mother had lost a second home.

It is hard to assess such a loss to a young and devoted wife, widowed with such suddenness at the age of twenty-six after less than four years of perfect happiness. There is little doubt in my mind now as I look back—that subconsciously I missed my unremembered Father badly. It came out in unmistakable ways. Lapped in feminine affection I grew up far too tender and sensitive in feeling. A Father would have made me tougher and more braced. Until I had learned at boarding school a certain hardening sophistication, I suffered untold agonies through sensitivity.

There was another thing. I liked male society — people such as my Mother's younger brother, my Uncle Willie Murray. Later when I went to school I was happiest at any rate in my younger days with boys who were considerably older than myself. What was this but an unrealised hunger for the father figure?

CHAPTER III

Very Young

AFTER DEAN Murray's death Mother and I and Eliza went to live with my Uncle John Williams at his house in Larne. He had a nice elderly cook-housekeeper and my Mother filled in many gaps. It was a pretty house with a large garden and stood nearly at the highest point in Tower Road sheltered by the Drumalis woods on the North and having delightful views of Larne Lough to the South and Island Magee and the Harbour to the East. My Uncle was kindness itself. He had insisted on my Mother bringing not only my nurse Eliza, but also our young Irish terrier "Jock". I mention Jock because I am pretty sure that the *first* thing that I really remember concerned him later on that summer. My Mother and Eliza were taking me out in my pram to go down towards the sea.

Just as we got to the garden gate there was a terrific crash and the whole middle pane of the dining room window dissolved into fragments. Jock miraculously unscathed had joined us for our walk. After that summer my Uncle began to think of moving out to Hill Mount, the old family home built by my great-great Grandfather George Hill. My Mother took a cottage at Galgorm, near Ballymena for a few months and Addie Young (her cousin and bridesmaid) joined us. After a round of visits we rejoined my Uncle out at Hill Mount where, still in a sort of go-cart, I enjoyed outings along the coast road and the lanes off the Old Glenarm Road and romping in the large gardens with the ever faithful and good tempered Eliza.

My memories of this phase include some highly unsuccessful first attempts at gardening—plucking and "planting" bachelor buttons and silver lambs tongues in a small flower bed specially allotted to me. My first doctrinal and theological problems date also from those days. I remember as well my Mother, still dressed always in black, kneeling by my cot after I had gone to bed and saying prayers with me and singing in a sweet low voice various children's hymns. My favourite was Mrs. Alexander's "Once in Royal David's City". I learnt also to say "Our Father which art in Heaven", etc. I also prayed for "Dear Father" who was also "in heaven". Were "Our Father" and "Dear Father" one and the same Person? The address of each was the same—"in Heaven". All very perplexing at under three. It was some time before I got all this sorted out. I think for a time I thought that I was indeed God's Son; but not in the way in which St. Paul or St. John used the idea. I also used to wonder why my Mother who was prettier than anyone else also seemed so much sadder. In a way Eliza was not entirely unlike her. Both had deep golden hair and large mournful brown eyes and gentle faces. I also remember my first two experiences of physical pain. Once when Uncle John's rather crabby old dog Tim, so unlike good tempered Jock, bit my face as I scrambled along on all-fours on the dining room floor. The other time was when my Uncle's young groom "Jamie" who used to pick me up and put me on the garden swing or carry me round the paddock on his broad shoulders, allowed me to come up to his living room over the stable and watch him shave. It was a great thrill until in the end of course I got hold of the cut-throat razor and sliced my finger. I remember to this day the frightened youth's horror and the deft way he washed and bound up my finger and carried me back to the house.

The gardens were sheltered by many trees. The winds generally came from the westward hills not from the seaward side. A gently sloping bank dropped to the coast road some fifty yards below. The view was interesting and beautiful (I realised that even then). At either end of the bay North and South stood a sentinel head-land. Some three miles out to sea were "The Maidens", two little rocky islands each crowned by a white lighthouse. We called these "The Maid" and "The Cook". The fatter and Northernmost had in its white tower a fixed light, the Southern, taller and slimmer, had a powerful revolving light which raked the horizon all night long. By day the dim grey-blue hills of Scotland were usually visible — sharper in both colour and form when rain was imminent. At night Scotland had vanished and only the faint flashes from Ardnamurchan Point on the Mull of Kyntyre were to be seen. Many ships passed mysteriously by. Even today when I hear at night the menacing note of a fog horn at sea I travel back to those childhood nights. I see my dim lit bedroom, where a reassuring night-light inside a shining china swan floated in a basin of water on the wash-stand. In the warm half-light I felt secure; but there seemed to be terror in the dark waters of the ocean.

Although I knew nothing about it, the situation grew rather difficult between by Mother and Uncle John. He wanted to marry her, but she, though fond and grateful, did not feel that she could ever accept. He was just the kindest of brothers.

Her health was badly undermined and Dr. Killen advised strongly against spending the coming winter in the North. We therefore went to Dublin, staying in rooms part of the time, then with the Edward Murrays, but mostly with Great Uncle Jack McNeill and his family in Leeson Street. How well I remember that beautiful and spacious house and all the sociability and the coming and going of the jolly young men and the pretty twins. Katie was always full of vivacity with her pink frocks and pink bows: Ethel, often resting on the sofa in the large pillared drawing room, a quiet echo, with her preference for blue. I suppose she was already falling into a decline.

I remember cousin Elliot giving me a "tie-clip" to keep in place a black silk tie, but I prefered to try its strong spring on my tongue unfortunately. As can be imagined there was a noisy sequel to this experiment! It was a great treat coming down at night in my dressing gown to dessert in the big dining room and being given ripe pears and chrystalized fruits and seeing all the ladies in their evening frocks and jewels. I also recall my first conscious visit to Church; St. Matthias — very crowded and a hymn which immediately depressed me with a sort of smell of death "Shall we gather by the river". I wanted to cry and to go out.

About this time Mother and I were photographed together; she in semi-evening dress, black, white and grey silk plaid, I resplendent in a crimson silk blouse with lace collar posed behind her with my arms round her shoulder: very Victorian. This photo still survives.

The following summer saw us back at Hill Mount on the Antrim coast and the following autumn Uncle John got married to Lettie Lyon. My Mother was back in Dublin this time in hospital with bronchitis and pneumonia. I was left behind with Eliza at Hill Mount. Uncle John and Aunt Lettie were more than kind to me. She was rather lovely, with her great deep violet eyes and raven hair; always about her were the scent of heliotrope and the frou-frou of her rustling silk skirts. I was very much made of and spoilt. I was her "little sweetheart" or her "little piccaninny". Every time they went up to Belfast they brought me back an expensive present. It was all right in the day time, but at night there were tears for "Molo" my special private name for my Mother, the most loving and lovely of all. Each morning I used to go and get into bed with my Aunt and Uncle at about half-past seven and the world seemed to cheer up again, as they talked and joked and told me little stories. I still had Eliza and my boon companion the young groom Jamie. The spring came, and with it my Mother returned, at last, quite blooming; rosier than I had ever seen her before.

She was looking for a house in Larne and until we got it we went to the Bank House with my Williams grandparents. It was a fine old house with a large walled garden at the back, full of old fashioned yellowy-white roses and lilac bushes. The house contained many lovely things; but the pièce-de-résistance was a new object of interest in its "smallest room". My grandparents were the proud possessors of what would have been called "a status symbol", if the term had been in use in the late nineties—a real Water Closet, the first in the whole of Larne! How proudly my Grandfather used to show it to visitors, putting it through its paces by pulling the handle up (not down) and provoking that magnificent snorting Niagara. The whole thing with its blue and white willow-pattern china bowl and wide mahogany seating accommodation seemed to rival the description of King Solomon's throne as given in that wonderful "Peep of Day" version of the Old Testament, so carefully presented to me by "Gran Pa". Alas, this impressive addition to the house's amenities did not mean so much after all. The whole drainage system of the old place was in a shocking condition and in a short time I was desperately ill in bed with a virulent attack of diphtheria. However I survived and was soon fairly well again.

Then we moved into "Bay Lodge", a double fronted detached house at the eastern end of Tower Road and close to the sea. Indeed it was so close that when the storms came in from the North-East the foam of the waves blew on to our windows and the wind got under the carpets and made them billow like a miniature ocean. It was exciting in stormy weather to be literally "rocked to sleep" at night as the whole house shook and vibrated and the gale scrabbled and tore at the walls and windows. The walled garden at the back of the house was strangely sheltered.

Addie Young paid a long and cheerful visit to us that summer. I spent hours on the sands between the Bank Heads and the "Round Tower" lighthouse, known as the Cheyne Memorial. I built and in my imagination peopled innumerable castles and towns. Gardens bloomed with bright green and pink seaweed and yellow and mother-of-pearl shells. I was beginning a phase of my life when I frequently retreated into a world of my own, a period which must have lasted until I was at least twelve or thirteen; a lonely boyish Arabian Nights entertainment.

It was about this time that Sir George White, the hero of Lady-smith (South African War), arrived by boat on his way home via

Larne Harbour. Half the town turned out to meet the Stranraer boat and give him a hearty welcome. The Harbour Station was all beflagged and there was a brass band which played "Here the conquering hero comes" and other suitable music and a reception was held. Sir George made only one other call in Larne before going on to White Lodge. He called at Bay Lodge on my Mother whom he had known since her childhood and I remember that he kissed her and called her "little La" (her childhood pet name). I was duly presented and at first rather over-awed. Soon I was sitting on the knee of this great and gentle soldier and he was telling us of some of his adventures during the Siege and Relief of Ladysmith. He had just been a visitor at Windsor Castle the previous week. He talked also of a small informal military parade at which he had been in command when my Mother and her brother Ion had been small children. To amuse them he had given the ferocious command "Fix Bayonets: Charge!" and my small Uncle had turned and fled for his life, but "little La" had merely clapped her hands and laughed.

Mother began to entertain again. She had now been a widow for between four and five years. Amongst the callers, and one who came more and more frequently, was a clean shaven stoutish Englishman, a bachelor of about forty. He was very pleasant and very kind. I noted that he was immaculately dressed and invariably smelt of soap and some mannish face lotion and powder. He bought me all sorts of presents, including that new wonder a "phonograph", the forerunner to the early gramophone. How weird and wonderful to hear the different voices singing when the various cylinders were inserted in that magic box!

It is amazing how children often *"know"* things about grown-ups. William Wright's presents and kindness gave me a curious second hand sensation. Although I was not more than six years old I felt quite sure that these presents were offered obliquely as it were. He was not thinking "I hope that this pleases you, little boy." He was really thinking—"There, what do *you* think of that, dear Mother of this little boy?" Not even his often reiterated variations of the theme of "There is no end to the things I could do for your boy", could make me think that anything to do with *me* was really his ultimate aim and object. No one really knew very much about him.

"William is a wonderfully kind man," said my Mother. "He simply loves *you*!" This was often and variously said. My technique was "No Comment". I was never so ready to think as well of everybody as my kind and generous hearted Murray relations. Neither my Mother nor Uncle Ion ever expected anyone to be much less than a Saint. Naturally they suffered many bitter disillusionments in consequence. As a whole for a family of Scottish origin, the Murrays were singularly unsuspicious and optimistic. It must have been the addition of the Southern Irish and Huguenot Blood.

Then it came. For my sake Mother was going to marry William Wright. He was kind, he was good. he was rich, I could have everything. One day on her finger, next to my Father's diamond engagement ring and wedding ring, she showed me a large and handsome sapphire and diamond hoop. I had never from the first thought that she really wanted to marry William, but curiously enough all my Father's relations formed an approving chorus. Money, security. Yes. Yes. You will come to love him. So good for the boy, too, etc.

They went to Paris for a three weeks' honeymoon and once more Uncle John and Aunt Lettie had me and Eliza the ever faithful, back at Hill Mount. Every day something arrived for me from Paris: a model of the Eiffel Tower, with lift complete, a box of dainty marionettes, a marvellous clockwork monkey (capable of great gymnastics according to the English instructions) but broken — oh what tears! Somehow it made me feel that something in my Mother was broken also. Last of all, especially alluring, came, a little penknife in the shape of the Eiffel Tower once more. It is with me still, safe on my writing bureau.

Back they came at last and back I went to them at Bay Lodge. Everything seemed all right — or did it? Often my Mother looked as though she had been crying.

William Wright and his partner (Dyson, Wright & Co.) had three offices for their flourishing accountants business; Belfast, Huddersfield and Leeds. About once a month he went over to Yorkshire for four or five days. Those were the best times. Mother had a letter from her unseen mother-in-law, rather a dear old lady one gathered. She was a widow and lived at Norton, Stockton-on-Tees. Years later I saw the letter. I recollect one passage which might or might not have meant very much. "I am so thankful that my dear William is settled at last and is married to someone who, I hear, is not only beautiful but a really good woman. I am sure that you, dear Ada, will be the salvation of him. I long to see you." She never did however as she died within a few months of the marriage. Her maiden name had been Merrywether and I fancy that she had been much better class than her late husband. Later we met William's younger brother Tom (married with two daughters). They were strict Brethren. Thomas was as unlike William as possible; thin and cadaverious with a scrawny beard, a violent teetotaller and a complete hypochondriac ["Don't shout, William. Remember MY HEART."] He was "pious" in an almost revolting exhibitionist manner. Needless to say they were all "saved". I soon gathered that to them all William was the very black sheep of the family.

The trouble of course was that William, the better looking, cleverer and gayer of the two sons had been spoilt. He had led a roving life not only as regards his business, but in his emotional interests and pursuits; and by the time he was forty he had the makings of a completely selfish and irresponsible alcoholic and idler. The meeting with my Mother had indeed straightened him out for a few months, but this improvement had not even outlasted the honeymoon.

At first, at least, he was still making some money and keeping the home, but the money was going out much faster than it was coming in as he began to neglect his business and quarrel with his very decent Belfast clerks. We moved in a few months to a smaller house. Only a few doors away was the house where my Williams grandparents were now living in retirement. Grandfather Williams had become an old and ailing septuagenarian, not taking much interest outside the narrow orbit of an invalid existence. Grannie was engaged in looking after him, but was able to be a very considerable comfort to my Mother. Eliza was still with us. When my Mother told her that she might not be able to afford to keep her much longer, the girl said that pay or no pay she would not think of leaving her at present. I had now been about a year at a small but excellent school. My Mother tried her hardest to shield me from her troubles, and I had many friends of my own age, including my cousins Ruth and Nora Killen. Ruth, a little older, was always my favourite. I used to have some lovely parties during the winter. Once we had a conjuror. Another time a Punch and Judy Show was brought down from Belfast. William was increasingly away at the Yorkshire end of his business, and the Belfast branch languished through his neglect.

In the late winter of 1898 he said that their Belfast branch office was closing and he must return to England. He had found a good house in Headingley, Leeds. My Mother's heart sank at the thought of leaving friends and all things familiar to go to a strange place where she knew no one. Still if the change would help William to pull together both himself and the business, and get him away from his very undesirable drinking companions in Belfast, she would feel bound to go.

How well I remember the thrill of the night journey from Belfast

Adelaide Williams (Murray) with Lewis, 1895

Oxford, 1912

to Fleetwood on that cold February evening and the early arrival in the darkness next morning. We got sleepily into a first class carriage on the train for Leeds. Then tragedy. Alas "Monk", my beloved toy monkey from Paris (more beloved because, as it were, "an invalid from birth") had been left in our cabin on the boat. I was reassured. A telegram would be sent. Monk would be restored to me. As my tears subsided the daylight struggled through the smoky atmosphere of the more industrial area around Manchester and other towns. I looked out at England and did not think much of it. My youthful verdict was "It looks dirty, and anyway there's no sea!"

My opinion of England however began to improve when we got to Burton Crescent in the more sylvan parts of Headingley. There was a good garden with lovely trees to climb. (Incidentally climbing then was about as good for one's clothes as clambering up a chimney would have been.) The house was large and impressive. On the ground floor basement I was to have a large playroom, where I could even ride my tricycle at a fair speed. There were spacious living rooms and bedrooms. We were to have two maids again, Eliza's sister Edith joining the staff. Before we left Headingley eighteen months later we at last lost our dear Eliza, as she married her soldier lover to whom she had held faithfully for some seven years whilst he was serving abroad. She was twenty-six years old when she married, just the age at which her mistress had been widowed. They went to live in South Shields, Co. Durham, and there we visited them twice. Eliza had a happy married life, but not a long one as she died of T.B. about seven years later.

The best luck of all in our new surroundings was the fact that the house was semi-detached and in the house next door lived three of the nicest people I have ever known—Julius and Frances Bennedik and their son Wilfred, one year older than myself.

CHAPTER IV

Preparatory School Boy

JULIUS BENNEDICK, who was in the woollen business in Bradford, was of German origin, but very Anglicised in his outlook if not in tongue. He was one of the most kind-hearted and completely amusing men that I ever met in my childhood's days. Frances Bennedik soon became one of my Mother's best and life long friends. She was an unusually attractive woman in all sorts of ways. Not strictly as beautiful as Mother, she was a delight to look at. Bronze wavy hair, a delightfully dainty and humorous nose and the most vivid green eyes I have ever seen. She was clever and witty and of sterling worth. She was also more completely and patriotically English than anybody I have ever known. I learnt from her far better than from the writings of Charles Kingsley (which she delighted to quote and to read to us boys)—what England at its best really stood for. Later I tended to equate her with Hypatia, for she was very learned and when Wilfred, for health reasons and extra cramming for an Army career, left Charterhouse, Frances learnt Latin and Greek with him.

Wilfred was my first real boy friend and for the next eighteen months while we lived next door to each other we were inseparable both at home and at school (Miss Harland's kindergarten—next door). In these days curiously enough we were not at all unlike, although he was dark and I was fair, and more than one person took us for twins. At last I had a brother. We had wonderful times. We had both just read Ballantine's "Coral Island" and a children's version of Robinson Crusoe. Our games took on a similar character and we began to long for the great open spaces. One day, having secretly saved up our pocket money for a few weeks we bought "iron rations" and ran away from home. We got out into the country (as it then was) beyond Far Headingley and "The Seven Arches" and we had a marvellous day. First of all we found ourselves a likely lair amongst the bushes which we made into a sort of hut with leafy branches and odd scraps of wood. The discovery of a dried up pool with reddish clay sides gave us further inspiration. We rubbed the clay on our hands and faces. I am not now quite sure what the object of this was—whether to make us look more like South Sea Islanders or for purpose of camouflage, probably the former. The latter would suggest rather more sophistication than we possessed at our tender age. About six o'clock we began to wilt a little, our food supplies were finished and the light of the spring afternoon was failing. We started for home and soon had a great shock. Two young policemen pounced upon us and asked our names and addresses. We had immediate visions of prison bars. However they became very paternal and we were taken home by them. We found two distracted mothers. Apparently the Leeds Police Constabulary had been alerted and many Police Constables had had a busy day. Had some awful accident occurred? Had we been kidnapped? murdered? By this time we were now rather shamefaced and weary little boys— forgotten even were the cannibals and sharks we had been sleuthing and dodging all day. Many kisses, hot baths and supper in bed was our fate at the hands of our forgiving mothers. No doubt a spanking and no supper would have been better.

In the August of 1899 my Grandfather Williams died and within a few weeks of his decease Grannie came to stay with us. With no one there any longer to tell her how delicate she was she began to take a new lease of life. Long walks over the fields through Becket's Park to Kirkstall were taken, instead of the stately one mile promenade arm-in-arm with grandfather to the top of the Bank Heads to inhale the ozone. One day we found a five bar gate (usually open) padlocked. The next thing I saw was Grannie in her long black garments and widow's bonnet climbing the gate with commendable competence, although not without making a liberal display of a maroon coloured pair of knickers. Henglers Circus came to Leeds. We saw the triumphal entry, and enticing circulars were left at many houses (including ours). My Mother was surprised and, I fancy, a little shocked, when Grannie (a widow of only some weeks standing) said: "I don't think the dear child should miss this. If you are engaged I can take him". Mother was engaged and off Grannie and I went together. It would have been hard to say which of the two of us enjoyed the outing more.

My first Christmas in Leeds was memorable for two things— first the Christmas Carols and music at St. Chad's, Headingley, where the Vicar, Mr. Stables and his wife had become very kind friends.

The other highlight was a visit to both the wonderful Leeds Pantomimes. The Grand Theatre's was always one of the most spectacular in the country. That at the Theatre Royal was usually one of the most amusing. That year it must have been at the very peak. We saw Dan Leno as "Sister Anne" in Blue Beard. I do not think that I have ever in my life seen anyone else as funny: Dan Leno as a child in a pram or as the char "lady" who comes to oblige: quite unforgettable.

In the meantime neither William Wright nor his business affairs were improving. The partner, Mr. Dyson, was in very failing health and it must have been apparent to anyone (except a small child) that the whole business was folding up. By the late Spring there was talk of selling up and another move. By the Summer of 1900 we had moved to a small furnished house in Grove Road, Harrogate. Some of our furniture was sold and my Mother, now taking entire charge of things, began to search for a suitable small house in that delightful town. This was found in under a year; but not before she had made some very good and indeed life long friends amongst the congregation of St. John's Church, Bilton. These included the Rev. D. M. Alexander and his wife and two daughters. Mr. Alexander had had a bad breakdown in his Manchester Parish and after several years "retirement" had, at the age of seventy taken on this growing Parish. He did remarkable work there for the next twenty-six years, celebrating twice and preaching twice on his last Christmas Day at the age of ninety-six, and dying a week later through an accident. To this day I can remember his fine handsome appearance and his marvellous voice. To hear him read the Advent Collect was in itself a religious experience. There was something Bronte-ish about the whole family: quite remarkable people.

I think that William Wright was probably at his very worst during that year in Grove Road, Harrogate. He and his work was mutually giving each other up and he seemed to spend his life between his bed and the hotel bars in Harrogate. His meals were mostly taken up to him on a tray. Sometimes they were eaten, often they were not. Not infrequently the food and trays were thrown on the floor or at my Mother. The amount of crockery broken was quite fantastic. We had some dreadful nights when he came in blind drunk: once he paraded noisily round the house with an open razor in his hand.

My Mother was now the financial mainstay of the home. William's financial activities were mainly confined to taking things out of the house and selling them. Mother however did her best to stop him taking things that had belonged to her and my Father and that one day should be mine. Even so some of my little treasures were taken and sold including in 1902 a complete set of gold coins, from a shilling to a five pound piece, bearing the head of the new King Edward VII.

In the Spring of 1901 we moved to Number 12 Leadhall Lane. Mother made it charming. She had kept all her nicest things. The furniture disposed of by William had been mostly what he had provided for the larger house in Headingley—a lot of pseudo "Louis Quinze" stuff all black and gold and spindly. We had quite a good garden. My gardening I am afraid consisted mostly in building mausoleums for defunct goldfish and things of that sort. I had recently been hearing about ancient Egyptian burial chambers and so on.

In the meantime I had started, while in Grove Road, at Balliol House School, Clarence Drive, run by W. E. Moore (M. A. Oxon.) and his partner and brother-in-law, S. H. Drinkwater (M. A. London) two excellent men and between them very comprehensive in their coverage of Preparatory School education. Mr. Moore was quite excellent for English, Latin and History, also Scripture. Mr. Drinkwater taught equally well Mathematics, Drawing and French. There were once a week a drill sergeant, a Singing and Music Master and an Art Master. Mr. Fall, the musician, intrigued us boys. He had long white hair and wore his steel rimmed spectacles on the very end of his big red nose. We discovered ultimately that there was a reason for this. With his glasses at that angle when writing at the blackboard with his back to us, he could see behind him. Anyone who began to fool and take advantage behind his back was immediately identified and called out. He was then usually made to sing the verse of some highly unlikely song, solo, whilst Mr. Fall and the other boys provided a very unappreciative (and sometimes highly critical) audience. In these ways the cunning old man got excellent discipline. No boy likes to be made a fool of before his classmates and this Mr. Fall could do as well as anyone I ever met. Years later when I (as extra War work) taught voluntarily at Kidderminster Grammar School for a year during my first Curacy, I remembered old Fall's technique. If any boy showed signs of giving me any trouble I took care to make him look foolish before his classmates. After the first week I never had any trouble at all and could safely be friendly and reasonably relaxed.

Mrs. Drinkwater (née Bertha Moore) was a host in herself and managed to be both competent and very sweet to the boys. It was a preparatory school for boys aged nine to fourteen. The number was about forty of whom half were boarders and the rest day boys. Mr. Moore made his own subjects enthralling to his pupils. The only trouble with him was that he had perforce to teach some elementary Arithmetic to the smaller boys. It obviously went against the grain with him and he taught it very badly. To say that he was hard to follow was a gross understatement. The principle trouble however was that in arithmetic periods he was almost always in a hideous temper. I shall never forget my woes when the subject was "long division". I came home very depressed one day.

"Don't you like your arithmetic lessons, Lewis?" asked my Mother.

"No, *I do not*". (a pause) "My only comfort is that I still know that there is a God above me."

This poignant comment was, I believe, later repeated to Mr. Moore. They were all great friends of my Mother's. Anyway my arithmetic periods became happier if not more illuminating. I think he hated teaching arithmetic as much as we hated learning it from him. I never saw Mr. Drinkwater lose his temper. His mathematical talents seemed to induce a calmer approach. His worst weapon was merely a gentle but corrosive sarcasm. I used to win with fair regularity the School prizes for English, History and Scripture (how suitable) and Drawing. My greatest triumph was (when I was twelve) to win the Drawing Prize. During the term I had broken my right wrist (in a cycle accident) and had to do all my work with my left hand.

However I am anticipating things. My first introduction to the School lives very vividly still. I was apparently going to be the youngest boy in the school by almost eighteen months. I was also going to be a boarder for the first few weeks as my Mother had to go to Ireland on business. Mr. Moore sent for the two senior boys of the School (both boarders, one the Captain of Football and the other of Cricket). They were large adolescent youths bound next autumn for Oundle and Uppingham respectively. They were told that I was very young and that they were in charge of me, to see that I was not bullied and to show me the ropes in a general way in the School. Never did a small boy have a more faithful and devoted Praetorian Guard. I believe they both regarded me as a new toy and they vied in petting and spoiling me. I was at once carried off to their "study". None of the other small boys had such a distinction. I was refreshed with cake and raspberry wine. I remember being carried on the shoulders of the footballer into the general room of the boarders and being confronted by about twenty pairs of surprised eyes.

You there, you little beasts! Listen, this is Williams. He is a very young kid and you are to look out how you treat him". "Billy says so (Mr. Moore) and we say so. If you touch him, we'll skin you alive". The point was taken. I had a royal time that term. Once a rather horrid boy of about eleven who got me alone (as he thought) was caught by the Cricket Captain, thumping me and pushing my head into a basin of water. He was very sorry and sore afterwards for the rest of the evening. Under the inspiration of the literary Billy Moore from eight years old I always had my nose in a book of some sort or other. It was soon after I arrived at "Balliol House" that I began to get immersed in Shakespeare. I started on Lambs' Tales from Shakespeare when I was eight which made me want the real meat and before I was eleven I had read all the plays (some of them many times). This of course did not include The Sonnets nor "Venus and Adonis" nor (fortunately) "Lucrece". I fell most heavily for the historical plays: nice and bloody. I am afraid my literary taste was not as great as my interest in history and blood and thunder. My firm favourite was Henry VI (Part III) and my great heroine was that courageous Queen and mother, only woman General in English mediaeval history, Margaret of Anjou. I was a violent supporter of the red rose of Lancaster. Indeed I used to make all the characters (coloured paper figures) and act the play of the Wars of the Roses, beheading Richard of York with great eclat after the Battle of Wakefield and displaying the dead Crookback Richard after Bosworth. It was curious to find sixty years later, when I saw the Stratford production of "The Wars of the Roses"—how familiar many of these episodes and speeches still were! If only one could remember as vividly what happened sixty days ago as one does what happened sixty years past!

In those days I lived quite half my time in a world of my own imagining. One of the effects of being an only child no doubt.

In my third term at school another small boy, a few months younger than I, arrived; little fair haired Gillie Lammin with his elder (and much less attractive) brother Jimmie. They lived in Bilbao in Northern Spain and Gillie's English was certainly not so good as his Spanish. He was a gentle jolly little chap and we became great friends. Indeed about three years later I spent the whole of my summer holiday with the Lammins (Don Arturo and Mrs. Lammin) at their summer home at Portugalete at the mouth of the Nervion river in Viscaya, one of the Basque Provinces of Spain. It was a wonderful experience, with the train journey through France and with a day in Paris into the bargain, each way. We did a lot of sightseeing visiting the mountains and San

Sebastian, as well as various old castles and show places and fairs. We also had the best bathing I ever knew until we went to Bermuda some fifty years later. The Lammin boys left Balliol House a little sooner than I did, going on to Hailybury. Poor Gillie had a very short life, dying quite suddenly at the age of nineteen, having while on holiday with some friends, just climbed to the top of Mont Blanc.

My other great friend at my Preparatory School was Arthur Solly, the clever eldest child of one of Harrogate's many doctors. My Mother liked me to have as many boy friends as possible to counteract the handicap of being a "one and only". Almost every week one or other of these boys used to come back to tea with us on a half-holiday, or else I went to the Solly's large house and met his brother and sisters.

Arthur Solly and I each possessed one of Pollock's Toy Theatres. Many were the melodramas and pantomimes we produced, with terrific (and sometimes) very noisy stage effects. It was providential that we did not burn our respective homes down with all our various green lights and red lights and "thunderclaps" etc. Arthur went on to Rugby after a short period at Mostyn House, and then to Cambridge. He too died young, being killed in an air crash just at the end of the War (1918).

We had one very quaint little boy at School with us — about eight months younger than I. He was the son of a local doctor with rather a "county" practice. They came from the Channel Islands. His chief distinction from the other boys was that he wore stiff white cuffs every day. The rest of us only wore them on Sundays with our "Eton Suits". One day some of us asked him why he wore these cuffs always. He looked at us very solemnly and then said in an impressive tone of voice:

"Well, you see, I belong to a very old family and we have to think more about keeping up appearances than the rest of you at this School". Naturally this amused us all very much. I suppose that he was about eleven then. He had not changed when I encountered him some seven years later when we were both at Oxford. Indeed he was more like himself than ever. Hearing that I knew a certain V.I.P. he begged me to ask him to lunch to meet the great man. I did so and I heard that he entertained this person the following week—though I was never asked back! Not quite an old enough family I suppose!

There was one unpleasant episode in my Preparatory School career. There was an older boy Edgar (another Day Boy) whom I did not encounter much until after my first year or so, at Balliol

House. He must have been about fourteen when I was ten as his younger brother who was charming, was two years older than I. This youth had the makings of a sadist. He used to waylay other and younger Day Boys (the small ones) after school and torment and terrorise them. Sometimes he would catch a lone straggler in the playground or the Gym and try out various methods of torture on his victim. I think he disliked his brother's friendliness to me and one term marked me down for special attention. I usually managed to avoid him, but one evening he caught me alone in the Gym: knocked me down, sat on my chest and alternated various tortures twisting my arms, pressing his thumbs into my eyes, and pinching my nose with his other great paw over my mouth until I nearly suffocated. After about ten minutes of all these delights he let me go, saying he would half kill me if I sneaked. Trembling with fear and fury I shouted at him.

"I hate you. I hope you'll soon be dead."

The awful thing was that I got my wish—four days later: sudden double pneumonia. I began to wonder if I had "the evil eye". I had recently heard of it in some book I had been reading and it made me rather solemn for a time.

My Mother of course wanted to send me to a good Public School and naturally thought of Shrewsbury where so many of my cousins were educated; but it was not possible financially. For some years now she had got rid of William Wright on certain terms. On condition that he stayed away she paid his lodgings in Manchester, where he had a few friends and occasionally earned a little money by doing temporary accountancy jobs. From time to time things went wrong in Manchester and he descended upon us, sometimes being sent off with hush money the next day, sometimes staying longer and finally staging some drunken scene. It was on one of these occasions that he and I had our final reckoning: I was about sixteen and home from boarding school at Worcester.

Mother used to let the house in Leadhall Lane, Harrogate, for anything from three to six months in the summer, but we used to spend our Christmas and Easter holidays there, Grannie generally being with us. In the summer holidays we went every year to Ireland staying usually in Larne to be near Grannie. Occasionally when Mother was busy Grannie and I joined the Blackwood family at Newcastle, Co. Down, and my cousins and I had great times together bathing and climbing and picnicing in the Mourne Mountains.

In the year when I went to Spain Mother very nobly and bravely went to Queen Charlottes Hospital, London and took the mid-wifery course there, a matter of some months. Incidentally she got higher marks in her final examination than any of the other candidates in her group. The idea was that if she did some nursing for five or six years the financial situation would be more possible. The home could be kept, my school fees met, and William Wright's lodgings paid for and a small allowance to him maintained. I felt it badly that my education should make this necessary and I felt it even worse that she should feel bound to support her worthless husband, whom she steadfastly refused to divorce.

I think that most people thought that my Mother was very plucky and unselfish to take up this arduous branch of the nursing profession and she got much appreciation and kindness from her patients. I can only think of two people whose reaction was different. One was a clergyman's widow in Northern Ireland, who together with her husband had received much kindness and hospitality from my grandfather, Dean Murray, when they had had a small country parish in the Ballymena area. She took to cutting us and not seeing us, when confronted with the sight of a woman who was now "earning her own living." She was just one of those pathetic old snobs that one still meets now and again. The other lady who disapproved lived in Harrogate and dropped us for the same reason. She was a great social climber who spent many years in trying to get to know the "county" people around Harrogate and did not wish to be encumbered by people who she thought no longer in a good social position. She just could not understand why she still met us in the homes of some of the "nicest" people she knew.

Actually my Mother did not keep up her nursing after I left School. As soon as I got my Scholarships to Oxford my Grandmother offered us a home with her in Northern Ireland. She was unhappy living with her other daughter-in-law, so she took a good-sized house in Larne and we took our furniture. All the time I was at Oxford and my Theological College at Salisbury, my home was once again in Larne. It was a very happy time for all three of us, and the contrast between Oxford and Larne was piquant.

I cannot close these memories of my preparatory school period without some reference to the Church of St. Wilfrid's, Duchy Road, Harrogate and its first Vicar, the Rev. W. F. Swann. The School attended the Church and Mr. Moore was one of the pillars and a churchwarden. Swann had been a Minor Canon of Ripon Cathedral and besides being an artist was very musical and possessed a magnificent voice both for singing and reading. Swann taught us the Catholic Faith and the place of dignity and beauty in worship. His sermons, perfectly delivered, were models of teaching. He was also a painter of word pictures and his sincerity and attractiveness were outstanding. I may have been very young and impressionable but I have never heard better preaching. Swann aroused great enthusiasm whilst the architect's plans for the great church were much on view in the little temporary building. He spoke of its future glory so realistically that we could almost see it. It was to have something of the sturdiness of Hexham Abbey in the exterior views; but the elegance of the Early English in the interior. All the boarders at Balliol House, even the most unlikely boys, attended the Church and seemed literally to enjoy the Services. My Mother and I, who lived about a mile-and-a-half away from Duchy Road, Leadhall Lane being at the southerly end of Harrogate, used to walk twice every Sunday to St. Wilfrid's and back. Neither snow nor rain kept us away. At that Church, even when it was only the poor little temporary building I felt a difference. Hitherto I had merely attended Church: at St. Wilfred's I learnt to worship, and to worship in the beauty of holiness. The Sung Eucharist was of the very simplest and was celebrated with a minimum of ritual; but everything that was said, sung and done, was the very best and carried out with the utmost dignity and care. People from a wide area and all strata of society were being drawn in to the life of the Church. Mr. Swann was a good friend to my Mother during very difficult days. He stayed long enough to see the fine nave of the Church completed. When the nave was first used we faced *west*, the altar being placed temporarily in the apsidal west end which was ultimately to be the baptistry. A very plain and uncompromising brick wall blocked the central arch at the east end of the nave. A certain rich lady one day complained to the Vicar about the hideousness of this wall and got the reply:

"Dear lady, I sincerely hope that everyone will agree with you about the wall. The uglier the better! The uglier it is the sooner you will all want to build the chancel and have it removed."

She took the point and a large cheque came along the next day. The Church must have cost well over £100,000 all told which was a large sum in the first years of this century. The builder gave the Lady Chapel as his contribution and thank offering. The way in which the bulk of the money came was strange indeed. Two elderly ladies (the Misses Trotter) were visiting Harrogate. One sister died there very suddenly and the other who then settled in Harrogate, before long became interested in the project of the building of this new Church, and gave large sums amounting to

£20,000 in her sister's memory towards the building fund. A second sum of over £30,000 came on the death some years later, of the second sister. Even we school boys were happy to give our sixpences for a 'stone' and the money rolled in. After some ten or twelve years Mr. Swann left, and after holding important secretarial and administrative positions with the Church of England Children's Societies and the S.P.G., he took a South Coast Parish. I do not think that he was ever as happy again as he had been in his work as the builder of one of the most beautiful Churches in England. When he died many years later he was very suitably represented there by a fine brass in the Chancel floor, which shows him in his Eucharistic Vestments in the attitude of prayer. It has always been a complete mystery to me that a man so dedicated and so endowed with all the talents never received even such recognition as an Honorary Canonry or a Prebendal Stall. To those who knew it his work in Harrogate alone was one of the notable ministries in the Anglican Church in the first half of this century. Strange and unpredictable indeed are the paths of promotion in the Anglican Church! Cyncicism suggests the idea that *whom* you know seems to be at least as important as *what* you know. I am naturally a believer in Providence; but I am sadly conscious that in this wicked world other factors are at work and cannot be overlooked or ignored. Even if barefaced nepotism is less apparent than in the eighteenth century—a "friend at court" (or at least a relative or friend in some strategic position at the right moment)—a capacity for attaining the limelight on committees or conferences—and sheer good luck—can still do wonders. I can think of one man who attained high promotion (not a Bishopric), who had been only about five or six years in Orders as a Schoolmaster and who had never even taken a baptism or a wedding in his life until after he had become a high cathedral dignitary. Nor was he some great scholar. Far from it: his religion was completely adolescent and "Public School". The solution? He met the right people at the right moment. With the inside knowledge chance has given me (as Domestic Chaplain to two Diocesan Bishops) I could tell some cynical tales. What angers me however is not only that so many mediocre people attain to important positions with which they cannot really cope: but that so many really good and able people are ignored, when if only given the chance, they could have done a splendid and really big job for Christ's Church. Preacher, artist, musician, administrator, organizer, (charmer) and saint—all of the highest order—William Fowell Swann should have been made a Dean or Provost and he would have built some great shrine which would have given fame and a soul to some great modern city. No doubt he now has his reward.

It was just before my time at Worcester Cathedral Kings School and when my Mother was doing her maternity nursing that she had a somewhat embarrassing experience. She was staying with Grace Rutherford (who once nearly became her step-mother) and had now moved from Windsor to Tunbridge Wells. On two or three occasions she met at some small parties a very courtly old gentleman, Colonel Lambe, a widower of about seventy. He was very lonely and I suppose that she was kind to him and listened to his woes. What was her surprise when she received one day a magnificent bouquet and a letter asking her if she would marry him—quite poetical—and "become the evening star of his life." Poor Mother: she had to write and explain that although she was earning her living and keeping her son at school she was not a widow. The Colonel who was very disappointed and overcome, wrote again with profound apologies. Four months later he died, leaving over £250,000. Mother got rather teased about this both by Aunt Grace and by me. Actually there were at least two others, who made the same mistake, one a Specialist in Dublin whom she consulted once or twice, another a retired Grammar School Headmaster, an Oxford M.A., who used to follow her into Worcester Cathedral and gaze at her during Service.

CHAPTER V

Public School

WHILE I was at my public school (1907-11) my Mother was working and letting our Harrogate home furnished but we always had our home available during the Christmas and Easter holidays. In the summer I was in Ireland with either my grandmother or my Blackwood cousins. If circumstances allowed Mother was there for at least part of the time. We kept closely in touch, writing to each other one long and one short letter every week. I think I realised what a wonderful Mother I had and not only how loving and brave she was, but how wise. To me as a boy she was unique: the best and most beautiful of women.

It was through some of her well-to-do patients that she heard of Worcester Cathedral Kings School. The fees were less than Shrewsbury. The school had a good tone and the present Headmaster, the Rev. W. H. Chappel was a man of outstanding goodness and ability. I was too late to sit the King's Scholarship examination that year; but I sat a private examination and was awarded an exhibition at the Headmaster's discretion (£40 per annum) and this helped. We had been put up by some kind friends of Mother's (also patients) who lived in Worcester and Mother became very friendly with Canon and Mrs. Chappel. Indeed she later came and stayed with them at the School House on two or three occasions. The whole set up of the School made an immediate appeal to a boy of fourteen with romantic and artistic tastes: the classical buildings of the Cathedral Close, the green lawns and trees, the great river Severn flowing by, the mediaeval College Hall (former Monastic Refectory) and the great guardian angel which I seemed to see in the superbly dominating Cathedral tower presiding over everything. There were also glimpses of the deep country across the river westwards to the blue line of the Malvern Hills.

Some enthusiasts claimed that the School dated back to Alfred the Great. No doubt the monks in Saxon times had their pupils in their well established Monastery; but the more soberly constituted were content to accept 1541, the date of Henry VIII's foundation of the School; after the Dissolution of the Monastic foundation. The King's words were ideal—"that piety and good letters may in our Church for ever blossom . . . for the glory of God and the advantage and adornment of the Commonwealth'.

(The letters "W.C.K.S." were emblazoned in white on our dark blue caps and we rather wished that they were not! "Worcester can't kick straight" was invariably the cry of all the local street urchins.)

I should say that it was an excellent minor Public School, run on Marlborough lines by a Headmaster who had been a Marlborough House Master. The propinquity of the Cathedral was a great asset as was the interest of the Dean and Residentiary Canons. The beauty of the building, the good music and the (usually) clever and stimulating sermons all helped. The Worcester Canons were Crown appointments and we got both ability and variety. Later, as a Prefect, I got to know several of them extremely well—Dean Forrest (a fellow Irishman who knew my great Uncle Sir George Moyers) and Moore Ede (friendly and humorous) —Canon Teignmouth-Shore (generally considered intimidating because of his very pointed little notes to other Close dwellers whose dogs barked "for nineteen (or was it twenty-nine) minutes last night", and so on.) He was stigmatized as "old Margate-Sands" by Dean Forrest. He was however always charming to me and interested in my efforts to start a School Dramatic Society. Another good friend was Canon J. M. Wilson (the Cambridge mathematician) who used to have me to stay in his lovely home. (Part of it is now the residence of the Headmaster). He was for one term (during Canon Chappell's illness) acting Headmaster and although well over seventy did the job amazingly. Everyone loved him and Mrs. Wilson. She was a dear and also, being a Sidgewick, an extremely clever woman. They had played since the early days of their married life an unending game of piquet. I remember her saying to me one time when I was staying with them:

"Don't ask the Canon the latest score at breakfast today, my dear boy. He had a bad night yesterday and I am now about ten thousand ahead. He is getting quite depressed!"

Canon Chappell (a First in Theology from Worcester College, Oxford) was a most saintly, scholarly and almost too conscientious man. Although an excellent organiser he nearly worked himself to death. In many ways he was too good for us boys, many of us being fairly pagan and cynical little animals. I think that it was in his illustrations in his sermons and his "pep" talks that he was least successful: just a little too Victorian. On one occasion he was speaking of the outstanding careers of some Old Vigornians. Two were mentioned who were specially held up to inspire emulation.

They had gone abroad (one to India, the other to Central Africa) and had done great and selfless work. One had died some five years ago at under thirty: the other still quite young was to be buried this very week. When we came out of the service one popular wit said:

"A bit ominous 'Daddy's' Sermon 'Whom the gods love die young'. I don't think I want to be too good. I want a good innings here!"

He was a very popular and delightful youth, captain successively of both cricket and football, a wonderful athlete and one of my very good friends. Curiously enough he too went out East on leaving School and died within two years of some tropical complaint. On another occasion in School Hall "Daddy" referred to a delinquent youth whom he had just expelled. He ended his poignant discourse with the words:

"Before I sent him away I flogged him with all the strength which God had given me".

It might have been put differently and to an audience of boys with more effect. These however were superficial things. The mere fact that the Head's nickname was "Daddy" showed that he was regarded with trust and affection and that we realised that he carried us in his heart. He certainly never spared himself and took endless trouble in individual cases which provided problems. I think perhaps he rather naturally liked best the docile boys who more or less conformed to a pattern. Those of us who were more individualistic and less easily guided or swayed by him got a more qualified approval. I remember when X and I were sent up to Oxford to try for Scholarships (X being one of his prime favourites). I was commended thus:—

"Well, Williams, I *hope* you will do well; but you have not worked as hard as X."

Afterwards when I had got a £100 a year Scholarship (in Modern History) at Exeter College "Daddy" said generously in a letter to my Mother:

"I must allow that I backed the wrong horse this time, but I am none the less delighted at your boy's success (he could not refrain from adding) although it was not in Classics but only in History."

Scholarships in History or Mathematics were not considered by the good Canon as being quite on the same high level as those for Latin and Greek. I cannot imagine that dear old "Daddy" would at all have approved the swing in the modern and scientific direction which has been the answer of even the most ancient English Universities to present day needs. I had just enough of Latin and

Greek to hold my position as head of Upper Fifth and Lower Sixth Forms and in the top Quartette of the Upper Sixth successively, to gain by Higher Certificate my Oxford matriculation. History and English always interested me more as being so much closer to life and to people today.

I was extremely fortunate to be in Castle House (no aspersions intended on either the School House or The Hostel). In those days it was certainly the best House in many ways. Practically all the School Cups were there and I think most of the more interesting amongst the boys. We also had a wonderful partnership in charge. Mr. T. E. Rammell (Trinity College, Oxford) and his much younger sister Miss Kitty Rammell were both excellent. "Tommy", without being fussy, knew just what was going on. A kindly and friendly man, he was always approachable; but not to be fooled. "Kitty" (as we all called her) was much adored and was undoubtedly a most outstanding and remarkable woman. She had exactly the right approach to every person and problem and her kindness to anyone who was in the house "Sick Room", had only one drawback. It made the patients prefer a lingering illness to a rapid recovery. After she left the School which she literally made her life, she still took an interest in all the boys who had been to Castle House in her time there. At a very wonderful ninety she was still keeping up with a number of us and remembering all sorts of details from fifty to sixty years ago. Tommy had always seemed to be a confirmed bachelor; but when he retired he confounded his colleagues by going off for a short holiday and returning engaged to be married. He only lived a very short time after retiring, in contrast to the longevity of his wonderful sister.

Other members of the staff had considerable influence upon me; but it was Fortescue, the Upper Sixth Form Master (a brilliant First in Greats from Brasenose College, Oxford) who did most for me intellectually and academically. It was his interest and encouragement that helped me to win my Scholarships to Oxford. The fact that I was not going to be a Classical Scholar did not damp down his interest in me and he told me that if I would work hard for a year I would get a good History Scholarship. He was an outstanding teacher and it was tragic that he died so soon and so young.

My three greatest friends were certainly, as far as intelligence and the arts went, three of the most outstandingly gifted boys in the School. Tom Bye was a Day Boy and a brilliant pianist, who later won a Musical Scholarship at Keble College, Oxford. Later he became well known in musical circles as an exponent of Scarlatti and did some broadcasting for the B.B.C. He spent a short time as Organist of St. Matthews, Westminster before devoting the rest of his professional career to Uppingham and after that to the Leys School at Cambridge. He never married (although many "were willing"); but had and has a host of friends. I valued him for his gentle artistic and humorous nature. He was an orphan and lived under the auspices of Canon Robert Wylde of Newland, Malvern. My Mother was very attached to Tom Bye also and during the latter part of our School days and throughout Oxford times he spent many summer holidays with us while we were living in Larne with Grannie. My Irish relatives and friends accepted him as one of the family. He was always a wonderful mixer. Our friendship has never changed and he is still one of our most welcome and favourite visitors. Now I think we value and amuse one another as repositories of so many bygone memories, adventures and jokes, which make us feel that we are still defying time.

My two other great friends were two boys of the same name but no relationship and as different from each other as possible, Hugh and Seiriol Evans.

Hugh de la Poer Evans (half French, half Welsh) shared a study with me and whatever form we were in we kept our places as top and second. We were known by Tommy Rammell as "the firm".

"Well, what answer has the firm got to that one?" Hugh (Guinea Pig—not entirely unlike one) was short and fat and exceedingly clever. His forte was mathematics. In these things he was my support and I his despair. Still I could help him with his classics as well as with history and English. His parents who lived in Stratford-upon-Avon, I scarcely knew; but he had a delightful half French aunt Miss Georgie Power, who lived in Worcester and was one of the leading archaeologists of the city: a woman with a first rate brain and boundless knowledge. We often went to tea with her and I for one learnt an immense deal from her. Hugh left school over a year before I went to Oxford. He passed very brilliantly into the Paymaster's Department of the Royal Navy and although for a time we had a typically desultory school boy correspondence, we never met between 1910 and 1918. When we did I was a rather intense young Curate and he a gay young man of the world in business. Because he never ceased to suffer from sea-sickness he had come out of the Navy immediately after the end of World War I. Miss Power stayed with us both in Ireland and in my Kidderminster and Harrogate curacies days; but she died very suddenly and I did not hear any more of Hugh. Efforts through the Navy as well as through the Old Vigornian Society failed to get me in contact with him again. Possibly my clerical aura in my early days in the Priesthood frightened him off! I often wonder what became of him. All his other old friends connected with the school lost track of him as completely as I did.

Seiriol Evans, my other great school friend was over two years younger but never seemed so. He had more poise and sophistication than many of his seniors. We were mutually attracted almost from the time of his arrival when I was already top of the Lower Sixth and a House Prefect. Curiously enough we found out that the original attraction was that we each thought the other the boy with the best manners in the House! For his age he had a considerable degree of culture. He had been a chorister (a soloist) at King's College, Cambridge, and between that and his father's hospitable Vicarage had met many interesting people and acquired social experience. We talked music, painting, architecture and our own futures on long walks together in a wet spring term when the School playing fields were well under the inundations of the swollen Severn.

It was also about this time that the general influence of the Cathedral and its atmosphere brought me to the decision that I wanted to be ordained. Actually Seiriol was away from the School a good deal during the end of my time there. He had, I think, two bad bouts of pneumonia. I went to Oxford and a year or so later he went back to King's, Cambridge, where I paid one or two delightful visits, dining at High Table and having the honour and pleasure of sitting next to the Provost, Dr. Montague James, the writer of the best ghost stories in the English language. I remember him talking about Icelandic and Norse Sagas and how he said that he got some of his inspiration and horrific touches from these ancient sources. I had just read his "Ghost Stories of an Antiquary".

In later years it has been a great delight to stay with Seiriol and his charming wife Selina (née Townley of Fulbourne Manor, Cambridge) both at their lovely medieval Rectory at Upwell in the Fens and later at the Deanery at Gloucester.

One other friend of mine at Worcester Cathedral Kings School I must mention because of his peculiar problems. He was a dark saturnine boy, a few months my junior. Although he was in the Lower Sixth and I in the Upper, we worked a good deal together during my last year as we were both specializing for the Oxford History Scholarship Examinations under Fortescue. I did not overwork and Leo Harvey did even less. He was a day boy and came from a curious home. His Mother, who was Dutch, was dead and the household consisted of a clever and eccentric old father (bearded and Southern Irish) who had been a Librarian at the House of Commons, an elder brother, Godfrey (later a contemporary of mine at Exeter College, Oxford) and a youngish-middle-aged housekeeper. Noticing Leo's consistent abstracted melancholy I eventually asked him what the trouble was. Imagine my surprise when this boy of seventeen burst into tears and then blurted out:

"I am married! I felt I should go mad if I did not tell someone!"

It was the housekeeper, a pleasant and attractive person, but a woman of thirty.

Godfrey, cool, fair and over twenty was as worldly-wise as poor Leo impulsive and imprudent. I soon got the whole story out of him. I introduced him to my friend Hugh Evans' wise old aunt, Miss Power and she did a great deal to help. Between us we got Leo to tell, first his father, then the Headmaster. There was going to be a baby. At first "Daddy", confronted by a new problem proposed to expel the wretched youth; but ultimately Leo stayed his full course, and came up to Oxford (St. Edmund Hall) the following year, although without any Scholarship. He was the only seventeen-year-old school boy I ever knew who was a married man and a father. Leo's future career was dogged by ill fortune. After Oxford he got a Professorship in one of the smaller Canadian Universities and later on exchanged this for a better paid post in the U.S.A. He now had a wife and two children to support. Before long came the terrible slump of 1929. Practically all Professors at American Universities who were not American citizens were dropped from their posts. Leo soon returned to England, parting finally from the wife with whom he had really little in common. Never again did he prosper and it was the kindness of his successful brother Godfrey which in future mainly provided for him. The old father had been dead for many years and Leo had a lonely life and much ill health. We renewed our friendship during his last years. These days all seem far away now. So many school friends were killed in World War I or have died since. Only Tom Bye and Seiriol Evans survive.

I suppose that on the whole my school career was reasonably successful. It was only in my last year at school that I was able to enter rather casually for the school sports and without any training. The three years previously I had always had some minor complaint (measles, influenza, etc.) which prevented my entry. My last year I entered just as a joke and was surprised to win (in 10.8 seconds) the Hundred Yards, also the Two Hundred and Twenty Yards and Long Jump and so be runner-up to the *Victor Ludorum*, another

Castle House boy. At least between us we kept the Inter House Sports Club for Castle House, I won the Schools Chess Cup each year of the four I was there beating various sixth formers and never losing a game in the annual tournaments. At sixteen when only in the Upper Fifth I won the Prize in the annual School General Knowledge Paper, beating the Upper Sixth Form Olympians of eighteen years of age, an event on which the Headmaster commented in Hall saying that no-one below the Upper Sixth had ever won this School Prize before. I enjoyed two years in the Upper Sixth and as a School Prefect. I was for a year the Editor of The Vigornian, so could publish my own few poems! I went on to Oxford with £200 per annum in Scholarships, which took a big load of anxiety off my Mother's shoulders.

The really brilliant boys of my period at Worcester Cathedral Kings School were C. J. Barker who won a Classical Scholarship to Christ Church and after a distinguished career as a Civil Servant took Holy Orders and became an Incumbent in Devonshire. The others were S. St. G. Kingdom, Senior Kings Scholar, a Demi at Magdalen, Oxford, later librarian at the House of Lords (who died in early middle age); and C. V. Hancock who became a Bible student at All Souls, Oxford and later an Editor of the Birmingham Post. I feel that we all owed a great deal to the Cathedral Kings School. Not only did it help us to get to Oxford. It showed us many things: the meaning of beauty and of history and how to learn and appraise things. Looking back I think that this school did as much for our little circle as any of the larger and more famous public schools could have done. If by some freak of fortune I had got to Harrow or Shrewsbury, where so many of our friends and relations had been, I would probably have gone to Oxford with far more extravagant ideas. As it was I was happy to find that I never had to ask my Mother for a penny in the whole of my time at the University. My scholarships and a small income from some house property in Belfast, left to me by my Father, paid for everything, including my fares to Northern Ireland and back three times a year.

School days were happy; but I have never sentimentalized about them. I always preferred home and the holidays. I suppose that I was always too much of an individualist to appreciate any kind of regimentation which is after all essential to any sort of community life. The freer life of Oxford suited me better than either a public school or a theological college. Also tutors at a University do not apparently feel bound to indulge at times in cant and clichés to inspire and indoctrinate their pupils. I was never a particular favourite of my Headmaster's, as I was far too independent minded; but we ended up by respecting one another. For my House Master and his wonderful sister I had a deep and affectionate appreciation. The man to whom however I owed most academically was probably our brilliant Sixth Form Master, Fortescue of Brasenose College, Oxford to whose tutorship and encouragement I owed my ultimate scholarship success at the University.

CHAPTER VI

Oxford

I CAN truthfully say that my three years at Oxford were amongst the happiest and most revealing of my whole life. To me Oxford will always be the enchanted city, the true inspirer of dreams and visions. It is not just the incomparable beauty of its ancient buildings and the companionships of one's contemporaries in all their rich variety. It is because there is an indefinable "something" which for want of a better phrase one might call a distillation of *history realised* together with premonition of *future felt*: the richness of stored experience blended with the freshness of forward-looking youth. There was the piquancy of contrasts: the tolerance and humility which come from deep and real knowledge meeting the impulsive confidence and absolutism of youth. My three years at Oxford were at the very end of the Augustan era—a Golden Age—before the blasting and bleakness, the sick humour and negativeness which the ghastly World Wars of this century have brought to Europe. The cost of a University career was less than half what it is today, but the richness of the whole experience was more than double. We know how estimable it is now that all students at University should work or get out; but in those more spacious days, although actual study perhaps claimed less of our day some things were learnt and valued which are just not there now: things that were not even then on the academic curriculum so to speak: but they were precious, perhaps priceless.

Knowledge can do two things. It can inspire and lead to fresh discoveries and it can sharpen the critical and appraising faculties. I rather fancy that if life is lived in too much of a hurry the second of these two gifts of learning is less likely to develop and there tends to be a certain loss of true culture. That is perhaps why there are so many fully primed products of Universities today who have little about them which suggests a generous culture, a general capacity for appraisal and a sureness of touch or taste, in spite of their specialisations.

Between eighteen and twenty-two in most cases a man's mind is still young enough to receive and retain impressions vividly and yet old enough to sift and evaluate, if he is not too impatient.

In my entrance form for the scholarship group in which I was successful I had given my first preference to Christ Church: but I I have always considered myself none the less most fortunate to have been elected at Exeter College. A smaller college has certain advantages, especially for a man with limited means. Exeter was a happy friendly society. There were some fifty-four freshmen in my year (the College total being about two hundred and twenty in 1911); so there was a strong probability that one would find at least a few kindred spirits and a variety which in itself would be educative. The general character of the undergraduates of my year was pleasant and sociable. There was a strong contingent of the sons of the West Country gentry. The College was attractive in many ways. The front quadrangle was pleasant and spacious. It had one of the most beautiful of all Oxford College Halls and gardens (through this latter was small). It had what I still maintain is one of the noblest College Chapels. Today of course it is the fashion to decry it; copies of previous styles of architecture being "out". In my second year I had one of the finest sets of rooms in the front quadrangle. It was first floor up looking straight across to the main entrance from the Turl. It was graciously proportioned, completely panelled and the bedroom and 'thirder' both had windows looking out on to the Fellows Garden. I had several well framed Medici prints and always flowers or flowering plants on my table. Indeed it was a room so fine that on one occasion it was the cause of an amusing incident. There was a rather timid tap at the door and I said "Come in". There appeared an extremely smart young man, a year junior to myself. I knew him by sight but I did not know his name. I had however heard that he was one of that year's Eton contingent (there were usually five or six each year) and that he was somewhat "upstage". However he seemed to be extremely modest and amiable and I asked him to sit down and offered him a cigarette. We talked vaguely but pleasantly for perhaps ten minutes. Then he glanced at his gold wrist watch and said rather dispassionately: "May I read you my essay now, Sir?"

His disgust when he discovered that I was not his tutor was most amusing. Here was a real "blood" who had piped down quite unnecessarily to someone who merely had an impressive room. Of course I had been enjoying his mistake for several minutes. I informed him with a bright smile that Mr. Barber's room was the one immediately overhead. Exit (without flourish of trumpets).

The personnel of the College contained many attractive folk and one gorgeous eccentric. For the first part of my time Dr Jackson who exhibited a certain superficial diffidence, was the Rector. The College joke about any interview with him on the part of any undergraduate had a fixed pattern. The scene was the large dining room in the Rector's Lodging, a room with about thirty chairs placed against the walls. You began by sitting on the chair immediately on the left of the door from the hall, the Rector sitting at a safe distance two or three chairs away. As you enthused or grew more intense on the subject of discussion (whatever it may have been) you moved one chair nearer. At the same time the Rector retreated in proportion to your advance. When he reached the *last* chair (to the right of the entrance door) the interview was considered to be at an end and you were bowed out. Mrs. Jackson was a wealthy woman and ultimately the College benefited by nearly £200,000 through her generosity. The Rector however had a life interest and as he lived on to be a nonagenarian the College had some years to wait for this welcome addition. It was probable that Dr. Jackson was less detached from the life of the College than appeared to be the case at first sight. One heard of many acts of kindness, interest and understanding on his part.

Dr. Lewis Farnell who succeeded him was also a most kind and sympathetic man and had a rather more progressive outlook. His tenure of the Rectorship was complicated by his also becoming Vice-Chancellor of the University. He got rather a bad press occasionally ("poisoned chocolates" and other trifling matters), but did well during a difficult period, the First World War. Mrs. Farnell, a keen musician and somewhat of a power behind the throne, was quite a character and a wit. I got to know her better actually when I was Vicar of Banbury (in the 1930s) and she most kindly helped us on various musical occasions. Dr. Marett, the genial Channel Islander who succeeded Dr. Farnell, I never knew personally.

Dr. Bernard Henderson, my "Moral" Tutor, was a very devout person, immersed in the study of Roman Emperors and the Boy Scouts Movement. The only time I had really much contact with him was when he once tackled me on a not particularly fundamental matter, namely the colour of a silk collar and shirt which I had once worn in Chapel. I got a lecture on sartorial correctness, delivered in staccato sentences without a single "R" sound in them. It was hard to keep a straight face.

Those I found most helpful personally were the Sub-Rector (Balleine) a truly delightful Channel Islander and a useful person, killed, alas, in World War I and A. B. Howe (the Bursar), affectionately known as "the Beefer", an old rowing Blue. He was everybody's friend: a man who would always listen to your troubles or problems. Further he always remembered old members of the College who came back years later to this function or that. The Chaplain, the learned N. P. Williams ("Nippy") was also always extremely kind and could be most amusing. He and C. T. Atkinson (our eccentric and my Tutor) had not much in common, "Atters" always referred to "Nippy's" room as "the bloody boudoir". It was noticed that if ever these two were alone at High Table at dinner they sat worlds apart and the conversation was nil.

C. T. Atkinson was a first rate Tutor, *if* he liked you. (He liked nearly fifty per cent of his pupils). I was one of the other fifty per cent although he must on the first instance have approved of my papers in the Scholarship examination—before he saw much of me. He used to look at me with great distaste and occasionally came out with such comments as "You're too bloody well dressed" or "Do you ever get your hair cut?"

Still there were others who roused his wrath to far greater heights. My friend Geoffrey Dennis (the novelist and later Head of the Interpreters' Department of the League of Nations) who took a brilliant First in Modern History was definitely his greatest *bête-noir* in those days. Geoffrey got one essay returned with the following inscription on its top corner in red ink:

"You have a mind worthy of a bloody Labour Member of Parliament."

When I read my essays to "Atters" in his somewhat grubby room he usually appeared to be suffering from corns and was either soaking his feet in hot water and soda, or else operating upon them with a murderous little knife. If one stopped, half mesmerised by his antics with this weapon, he used to growl at you:

"Get on. I have not got all day to listen to you". His comments on my work were short and uncomplimentary as a rule, only once do I remember him saying:

"Yes, that's all right".

Usually he was laconic.

"Don't agree with your point of view". "Your trouble is that you are not working hard enough. Going to be content with a Second Class I suppose".

Ultimately, at the beginning of my last year I was transferred by the Rector, Lewis Farnell, to the more sympathetic and interested tutelage of Lelio Stampa (a brother of the Punch artist) of whom it was said:

"If you can reproduce everything he tells you, you'll get a B+ on every paper!"

I think that I was not particularly fortunate in my tutors for my History Finals and I got the prophesied Second Class in the end, although achieving a few "alphas". Of course many of "Atters" cruderies, not to say "ruderies" became quite famous. Although Exeter College, when he was a Tutor, provided his livelihood for many years, he always remained a dyed-in-the-wool Magdalen man. I remember one Eights Week when the Magdalen second boat once pressed the Exeter first boat as sandwich boat and head of the Second Division. "Atters" ran with Magdalen crew shouting as he plunged along the river bank:

"Come along Magdalen, you've nearly got the blighters now."

This did not go down too well with the Exeter crew and Anthony Slingsby (the captain of Boats) suggested to "Atters" that the next day he should absent himself from the river bank, or else he might end the afternoon by taking an impromptu bath.

He loathed women coming to his lectures and used any means to get rid of them. His adjectives were forceful and freely interspersed. On one occasion he announced as an introduction to his lecture:

"I got wet on the way here. I warn the ladies present, I am going to take off my trousers and hang them near the fire."

There followed the desired rush for the door by the alarmed female seekers after knowledge. Actually in later life "Atters" and I became quite friendly. The last time I saw him was dining in Hall and I sat next to him at High Table, I had now become a Bishop and we had a delightful chat. He even hoped that I would have time to come and visit him at his home address. He was then well on in the eighties and had mellowed beyond all expectations. He had been a widower for many years and I think that he was really a rather lonely old man. People spoke of him with affection.

Lectures of course are as an important a part of the Oxford educational system as "tutorials". In my case they were more so, as I and my main tutor were mutually uninterested. Some of the lectures I went to were brilliant, inspiring and helpful. Men like Barker of St. John (later Professor at Cambridge), A. L. Smith of Balliol and Grant Robinson of All Souls, who was quite wonderful at making certain periods such as the Reign of Queen Anne, come to life again. I shall never forget his thrilling lectures on Bolingbroke and the chances of a Jacobite Restoration in the last months of Queen Anne. It would be unkind to mention names — but there were on the other hand some lecturers whose dullness was almost past bearing. I remember going to Lincoln College for a subject which I badly needed. At the first lecture there were forty to fifty of us. At the second there were nine. The third time there was a black man, a girl with thick glasses (who took down with heavy breathings every word as the learned man droned it out) and myself. Whether there ever *was* a fourth lecture in this series I do not know as I could not bear the prospect of another hour of such inexpressible boredom. The excellent man gave three impressions: first that he was really a bumble-bee, secondly that he could not read his own writing, and thirdly that he had out-Gallioed Gallio, and not merely "cared for none of these things", but that he positively loathed them. Actually outside the lecture room he was a very genial old gentleman.

I had a fairly wide circle of friends—mostly other Scholars or athletes: mostly also members of Exeter College. Except for Tom Bye, now Musical Scholar of Keble and Arthur Forrest, formerly Head-Boy of Sherborne and then a Scholar of Corpus Christi, all my great friends were at Exeter College. O. A. Staples (a Rhodes Scholar from South Africa) was a charming and magnificent creature, who played Rugger and read poetry. There was a strong bond between us and we would undoubtedly have liked to see more of each other; but our work and our different athletic interests did not make it easy. Allpass from Felstead (the German Scholar of our year) the son of an East Anglian parson was another friend. We lunched together one day every week. He was a charming youth but had one of those very reserved temperaments which often go with extreme blondness. He could never quite relax and really be himself. His greatest friend was another member of our set, a curiously different type, Cohen (English Literature Exhibition) a Jew from St. Paul's School. He was very Oriental looking with smouldering black eyes, and a quite brilliant brain. I will never forget a paper he read to our College Literary Society on the work and genius of Oscar Wilde. His powers of expression and of epigram were almost on a level with those of the writer whom he was discussing. Of course none of us really quite knew him, much as we liked his quiet kindness and admired his intellect. He would undoubtedly have taken a brilliant First in English: but he came to a sudden and tragic end. He shot himself. I have a suspicion that Allpass knew the reason why; but none of the rest of us did, at any rate at the time. Another friend of a very different type was Robin (A. E. D.) Milton, my next door neighbour during my first year, and a most genial and amusing person. He was a man of simple tastes (a mountain climber and a bird watcher) who curiously enough seemed to spend most of his vacations either climbing Welsh mountains or staying with one or other of the various Peers of the Realm (mostly Marquises) whom he knew.

My two greatest friends were Eddie Hudson (the French Scholar of my year) and Geoffrey Dennis (one year my senior). Geoffrey was a Commoner, but probably the cleverest undergraduate in the College at that time. Eddie Hudson did more to educate me psychologically than any other person of my own age and I am grateful to him for certain lessons which I have never forgotten. In short he taught me the art of self criticism. He showed me often by his analysis of himself—where I was in danger of being terribly egocentric, vain, over sensitive and furiously full of a sort of pride. I remember once he said to me, not at all offensively, but quite kindly:

"It would do you good to avoid using the words 'I', 'Me', and 'My', for even a week."

The revelation that gave me was like a blow in the face (though a friendly one). I began to realise something of what it had meant to be an adored and only child ever since I had had a conscious existence.

Eddie had an extraordinary clear and perceptive mind, good-looking in an ascetic manner, very tall, dark and thin with a sharp and knowing nose; he had the most penetrating eyes, he could look right through people. Yet he was never really unkind in spite of his gift for sparkling sarcasm. He had a tremendous sense of humour and that lovable quality of being able to laugh at himself. He and I were both hoping to be ordained and in spite of a surface pose of flippancy he was deeply devout and religious. He was also completely unselfish. One day we were together with five or six of our more intimate friends in Cohen's rooms and we we all in turn saying what we wanted to do with our lives. Eddie Hudson had sat there without saying a word. Then someone (I forget who) turned to him and said:

"What's *your* ambition, Eddie?"

Quite simply and quietly he said:

"To be a Saint."

A silence fell on us all.

Actually I think he succeeded although he died of wounds at the early age of twenty-five as an Army Officer in the Balkans Campaign in 1917. Eddie was bilingual. Indeed he said he spoke French better than English. He could probably have taken a First in the Final Honour School at the end of his first year at Oxford. He had more or less grown up in Brussels, where his father had been the Anglican Chaplain. Needless to say he got a brilliant First when he did take his Finals. His knowledge of French literature was tremendous and he introduced me to writers who have been firm favourites of mine ever since — Montaigne, Balzac, Flaubert, Victor Hugo, Merimee, Moliere, St. Simon and many others. I never, however, could emulate his enthusiasm for Racine, still less for Corneille, no doubt because my knowledge of the French language was on so much lower a level than his. I feel that it is still his influence that has led me on to enjoy French writers who have come to the fore since his death, such as Proust, Mauriac and Maurois. We used to take tremendous walks in the still unspoilt countryside in areas immediately outside Oxford such as Hinksey, Wytham, Eynsham, Cassington: and discuss an infinite number of subjects. He almost always had fresh and original things to say. The only subjects on which he so to speak, sat at my feet were all questions of art and architecture and perhaps in regard to English literature of which he knew little in comparison with his wide knowledge of French. We planned ahead wonderful trips we would take later in the less known parts of provincial France. Alas, it was all never to be. I remember the last letter he wrote to me in 1917 from Macedonia, asking for a copy of Meredith's poems. "I find that poetry suits my mood and circumstances these days" he wrote. I sent the volume after a little difficulty in getting it and I never knew whether it reached him before that Bulgarian's sniper's bullet cut off one of the most promising young lives of that agonised generation. I often wonder what he would have done if he had lived. He still had his firm vocation to the Ministry of the Church and I am sure that he would have come to occupy a position of eminence from which to influence many minds—perhaps a Canonry at Westminster or St. Paul's. I think that it would have bored and even cramped him to have become a Bishop and have had to cope with endless administrative problems and routine. He was definitely one of those by whose early death England lost much. Some of his ejaculations and sayings still live in my ears, such as:

"Oh, the invincibility of stupidity!" How often have I realised the truth of that saying of his.

My other great friend Geoffrey Dennis (who took a brilliant First in Modern History) was as different from Eddie Hudson as it is possible to imagine. Geoffrey had not Eddie's gift of summing people up. He saw them subjectively and did not often stop to think of what his impact on others might be. Apart from this there was little that he could not do. He had an immense sense of humour—bizarre at times, and was the most brilliant talker I have ever known. It was pure entertainment to sit and listen to him, although I frequently ended up by disagreeing with his conclusions, if not with all his premises. To illustrate his wit I could cite some of the questions and answers to his viva voce exam after the Civil Service Examination which he sat after World War I. He was one of the first four or five candidates in the final list of many hundreds.

"Mr. Dennis", said the examiner, turning over a little pile of references, "your former Tutor at Oxford, Mr. Atkinson, says that you have several peculiar ideas. What do you think he meant by that?"

"That my ideas did not coincide with his."

"Mr. Dennis, who would you place as the outstanding politician in Europe during this century?"

"Lenin."

Geoffrey had contributed to "Oxford Poetry" in 1913. He was later to win considerable appreciation for such of his novels as *Mary Lee* and *Harvest in Poland*, and his weird but clever *End of the World* which won him the Hawthornden Prize. He was a born linguist speaking with amazing fluency French, German, Italian and Spanish. In the last decade of his life he also acquired Dutch. He was, until the whole organisation sank under his feet, Head of the Interpreters Department of the League of Nations. Later he worked (during World War II) for the Ministry of Information and was sent on confidential missions to Spain where he saw and interviewed such people as General Franco and Cardinal Segura (Archbishop of Toledo and Primate). He also participated in the political broadcasts to Italy as well as to Spain. Later, until he was seventy, he took part in the meetings of U.N.E.S.C.O. in Paris and The Hague in a secretarial capacity. I do not think that he enjoyed retirement. He was, altogether too restless even to settle to writing, when he had nothing else he must do. In spite of much success, Geoffrey had much sadness in his life also. He never considered himself really successful. In his last years he used to say:

"I have been a failure! Look how successful you have been: a Bishop with a D.D. conferred on you by a respectable University."

It was no good telling him that he had had a wonderful career. He possessed a quaint old house in Woodstock; but he did not like it, infinitely preferring ours! Perhaps he had a "divine discontent". He died in 1963 and left quite a considerable amount of money but he always spoke of himself as a very poor man.

His first wife, Christine, was a most attractive girl. Vivid was the word. She had a fine brain and a brilliant academic career at

Strasbourg University. They came and stayed with us in Yorkshire when they had been married only a few months. She had glorious red gold hair and her clothes were exactly right. She sparkled and laughed and we all thought her completely delightful. Another few months and she and her baby boy were both dead. It took Geoffrey a long time to get over this, if he ever did. The League of Nations were very good to him. He was given three months' leave with full pay and he went to the U.S.A. with introductions to a great many of the most powerful and interesting people of the day in that country.

After a few years he married again another attractive person, Imogen Rossetti-Angeli, partly English, part Italian. She was of most interesting descent being the grand-daughter of William Michael Rossetti and the great-niece of Dante Gabriel and Christina; the only child of her clever and charming Rossetti Mother. We never met Imogen until over twenty years later, as they lived almost entirely abroad but when we did we were immediately charmed. They had two clever and handsome children, Edward and Helen. Edward following a career at Blundells and at Exeter College, Oxford, inherited his father's gift for languages. Geoffrey can never have been easy to live with, although the best company in the world. I can imagine that Imogen had a certain amount to put up with at times: but it was nice to see them in their pretty home at Woodstock. They had differing opinions and wordy battles about all sorts of subjects. I think that they were really very proud of each other. I was much amused when Edward said to me (shortly after we came to Woodstock and bought our present charming old house only four doors away from Number 15 Park Street) :

"You are one of the very few people who can manage my Father."

If this was true I think it was because I still saw Geoffrey as a highly intelligent and playful "infant terrible". I could still say :

"Don't talk such rubbish, Geoffrey! You know you are only trying to amuse yourself—and to shock poor old X."

In matters of down to earth common sense he often seemed quite happy to take or at least to listen to my advice. For all his brilliance he never quite grew up. A certain impishness survived from early days.

In the year of the abdication of Edward VIII, before the storm broke and everyone was preparing for the Coronation of a bachelor King, Geoffrey Dennis produced a most excellent book on the history of the Coronation Service with its implications and links with English history. The manuscript was shown to Queen Mary, who was graciously pleased to give a most appreciative approval. Then came the episode of Mrs. Simpson and the Abdication. Most unfortunately Geoffrey, in adding an *ad hoc* chapter, inserted a sentence about the lady which was taken exception to by the Duke of Windsor. The book which had had some excellent reviews was immediately withdrawn and the Duke took an action for libel. Damages were awarded. All this drove Geoffrey nearly frantic. He was always prone to worry and here he really had something to trouble him. As so often he had not been thinking about other people's possible reactions. I was glad that after all this Geoffrey got such responsible work under the British Government during World War II. In a way it gave him some sense of rehabilitation. In our Oxford days he was one of the more striking and amusing of the speakers at the Union and was noted for his studied verbal effects.

On one occasion an earnest athlete who represented the University in one of the great Inter-varsity Sporting events, made a lengthy and extremely dull speech, and the house emptied visibly. Then Geoffrey got up to reply.

"That was rather a Bolt from the Blue . . ." were his opening words and the rest of his sentence was lost in roars of laughter. He worried dreadfully over the Union. At election times he was like a herring on a griddle. One day in election week we were walking together down the narrow length of the Turl. A noted Union figure (a member of Balliol College) passed by on the other side of the road. Geoffrey clutched my arm and said in a stage whisper (which could have carried easily forty or fifty yards):

"Do you see that man? He hates me! He will be doing all he can to get his College to vote *against* me!" The man could not have helped hearing. I do not imagine that the episode proved a vote catching gimmick on Geoffrey's part. Geoffrey did achieve the post of Junior Librarian: but the Presidency of the Union eluded him. He would undoubtedly have made an outstandingly entertaining and brilliant President if things had gone otherwise.

I never thought of Tom Bye (Musical Scholar of Keble) as one of my "Oxford" friends, so much as one of my school friends. I suppose because we were such friends before Oxford days and also because for so many summers he used as a boy to visit us in Ireland and was accepted really as one of the family. We always saw one another two or three times a term; but in Oxford our paths did not naturally cross very much. He was immersed in the work of the Musical Club and the Musical Union. He was also Organist of Trinity College and often helped the Organ Scholar at Keble (Douglas Fox) in organising things.

Arthur Forrest of Corpus Christi College was another good friend. He had been Head Boy of Sherborne and his Mother who was the daughter and heiress of Sir Osborne Bunbury, an Irish Baronet, lived in Bath. I used to stay with them for the Duke of Beaufort's Hunt Ball and other gaieties. I was interested to meet amongst their friends the Countess of Charlemont, as I had always been impressed by the part which the first Earl of Charlemont and his family had taken in the cultural development of Dublin in the eighteenth century. Ivy Forrest's twenty-first birthday party and dance were more highlights. Alas, how soon they were all dead. Arthur, early in the First World War, Ivy still only in her twenties and the handsome Mother soon afterwards. Arthur Forrest had a great interest in music, though not the gifts of Tom Bye or Douglas Fox. His solemnity was a target for the good humoured darts of Eddie Hudson's wit. During his last year at Oxford he spent a good deal of time in Sweden where he got engaged to a charming Swedish girl. There was no chance for them to get married—just another of those war tragedies. Eddie Hudson, Arthur and I took a house together in Wellington Square for our last year at the University, each of course having our own suite of rooms.

I am afraid that I never let my work and studies spoil my social experiences of Oxford, nor bring me to the edge of a nervous breakdown as did three or four of the "First chasers" I knew: men who worked twelve to fourteen hours a day during their second and third years. I never worked after eleven at night, whereas Eddie Hudson rarely worked before that hour. He never seemed to need sleep. I have always been a "sleepy Williams", though not like my grandfather Alexander, still able to sleep the clock round when over seventy.

During my first two and a half years I went in for a good deal of sport. My first spring term I rowed (not very successfully) in our Second College Torpid having been in a winning four in the Michaelmas Term. All summer we played tennis hard. Then in the autumn I took to the running track and won about £30 of prizes in University races: Hundreds, Two-twenties and Quarter Miles. At one time I had vague hopes of becoming Oxford's second string for the Hundred Yards against Cambridge; but the arrival of one or two American Rhodes Scholars from California credited with impressive "records", put an end to that—although incidentally these Trans-Atlantic athletes never equalled their Californian performances in England. For two seasons I was President of the Exeter College Athletic Club and arranged a very pleasant Sports Fixture (and Dinner) with Corpus Christi College, Cambridge, their President, the sprinter Abrahams being their leading athlete and a Blue. The match was a draw which gave pleasure to both Colleges. They invited us to come to Cambridge for a return match the next year, little thinking of what was coming and that there would be no more sports for about six years. After the War the link I had forged was not renewed with Corpus but one with Emmanuel substituted.

It was in the winter of 1913-14 that I began to have trouble with my health, a trouble from which I was not to be free until I was well over thirty. I had had a "grumbling appendix" since I was in my teens (I ultimately had the operation in February 1918) but the principle trouble was a most unpleasant form of dyspepsia with bouts of sickness and pain. Looking back I am pretty sure that I had something in the nature of a duodenal ulcer. I saw several specialists and tried various treatments; but it was not until at least six years after my appendectomy that I could eat what I liked with impunity. It was this trouble which made me twice fail the medical when I tried to join up in 1914 and 1915 after the War had started.

I inherited from my Murray Grandfather a love of the theatre and although I never found time to think of joining the O.U.D.S. I did a certain amount of amateur theatricals in Northern Ireland during the vacations. In Oxford the opportunity for seeing good plays were considerable. I saw the whole of Gilbert and Sullivan more than once, several operas and many notable straight plays before their London production. This put me on to reading all the dramatists I could lay my hands on. All this I felt was a part of my education. I fear that I read little poetry—apart from Shakespeare's Sonnets, and the whole of Keats. I tended to read far too much general literature whilst I had my schools in view, and I read the whole of R. L. Stevenson, Thomas Hardy, Charles Dickens and Thackeray. (I never could get on with Dickens as a boy—except for *A Tale of Two Cities*). Eddie Hudson was, as I have noted, my discriminating guide in French literature. I also read Tolstoy, Turgenev and Dostoievsky. I suppose I should have spent more time on my Anglo-Norman French Chronicles (St. Alban's and the like) and on Stubb's Charters, etc. When my Finals came along my "Special Subject" was one of my weaker papers.

Oxford did not do much for me in my religious life. No doubt this was my own fault. I had been deeply influenced by the first Vicar of St. Wilfred's, Harrogate, who had taught me something of the Catholicity of the Anglican Church and to worship in a building where there certainly was the beauty of holiness. Worcester Cathedral and its clever Residentiary Canons had also helped. I did not meet any equivalent influences in Oxford. Dr. Darwell Stone of Pusey House definitely intimidated me and did not inspire confidences whilst the "church's gang" did not appeal to us. Dr. N. P. Williams, the Chaplain of Exeter, was kind and interesting but very reserved. The Chapel Services were rather "Public School". Eddie Hudson and I wandered round the Oxford Churches: St. Aldates (too Low and too hearty for our sophistication), St. Clement's (too dreary), St. Barnabas (too stereotyped). We were happiest at Christ Church Cathedral. The Services at New College and Magdalen were vaguely beautiful, but heaven seemed remote. One was "in the audience" there. The College Church Society was, like the hymn, a case of "Once, only once and once for all". During our time it was in the hands of extreme Evangelicals—good and earnest fellows no doubt. It is so easy for the young to be critical.

If I had to say something in answer to the question: "What did you get out of Oxford?" and put it as briefly as possible I should say something like this.

I learnt a lot but probably more outside my special studies than inside them. I think that I left Oxford as a moderately well read young man in English, French and Russian literature, and also with a very fair knowledge of art (painting) and architecture. I had also learnt a great deal more about human nature, and I hope about myself. Something was done to modify the awful effects of being a one and only child, brought up in a home without any male parental influence or guidance. Perhaps the most useful thing which Oxford taught me was how to *use* my mind and powers, such as they were: how to collect and marshall my facts and how to systematise my work. All this was quite invaluable when I got into large and busy parishes. When one was successively Vicar of such large parishes as Banbury and Bournemouth, with large Rural Deaneries to manage also and thirty to forty Committees, there was no time to waste and the choice was between "streamlining" and floundering.

Perhaps Oxford with its beauty and culture, its blending of history and stability on one side and of novelty and change on the other, also helped one to get a fairly clear set of values and a good perspective on life. I do not think that I have often chased or mistaken shadows for substances, or been badly taken in by charlatans. Unlike some of my amiable Murray relations I have never taken it for granted that everyone I met was bound to be what they wished to be thought.

It has been my good fortune to meet and to get to know some of the very best and most outstanding people of Britain in the first half of this century. Of these Dr. T. B. Strong, Dean of Christ Church and twice Vice-Chancellor of the University was one of the greatest, the most brilliant and attractive. It was not however until later (1920) that I came into such close contact with him, so that I will not mention him any further during my references to people I met in my Oxford days. He comes later.

North Oxford, the abode of anxious mothers with eligible daughters, was rather a corney joke in those pre-war days—"the great unvisited". Our set at Exeter were fairly detached from anything in the way of romance or feminine entanglements, except perhaps Arthur Forrest. Occasionally one was introduced to ladies with houses in that "great unknown". I remember at all clearly only one such episode, when Eddie Hudson, Arthur Forrest and I were invited to dinner and to spend the evening by a certain determined matriarch. To begin with I thought it odd. There were no other guests (no female competitors). She had a rather pretty, slightly faded only daughter of perhaps twenty-six, (anyway much too old for any of us). Everything was beautifully done, the dinner, the silver, the china and Hilda's silvery evening frock. I noticed the gentle kindness of the lighting: nothing but candles in every room—so flattering. Arthur Forrest incautiously mentioned his specific interests in Sweden. At that period he could think and talk of little else. One noticed with amusement that after that disclosure Eddie and I were the sole targets of the two ladies. A little later I was asked by Mother in what part of Ireland my people's "place" was. I replied that my Mother and I were living with my grandmother until I was ordained. I think that after that Mother preferred Eddie, although I was perhaps vain enough to imagine that Hilda was definitely concentrating increasingly on me with those large flashing eyes and side long glances! I had them once to luncheon in return and then refused all further invitations. I have occasionally wondered what became of Hilda. She was remarkably like one of those rather tubercular looking young women Rossetti used to portray. I suppose all this sounds very old fashioned these days. I wonder how many (if any) young women would now languish at home whilst Mother brought in possible young men. The modern miss (in her jeans) would go out hunting on her own in her various circles and her parents would usually be quite out of date on the subject of her contemporary interests and matrimonial intentions.

I had when I came up to Oxford in the autumn of 1911 an introduction from a friend to Dr. Spooner, Warden of New College, of "Spoonerisms" fame. Although I was neither a Wykhamist nor a member of his College and he must have had an enormous number of young men on his busy hands, he showed me considerable kindness and entertained me more than once. He gave one the impression that people of the albino type often do—that they do not see you very clearly; but unlike so many short-sighted people he certainly had no difficulty in making contacts and finding his way to the understanding of both your point of view and of you. I never myself heard an original "Spoonerism" while conversing with him, although of course Oxford was full of such stories. However I was to be provided some years later with a genuine one by Bishop Tommy Strong when I was his Chaplain and Secretary. Bishop Strong when Dean of Christ Church occasionally took a walk with the Warden of New College. It was a period when there was a good deal of unemployment and "the House" was trying to find work for some of the unemployed, by having stone flags placed in some of the paths in Christ Church Meadows. As they passed some of these men at work Dr. Spooner waved his stick in their direction:

"One of the employments of the unimproved, I suppose."—not quite on the lines of "Kinkering Kongs" or "the Shoving Leopard"; but nice.

I also had the pleasure of meeting Dr. Daniell, the Provost of Worcester College. The circumstances were, I felt, a little awkward. I had been elected at Worcester to an Exhibition (Modern History) of £50 a year on one of my trips from School to Oxford Scholarship Examinations. When I was a little later awarded a Scholarship of twice the value at Exeter, I called to resign. Dr. Daniell was charming and put his arm round my shoulder and said:

"My dear boy, of course we will be sorry to lose you; but you would be foolish not to resign here and accept what Exeter are offering you. I only wish we could say that we could double your exhibition here."

He showed me his famous printing press and some of his beautiful books from it. He had a rare warmth and charm.

One of the interesting (and strangest) people I got to know

during my Oxford days, but whilst on vacation in Larne, Northern Ireland, was Sir Roger Casement. The Casements were old friends of my Murray grandfather, the old Admiral having been a particular friend. They were of Scottish and Manx origin, *not* Irish, curiously enough. Roger was left an orphan in his teens and my grandfather was one of his Guardians. There were relatives at Ballycastle, Co. Antrim, and the boy used sometimes to spend part of his School holidays at Ballymena Rectory. My Mother described him as not only strikingly handsome but as an intelligent, sensitive and gentle youth: always ready to champion the weak and the downtrodden, loving animals and abhorring cruelty to them. He was very popular with her and her brothers as well and with the King boys (the sons of Dr. King of the Ballymena Academy). I was about nineteen when I first met him. He had just (1911) received a knighthood from King George V in recognition of his fine humanitarian work over the Putowayo atrocities. He came and stayed a night and I thought him one of the most interesting and delightful of men. Much of his conversation with my Mother was of course over "old times". It was nearly twenty years since they had met; but he told us a good deal of his travels in Africa and South America and was most modest about his own achievements. He was full of wit and fun. About a year later he came to see us again. We both noticed the enormous change. Gone was all the sparkle and brightness. He looked ill and worried and after he had left Mother spoke sadly of him to me.

"I have never known anyone change so in such a short time."

She went on to say that she hoped that his mind was not becoming affected. There had been something of that sort of trouble in some branches of the Casement family. As an illustration of all this she added:

"Do you know he actually told me that he was quite convinced that the British Government was trying to take his life! He had found out that his valet had been approached and offered money to poison him! It sounds absolutely mad."

We never saw him again. We returned to England to live at Kidderminster where I had my first curacy at St. John's Church in 1915.

Meantime Roger had passed out of our ken. Although we did not know it, he had been in the U.S.A. and then in Germany for some time and was getting very involved in anti-British schemes. The story of the fiasco of his landing in Southern Ireland in April 1916, just before the Easter Rebellion in Dublin is too well known for me to need to describe it. The obvious point was that the

Germans had at last realised that he was too mentally unbalanced to be of any practical use to them and they were anxious to get rid of him. He was cynically deserted by them and was a prisoner within a few hours of his landing. In my opinion his trial was not a thing that English people have much to be proud of. He should never have been condemned and hanged: he should have been certified and put into a mental home. Dr. Randell Davidson, the then Archbishop of Canterbury, I know, thought that Roger Casement was mentally affected as did Lord Bryce. However the War was going badly. Scapegoats were wanted and here was someone who was expendable. Actually if he had been put under protective detention and given psychiatric treatment the name of Britain in the U.S.A. would have shone more brightly, and perhaps the American legions might have appeared on the European scene rather sooner, stopped the slaughter and brought the War to a speedier conclusion. Anyway enormous anti-British propaganda was made out of this case in the U.S.A. and in other parts of the world. There were two particularly mean aspects of the whole affair. Accusations of moral perversion were sedulously spread. Whether the so-called Black Diaries were genuine or not was beside the point. He was *not* on trial for questions of personal morality. It was all raked up to smother sympathy for a mentally unbalanced man who honestly believed himself to be a patriot however open to criticism for his way of showing it. The deprivation of his knighthood also just before his execution was shabby. The knighthood had been given for good work done in the past —a work which was not undone by what happened later. My Mother who had known him so long certainly did not think the man was really responsible in his last few years. It was a horrible tragedy. The whole technique was rather like taking a sledge-hammer to kill a fly.

CHAPTER VII

Salisbury

AS I had been rejected for Military Service because of my digestive troubles, after leaving Oxford I went to Salisbury Theological College at the beginning of 1915. It had been arranged that when ordained I should start my work in the Worcester Diocese, as the then Bishop of Worcester, Dr. Yeatman Biggs, had a preference for this particular college. One reason for this, I gathered, was that the tone was "neither too High nor too Low". Another was that the training given had a practical side which few, if any other of the theological colleges in England gave at this particular period. The students "ran" various little Mission Churches and Chapelries in Salisbury and district. A senior student (under supervision) was "the Vicar" and a junior "the Curate". They visited, took Evensongs, and preached. The experience gained in these ways was most valuable. Stage-fright and some of the cruder failings of the green young curate were got out of the system before ordination. Our critics were our fellow students and forthright and to the point they could be! I shall never forget my tremors before my first pulpit performance. I was allowed to choose my subject together with appropriate lessons and hymns, etc. I chose to speak about "Christ as the Good Shepherd", and had the Twenty-third Psalm, and of course the parable of the Good Shepherd. The hymns were "The Lord my pasture shall prepare" (Addison's lovely poem and still my favourite hymn) and "The King of love my Shepherd is". I was as nervous as on my wedding day and the same thing happened on both occasions. I do not remember any single detail of either occasion. I know that several of my fellow students came and sat in the two front pews: but that is all. However the agony of my first sermon bore one fruit.

I never really felt nervous again, not even when I preached my first sermon in a Cathedral at the ripe age of twenty-eight, in the presence of a Dean and three Canons, and of a large though typical Cathedral congregation of bald heads and nodding bonnets.

We were lectured on teaching and had to take classes in some of the Church Schools in the city. This was sometimes under the "awful eye" of the famous and redoubtable Miss Forth, the Principal of the Church of England Training College in the Cathedral Close. In addition to these very practical advantages Salisbury Theological College had at that time an exceptionally strong staff. The Rev. C. T. Dimont (later Canon and Chancellor) was our Principal, the Vice-Principal was the Rev. Eric Graham (later Principal of Cuddesdon and the then Bishop of Brechin). Our third lecturer was none other than the Rev. William Wand (later Archbishop of Brisbane, and then successively Bishop of Bath and Wells and of London). We were indeed fortunate.

Chancellor Dimont, as he was later to be, was a likable, wide-awake and challenging personality. His burning desire for social justice earned him (at any rate in those days in the Cathedral Close) the reputation of being "rather red". He had sarcastic remarks to make about septuagenarian Deans and Canons who stuck like limpets to their emoluments and positions. Later his ideas must have changed or mellowed as he himself died as Chancellor and Residentiary Canon well on in his eighties. His lectures were clear, emphatic and Catholic (very Anglo- and not at all Romano-) and to the point. He had some considerable anti-Roman attitudes. We had amongst our students a curious but attractive little Englishman named Eustace Virgo, who had lived for many years in Rome and had been of the Roman Catholic faith. Perhaps it was a too close proximity to the Head-quarters of that Church, or the glimpses which he had got behind the scenes, which made him enter the Anglican Church when about fifty years of age. Actually he never got ordained. Some-times when the Principal brought out some of his illustrations of the errors or extravagances of Rome, Virgo used to jump to his feet and cry:

"Pardon me, Principal, but I must point out that what you are saying is not really so."

There would then ensue a fifteen minutes wrangle, whilst the rest of us would sit in silent amusement. Neither ever gave in and ultimately the Principal would glance at his watch and say,

"Well, I think that it is *I* who am supposed to be giving this lecture, so I will NOW resume."

Dimont was a keen chess player and was reputed never to have suffered defeat at the hands of any of his pupils. One wet Satur-day he asked me if I played and on my admitting that I did occa-sionally we had three games. I am afraid that I won them all. His chess playing went on; but I was never invited to play with him again! He had a dry sense of humour. Many amusing anecdotes from his contacts with blunt Yorkshire folk in his former parish in Halifax spiced and illustrated his Pastoralia lectures. Remembered, they acted like "cautionary tales", when I went visiting on my Kidderminster Curacy and I avoided many pitfalls.

Eric Graham was an entirely different type. A most saintly man, he also had a delicious, not to say more subtle sense of humour. After W. F. Swann, first Vicar of St. Wilfrid's, Harrogate, I think that he was one of the greatest influences on me spiritually, in my earlier and more impressionable days. One of his most saintly qualities was his genuine humility. Hard on himself, he was often lenient to others, although he could turn the searchlight right on to people's weaknesses if he thought that it was needful. He could also puncture pomposity with the sharpness of his wit as well as anyone I ever met. The more intelligent of the students deeply appreciated him. Some of the more stolid and less easily "air-borne" specimens just did not "get there". One of his best remarks came to me some years later when William Wand succeeded him as Dean of Oriel at Oxford. Wand had been at Oriel perhaps two terms and they were comparing notes. Wand said:

"I feel rather like a bull in a china-shop."
Eric Graham retorted:
"I often felt more like the china"!

It was a great thing to be brought into contact with William Wand. Actually it was later than during my time that he did much at the College; but we were privileged to partake also of his very considerable gifts. To his most charming and very living personality he added all the gifts which go with a powerful mind which at once grasps the essentials of any situation or problem. The Wands were both extremely kind and hospitable in welcoming me to their home and we used to lend each other books. I remember him thanking me for introducing him to the poetry and writings of William Blake which he had not previously encountered.

Quite candidly after Oxford I found the general social and intellectual life of the College a little dull and stuffy, and greatly enjoyed escaping to the Wands, to the Deanery and the Archdeacons Carpenter's and Buchanan's homes. About twice or three times a term Eric Graham and I, who were the only two possessors of motor cycles, used to go out on a "Church crawl", visiting many of the finer churches of that part of England—Sherborne Abbey, Christchurch Priory, Wimborne Minster and

Romsey Abbey, as well as some of the outstanding Parish Churches in the area. We had a common interest in architecture. Our greatest love was Wells Cathedral, which I still think has strong claims to be considered the most perfect ecclesiastical building in England.

Some years later I was staying with Bishop T. B. Strong at Cuddesdon Palace, and Dr. Seaton had just left the Theological College for Wakefield. Dr. Strong was worried about finding the right man to be the new Principal of that most important of English Theological Colleges. He mentioned various names, adding that in spite of many outstanding qualities none of those whom he had named seemed to be quite right for this position. Remembering the wonderful work and influence of Eric Graham at Salisbury, and all that he had done for me and many others I ventured to say:

"I know whom I would put at the top of the list if the responsibility for this appointment were mine."

Bishop Strong pressed me to say whom I had in mind. I replied:

"Eric Graham seems to have the right qualities."

The Bishop at once exclaimed: "Now that *is* an idea! "

How delighted I was to see the announcement of this appointment only a few weeks later.

After Bishop Graham's death in 1964 the obituary article in The Church Times acclaimed this appointment of Dr. Strong's as one of his greatest benefits to the Church of England.

Naturally I entirely agreed!

The interior of Salisbury Cathedral left us both rather cold. It was not then anything like as attractive as it is today, with the removal of much Gilbert Scottiana and its restored long vistas. Dean Page Roberts of Salisbury was in those days that city's greatest "character". He was extremely friendly to me although on the whole he did not appear to get to know many of the college students. I was asked alone to the Deanery sufficiently frequently for the Principal to remonstrate. The Dean could be amusingly naughty and did not mind blowing his own trumpet. Two or three of his conversations with me are still well remembered. He did not like what he called High Church "fal-lals"; but he certainly should never have made the following remark to a young ordinand.

"Our Bishop of Sarum is a dear good little man; and he is always more than welcome in my Cathedral—as long as he leaves his 'man-millinery' outside". (Cope and Mitre). Of himself, he once said to me:

"I have been considered no mean preacher. When I was in London at Vere Street Chapel I used to look down the crowded congregation and see Admiral Lord Fisher, Mrs. Humphrey Ward and usually one or two Cabinet Ministers, as well as many others prominent in Society in those days". He told me also how he normally prepared those wonderful vintage sermons, which were always such "finished" performances.

"On Monday I take a text for the next Sunday. On Tuesday I select and lay out my subject after a conversation with my wife. On Wednesday I read the draft to Mrs. Page Roberts and discuss it with her. On Thursday I write it out again. On Friday I read it again to my wife. Sometimes she has some valuable little suggestions. On Saturday I read her the final version with the inflections and entire manner of the actual delivery as to be used in the Cathedral."

The Hon. Mrs. Page-Roberts was obviously a very Christian and patient woman.

The Dean had two boxes of cigarettes, one for the generality, and a much more exotic brand for himself and the favoured few. I was always offered the latter—with a wink—when alone with him.

The work at the College I found interesting—The Old Testament, The New Testament, The Prayer Book, Church History (Early and English), Doctrine and Pastoralia. We also had a set book for our ordination examination. My one was Galatians and I worked at it hard. Imagine my feelings when the papers came and the questions on "the set book" were on Colossians! I firmly refused to do it and succeeded in getting one in Galatians in the end! On our terminal examinations we were awarded "Firsts", "Seconds" and "Thirds". E. W. Sara (later Assistant Bishop in Jamaica, Bath and Wells and finally in Hereford) Tom Chamberlain (a very studious Londoner) and I usually got "Firsts". I fancy that the marking of papers was not unkind!

Some of the other students were quite interesting. All were very kind friendly folk. One or two were men who were obviously never going to pass any ordination examination. One dear soul who had already been three or four years at the college (and was no nearer the possibility of passing anything) was the most amiable of men; but a sad victim of clichés. Apparently he also (like some others one meets) found it impossible to listen to what anyone else said. His two great comments on other people's remarks, as he brushed them aside, were:

"Splendid, splendid", or "How nice, *how very nice*".

One day when he was visiting a young woman in his "district", the following conversation took place:

"Oh, Mr. X, I am in such trouble, I have just heard that my brother out in France, is reported missing."

Pat came the answer:

"Splendid, splendid. How nice, *how very nice*". The effect can be imagined.

Tom Long (who would have been better named Tom Broad) both because of his breadth and bulk and the width of his sympathies, was I think, the nicest and best man in college: over forty and with a warmth of kindness and understanding, beyond us younger ones, he made an ideal Senior Student. Ordained in the diocese of Salisbury he later became a much loved and devoted Vicar of Brixham. Unfortunately for his friends and parishioners he died quite suddenly in early middle age. I suppose that he had been dead well on to a quarter of a century when I visited his former Parish Church, and I asked one or two of the people there if they remembered him. There was only one opinion about him.

"Indeed we do remember him. He was one of the best and kindest of men. He wore himself out for others." A fine epitaph.

Eric Graham taught us something of the rich mysteries of meditation. William Wand stimulated our minds and sense of vocation. The Principal gave us a very good working idea of the kind of problems we would be up against when we got out of the sheltered (almost cloistered) atmosphere of our seminary, into the wicked world. The routine life taught us the merits of regularity in our devotions.

What more could a University graduate gets out of the somewhat muted life of a Theological College after the so much more colourful surroundings of three years at Oxford?

As at Worcester Cathedral in my schooldays, so at Salisbury I met personally with much kindness from the Cathedral dignitaries; but the music and services at Salisbury were poor in comparison with those at Worcester, where Choir, and Organ, and preaching had all been of the highest quality; and the congregation had been the largest that I have ever seen in a provincial Cathedral.

During my time at my theological college I was still living at Larne in Northern Ireland with my Mother and Grandmother. The contrast between the two atmospheres was amazing. At Salisbury there was work and worship against the immediate background of the peace and beauty of the Cathedral Close, assuredly one of the loveliest in England; but outside that oasis the war, increasing continually in its pressure on people's lives, was becoming clangorous. The whole of Salisbury Plain was a seething mass of troops and manoeuvres. People were beginning to realise that Britain was up against it and in for an experience which she had never had before and which she might perhaps not even survive.

In Northern Ireland the war seemed much further away. The glorious Antrim countryside was quiet and calm. Although recruiting in Northern Ireland was as good as in any part of the British Isles, people were not becoming obsessed with the anxieties which were beginning to wear down their brethren across the Irish Sea. The cool Protestantism of the Church of Ireland in Larne was still as calm and unruffled as it had been a generation earlier. The learned and eloquent Rector of Larne and Inver, Mr. Andrew Boyd (ex-Presbyterian Schoolmaster and Minister) was still preaching little literary gems on the poems of Robert Browning. During my vacations my Irish girl cousins (Ruth and Nora Killen) and I were still having our picnics on the Antrim coast and Larne was as full as ever of its modest social gaieties. It was a confusing experience to be backwards and forwards three or four times in the year between two such different atmospheres and tensions.

In the late autumn of 1915 I went to Dudley to be interviewed by (and to interview) the Vicar of St. John's Church. He was a large domineering man, with a sense of humour which seemed to me to be like that of a rhinoceros (if such an animal has one). Whenever he spoke he shouted and was better at asking questions than answering them. He said that it was a pity that I had been to Oxford instead of to Cambridge. (Need I say that he was a Cambridge man.) I asked about the work of the Parish. His reply amounted to "Wait and see"! I met a poor down trodden little curate who in the two minutes during which he and I were left alone together, said to me in a whisper,

"Oh, I do hope that you will come. I should enjoy working with you until you were priested *and then I could get away*".

When I was leaving Dudley the next morning the Vicar slapped me on the back and roared:

"Well, I think perhaps you might do; but I will be writing to your Principal first, so don't expect to hear from me for at least a week."

Actually he heard from me two days later. I said that I did not think that I was cut out to work with him and that my instinct was that I had better say so at once. I added that I had discussed the question with the Principal on my return, and that he had agreed that I had better look elsewhere. I got a scorching reply. It was quite plain that I was workshy and afraid of coming to a Parish with *eight* thousand people in it, etc., etc. The noisy tone of his letter confirmed my view that I had made a wise decision. A few weeks later I went to see the Vicar of St. John's, Kidderminster, the Rev. R. W. D. Stephenson, who, although not having had the advantage of being at Cambridge had taken a First Class Honours degree at Oxford and was an Examining Chaplain to the Bishop of Birmingham. He was also a charming, modest and pleasant man and obviously had some consideration for other people's feelings. I met both his Curates who spoke warmly of him, although they were both on the point of going off as Army Chaplains. I was happy to receive the offer of a Curacy from Mr. Stephenson. As I had not yet replied to the furious letter from Dudley I did so now, saying that I had duly received his communication and that I was sure that he would be pleased to hear that I was going to work in a Parish which had nearly *twelve* thousand people. I also said that I thought that Mr. Stephenson would be a most helpful and understanding first Vicar to work under. I got no reply; but when the reverend gentleman and I met later at Diocesan gatherings the rencontres were invariably aimiable.

There were seven or eight deacons and three priests at the Ordination at Worcester Cathedral on St. Thomas' Day 1915. I had the honour of being Gospeller. I had a curious little interview with Bishop Yeatman Biggs the previous day. He asked me if I had made my confession. I said: "No."

"Why not?"

"I am not sure that it would be helpful to me—at any rate at present."

"Well it is a question of—of. . . ."

"Temperament?"

"Certainly not. That is exactly what it is *not*. It is a question of whether you have anything to confess." He paused.

"All the other candidates have made their confessions."

"I am afraid that I am then going to be the only one who has not, my Lord." There was a long silence. Then he said:

"The other matter I wished to discuss with you is the question of marriage. I insist that you promise not to get engaged to be married until you have been two years in Orders."

"I have certainly never yet considered the question of matrimony. I imagine that it will be many years before I could contemplate it: if ever.”

“That is not exactly the point. I desire you promise before your Ordination.”

“I would rather not promise, but—”

“I insist.”

“Then I do so; but only under pressure and with protest.” Another long silence. Finally the Bishop continued:

“There is a third matter of which I hoped it would give me great pleasure to speak. It does not do so quite so much now. None the less your examination papers were so definitely ahead of all the others that I cannot do other than invite you to be the Gospeller at the ordination tomorrow.”

“Thank you very much, my Lord. I shall feel greatly honoured.”

After affectionate and human Archbishop Crozier of Armagh, one of my Mother’s Godfathers, this handsome and wealthy prelate seemed somewhat absolute and baronial; but later on I got to like him very much. His daughter became rather a friend of my Mother’s, and some months later they both came to tea with us in our little house in Manor Avenue, Kidderminster. The Bishop who was more than friendly was looking with great interest at my Mother’s glass-fronted china cupboard.

“Why,” he said, “you have a very early Worcester teapot there—h’mm—crescent mark. Do you know that I have the whole tea-set to match—all *except* the teapot!” I ventured to suggest that we might try the Apostolic technique of drawing lots —our teapot against his tea-set; but the Bishop smiled and shook his head.

CHAPTER VIII

Two Curacies

a. Kidderminster (1915-18)

OUR MOVE from Ireland to Kidderminster was complicated by a dock strike in Belfast. This meant that our furniture did not arrive until two months after we did, and we had to go into rooms for eight weeks. My stipend according to the current rates began at £120 per annum; to rise to £150 per annum when I was priested.

My Mother and I arrived at St. John's, Kidderminster on 22nd December, 1915. Christmas Day provided my first experience in taking part in the Services in a really large Church and as an ordained member of the staff. I had one little *contre temps* at Matins when I sang the service and the Vicar preached. After the Benedictus I turned to the East and began to intone the Apostles Creed "I believe in God". (I have never approved of clergy singing merely and vaguely "I believe" . . . and leaving the rest hanging in the air). Immediately from the Vicar's stall and on the same note came a remonstrant rejoinder:

"No. No! Whosoever will be saved! "

I had forgotten in my newness to everything that Christmas Day was one of those on which the Prayer Book rubric enjoins the use of "The Athanasian Creed" (so-called). I do not think that I had encountered it twice in the previous ten years of my church going. Doing my best to recover from the shock I carried on. My Vicar was strictly Prayer Book; but I doubt whether ten years later he was still insisting on an effusion of faith, if not entirely of charity, which was neither a Creed nor by St. Athanasius.

In the long vacation which I had spent in Northern Ireland the summer before my ordination, I had some singing and elocution lessons in Belfast from a lady (a Mrs. Wale), who had been for many years with the Doyly-Carte Opera Company. She was a good teacher and we got on famously. The last time I visited her she surprised my by telling me that she had "second-sight" and she would tell me a few things about my future, if I liked. Who could refuse such an offer at twenty-three? Here are some of the things she told me in a very simple and straight forward way as she looked unemotionally into her crystal.

"I see you in your first curacy. There is a curious looking Church. The spire is small and black, the Church large and red. Inside there are three lancet windows at the East End, only the centre one has stained glass." This was three or four months before I had even fixed up to go and look at St. John's, Dudley and its redoubtable Vicar. It was also a very accurate description of St. John's, Kidderminster, where a large red stone building was fitted on to the small spire of the original little blackish brick church. I never saw this Church until after I had told the Vicar that I would be happy to accept his offer of the curacy. When I did visit it the next day I had a most curious sensation, as may be imagined. Is there such a thing as Time? Or is it a sometimes convenient convention? Such experiences provoke such questions. The lady also told me many things about my future life—my marriage, my family and my future appointments which were all curiously fulfilled during the course of the ensuing years. I do not indeed recollect anything she foretold which has not since come about. I would be closely associated with many very important people. I would not marry the first time that I met someone who interested me. I would have several daughters but only one son. My daughters would supply many grandchildren. I would have a long and happy married life. Rather late in life I would have the highest promotion in an opportunity of working abroad. This would be after I had been Vicar of a large church with a lofty spire. This church would be in the middle of a large town which appeared to be in some sort of holiday resort or seaside place. There were several large shops or stores round about this church. (This of course was a good description of St. Peter's, Bournemouth which I never saw until twenty years later.) She also told me that as I grew older my health would improve. Finally she saw me as an old man, white headed, active and a little deaf. Every one of these statements has been substantiated.

When I got to Kidderminster some four or five months after her description of a church that neither of us had seen nor heard of, I sent her two photographs, one of the outside of St. John's with its odd little blackish brick spire and the other of the east end of the interior with its *one* stained glass lancet between the two plain ones! Now of course all three lancets are filled with stained glass; but this was not so during my time there.

The large church of St. John the Baptist, Kidderminster, had a daughter church, "The Holy Innocents," in the growing Foley Park area. St. Mary's was the old Parish Church where Canon

L. B. Sladen reigned for so many years; but St. John's, for all its twelve thousand industrial parishioners, yet boasted the main residential areas and the residences of many of the local elite. There was plenty of work for a Vicar and two or even three Curates, with three Churches to serve and practically every known organisation that was fashionable in large and live Anglican Parishes at the beginning of the twentieth century: a Boys' Club (duplicated at Holy Innocents), a Girls' Club, three large Sunday Schools, a Parochial Scout Troop, a Men's Bible Class, a branch of the C.E.M.S. and of course, also the Mothers' Union and the Girls' Friendly Society (these last were however, considered taboo for all but the Vicar and the Senior Curate). The Senior Curate left a few weeks before I came. The second man, the Rev. D. H. S. Mould, an energetic Durham University rugger player, and a delightful and uninhibited person, went a few months later, but not before we had become very good friends.

Both went off as Army Chaplains. Mould used to write me amusing letters in which, even after he got to Mesopotamia, he was still wishing that he was back at his tough but happy job in the Parish instead of being, as he put it, a purveyor of cocoa and entertainments to the troops. For the next two years and eight months the Vicar and I kept all the organisations going, besides house to house visiting, dealing with long lists of sick people and two large Hospitals, one a Military Hospital. I soon also became Curate-in-Charge of Holy Innocents Church, where we had a flourishing Choir, a large Sunday School and a good congregation, characterised (in spite of wartime) by the notable preponderance of men and youths over women on most occasions. Early in my second year I taught for the Summer term at the Kidderminster Grammar School — Mathematics, English and History. I was certainly not qualified to teach the first of those subjects; but the boys apparently never found out. One at least never had a dull moment. Indeed it was quite fun. My Mother ran our little home admirably with the help of a nice young Irish maid from Larne (brought with us). She did a considerable amount of entertaining, and also taught in the Sunday Schools (boys only) and helped in many other ways. My Grandmother lived with us most of the time we were there and made many friends. She was now eighty-four; but extremely active and interested in everything. One lady, a Miss Chillingworth, a near neighbour and a member of a very old Worcestershire family, used to take my grandmother for drives. Grannie was properly appreciative of these kind attentions and consequently very vexed with herself because the lady's name often eluded her. I tried a little Pelmanism to aid an octogenarian memory:

"Grannie, the name is *Chillingworth*. Think of a *shilling's worth* of something and that will get you there."

"Splendid," she cried. The next day I heard her profusely thanking her friend at the garden gate on the return from a nice country outing.

"So very kind of you, dear Miss *Pennyfeather*." When I pointed out her mistake, she said:

"Well it's really your fault: making up all that nonsense about money."

The Kidderminster people were amazingly friendly and hospitable. To this day I am still in touch with some of my then chubby rosy scouts and cubs, now grey haired fathers; but most of the other friends have now passed on to a better world. One of my most intellectually stimulating friends was Mrs. Preen (née Sybil Brinton), a Jane Austen enthusiast and the author of an excellent novel in the Jane Austen manner, "finishing up" the lives of some Jane Austen's characters left unaccounted for or at least uncoupled in her own inimitable stories. In *Old Friends and New Fancies* Sybil Brinton was extremely successful in maintaining the style and atmosphere of the original novels and providing plots which were neither too original nor too closely fashioned after the fortunes of Elizabeth Bennett, Emma or other Austen heroines. Alas, not long after we left Sybil was knocked and killed by a passing car.

The clergy of Kidderminster and district was most sociable and friendly. I got a little half humorous criticism from the St. Mary's Curates (amongst who I had several close friends) because Canon Sladen, who never played golf with his own curates, used to play with me on various occasions. I pointed out to my critics that the sky would not fall if their august Vicar were beaten by some other incumbant's accomplice, although it might not help local discipline if he were too often worsted by his own!

The work of the Parish was unending and relentless, although extremely rewarding and happy. There were many sad incidents which seared one deeply. War casualties took young husbands, only sons and so on. In my sick visiting I worried terribly over the sufferings in both mind and body of many of my "chronic" cases. It is hard to soften the pains of those suffering from painful and incurable diseases, by speaking of the mysteries of suffering and the spiritual enlightenment which they can bring.

One could just go on praying and sympathising and being as cheerful as one could or perhaps as one dare. At least one was rewarded by an amazing response of gratitude and affection. The illness and deaths of some really charming young people from T.B., etc., were productive of some precious friendships and considerable heartbreak.

After a strenuous two years I finally, in February 1918, succumbed to my continuous and often painful dyspepsia and had to have my appendix removed or risk peritonitis. The operation was performed by Dr. Charles Hyde Cosens, our old family friend, who twenty-five years before had spent practically the whole of three days and nights at my father's bedside in Norfolk. I went to the Hyde-Cosens' home in Hitchen where he was then practising and was marvellously treated and cared for by the doctor and his wife. Two nurses were provided. Mother was also there. Apparently I was extremely exhausted and anæmic and took an alarmingly long time to come round after the anæsthetic. However after ten days in bed I made a good recovery and returned to work in just under a month. Unfortunately both my doctor friend and a Birmingham specialist insisted that I should leave Kidderminster and get to a place where the climate would suit my health better, and, if possible, provide a slightly less strenuous job. I found the former of these two requisites (but not the latter) in a Curacy at Christchurch, Harrogate, where the bracing champagne-like air soon built me up, and I was eagerly tackling a situation with at least as many demands as that in Kidderminster. I got the Harrogate Curacy against the competition of five or six other men through a rather curious coincidence. I gave amongst other references the names of two of the other Harrogate incumbents. One was dear old Mr. Alexander, the Vicar of St. John's, Bilton, now aged ninety-two but still amazingly alert and active. The other was the Rev. W. F. Swann, Vicar of St. Wilfrid's. Both, said Canon Guy, spoke well of me and had known me since early boyhood. These two gentlemen were rarely in agreement on any subject and hardly even on speaking terms, the first a firm Evangelical and the latter a definite Anglo-Catholic; but they did agree about me, Canon Guy therefore thought that he could safely decide on appointing me.

I think my Mother and I were both extremely sad to leave friendly Worcestershire and the kindly people of St. John's and Holy Innocents, Kidderminster. We departed on the 31st October just before the Armistice, laden with gifts which included a "very useful" cheque.

I had learnt a lot about pastoralia and human nature in my two years and nine months in that large Parish. My kind and learned Vicar had perhaps hardly been an instructor in the direct sense of the word. Only once when I was first due to preach did he ask to see the manuscript of my proposed sermon. Whenever he gave advice or comments on my preaching they were always kind and constructive suggestions rather than criticisms. His advice on current problems came not gratuitously but when asked for, and was always gentle, wise and Christian, not unmixed with humour. I liked him very much and sympathised with his many troubles. A clever though shy man he had succeeded an extrovert old bachelor parson who had been a popular "father-figure" in the Parish for years. Rex Stephenson was never appreciated there as he should have been. The many spinsters who had had hopes of Canon Kershaw up to the day of his departure, were inclined to be critical of him from the first. A married man with a large family was much less interesting to them. Mrs. Stephenson, rather worn down by motherhood was not particularly tactful. "Curt Gert" was her nickname amongst the congregation. I remember one unmarried and hard working lady say of her:

"The trouble with Gertrude Stephenson is that she appears to regard her husband's Parish as a distasteful appendage to a house and five hundred pounds a year." This was rather severe. I think that they were not without financial anxieties. He was a marvellous gardener (too much so said the Parish); but he grew all the vegetables the Rectory needed—no mean task with such a large family to feed.

Amongst the curates at St. Mary's of whom I saw most was Reynolds, a Cambridge Rugger Blue who confided in me that the first time he "took" Baptisms at the Parish Church he had to deal with eight squalling babies. Having some fear that the sacrament might be invalidated by inaudibility he attempted (unsuccessfully) to shout them down. His final comment was:

"I sweated more than during the Varsity Rugger Match."

I do not think that I have ever worked harder or with more appreciation than I did at Kidderminster. It was a twelve hour a day proposition rather than an eight hour a day job; and the work was extremely varied. It was odd as a deacon of four months standing to become practically "Vicar" of an area with over three thousand people and quite a large congregation with as many organisations as are to be found in most busy Parish

Churches. However it was wartime and one never refused any responsibility. When one learns by "trial and error" the lessons learnt are not forgotten. What had seemed alarming at Kidderminster had become routine by the time I got to Harrogate. I had certainly learnt not to waste time nor to be unsystematic in my work. It was in Kidderminster that I met the nice girl with whom I played tennis, but whom I did not marry. If I had, I should definitely have suffered considerably from mother-in-law trouble. Enough said.

b. Harrogate (1918-20)

ECCLESIASTICALLY, HARROGATE was a somewhat amorphous place. Unlike its great neighbour, Leeds, it had no "Vicar". In my days however there were three clergy anyway who had ambitions. They were the Vicar of Christchurch (my Vicar), the Vicar of St. Mary's, and the Vicar of St. Peter's. Rumour had it that there was a register in a certain Swiss hotel which all three had signed at different times, adding after their respective names "Vicar of Harrogate". If this was not true in fact, it was not far off the mark otherwise. The Vicar of Christchurch could and did claim to be Vicar of High Harrogate; the Vicar of St. Mary's, Vicar of Low Harrogate; whilst the Vicar of St. Peter's could say that his church was in the very centre of things and was *par excellence* the "Town Church" of this very pleasant place.

My mother and I arrived in Harrogate in October 1918 and duly installed ourselves in a roomy house in Christchurch Parish, No. 81, East Parade. My Grandmother was with us nearly the whole of the two years and three months we spent there. Mother was asked almost at once to take on the Superintendency of the Senior Boys Sunday School.

My Vicar and his family were quite interesting people. Mrs. Guy was rather an invalid and was unable to take any part in the work of the Parish; but she was a kind and charming woman and invariably nice to us. She had a brother who was a Residentiary Canon of Canterbury and the Vicar's views were not always her's. They always took their holidays separately, she visited relatives and friends, he usually went after Christmas to Switzerland. I remember my surprise when I once visited her and she said to me "How would you like it if you were me, and you came back from your Summer holiday and found that your husband had taken your lovely sunny drawing room and made it into his study during your absence?" I had to do some rapid thinking before making a reply that was at once sufficiently sympathetic and non-partisan. It was a revealing moment. I had unwittingly opened the flood-gates by saying quite innocently, "I hope that you are glad to be back home." The family of five daughters and four sons were all nice and capable people.

The Reverend Douglas Sherwood Guy himself was a "character", almost on a level with Sir George Sitwell, immortalised for his eccentricities by his gifted son Sir Osbert. A scholar of Trinity, Cambridge, with a First Class in Theology, he had been a member of the "Auckland Brotherhood" under Bishop Westcott at Durham. He had thus been one of a group of promising young clerics who, with the exception of himself had all gone far in the Church. When I came to him in 1918 he was a small red faced bald headed man with a curiously sing-song manner of speech. He must have been in the late sixties; but it was not until I was leaving at the end of 1920 that he achieved an Hon. Canonry of Ripon Cathedral. There was no doubt that Canon Guy had in certain ways an active and resourceful brain; but he had a tortuous naivete of mind which defied prediction. "One never knew where one had got him," was the verdict of one of his most outstanding curates, Chancellor Harrison of York Minister. This was endorsed by many others. I had applied for "the Senior Curacy of Christchurch Harrogate," as advertised in the *The Church Times* and had been duly appointed. I suppose that I therefore fondly thought of myself as Senior Curate, although for the moment I was the only one. However, when I had been just about a year in the Parish, grappling with at least as much as I had ever shouldered in Kidderminster, one of the great ladies of the congregation stopped me in the street and said:

"I can't tell you how sorry I am to see in the paper that you are leaving! "

"That is very nice of you, Mrs. ———, but I am *not* leaving! "

"Oh, surely! Anyway I see that the Vicar has an advertisement in *The Church Times* again, seeking for a *Senior Curate,* so I thought it meant that we were losing you."

Thinking that I ought to find out the true inwardness of all this, I called the same morning at the Vicarage and asked for an elucidation of the situation. The following is what I got.

"Yes, of course, I am more than satisfied with your work; but you *look too young,* Williams. You are twenty-seven no doubt, but you look a mere boy! I must have someone who *'looks* the part' more. I know that my former advertisement which you answered said 'Senior curate'; but how was I to know that you would look so young?"

I replied that I thought that if I was fitting the bill my appearance was a secondary consideration. The Vicar's final plea was:

"Be a good Christian my dear boy. Stand down this once and I solemnly promise that I will never, I repeat *never* pass you over again."

In a short time a new Senior Curate arrived, five years older than I, very bald and comparatively venerable looking, but alas, poor man, almost completely deaf. He was an excellent and able person, a First Class Honours man from Cambridge, a former Theological College Vice-Principal at Westcolt House. More recently he had been Senior Curate of Wakefield Cathedral. We became very good friends and when he married a few months later he asked me to be his best man. He was the Rev. Frank Conquest Clare and the wedding took place at St. Michael's Church, Wakefield.

About the same time a third curate arrived, the Rev. Basil R. Buchanan, late of Trinity College Cambridge and Ripon Hall, Oxford, and he also became one of my closest life long friends.

Unfortunately, neither Clare nor Buchanan, although such very different types, remained on friendly terms with our excellent Vicar for very long. Buchanan wrote some quite able letters in the Yorkshire Post which attracted a considerable amount of attention. Guy was not pleased. "Deacons should be seen and not heard." The Vicar was a more suitable person to write letters in the papers. There was a great row and Buchanan left to become Curate to R. H. Malden, the very outstanding Vicar of Headingley (later Dean of Wells). As the confidant of both contestants I had a difficult time in maintaining a benevolent neutrality.

Nor did Clare remain for long on good terms with the Vicar. Guy went shortly after Christmas for his usual lengthy holiday in Switzerland, where he financed a ten or twelve weeks sojourn abroad by taking a Chaplaincy. Clare and I were left together to grapple with Lent which came early that year. We (mainly Clare) planned a spiritual marathon: special articles in the Parish Magazine, extra Lent courses of Addresses, etc. Imagine Clare's righteous indignation when he found, when the February issue of the Parish Magazine appeared, that his carefully devised spiritual uplift article was entirely omitted (owing to shortness of space) to make room for the Vicar's racy letter from Switzerland, expatiating ad lib on the quality of the food in the hotel in which he was housed, the number of V.I.P.s he was meeting and how no less a person than the Queen of Greece had informed him that she had never heard the Scriptures more beautifully rendered at Sunday Matins than by himself! Clare took care that in the Church Magazine there were no more menus or social chatter from the Alps, and that his own articles went in in full. Score one all! The Vicar arrived back on Maunday Thursday and before Easter there was war. The Vicar told Clare that he was insubordinate and impossible. Clare told the Vicar that he could no longer work with a man so lacking in all spirituality. He too left.

I was sorry to lose the companionship and help of my two colleagues; but at least I was again Senior Curate—or was I? Back came the advertisement in *The Church Times* "Vacancy for Senior Curate at Christchurch Harrogate." I expostulated and reminded the Vicar of his explicit and solemn promise not to pass me over again. "Ah, but Williams, when I made that promise I did not know that Clare would stay a bare year! Besides, you don't look any older! " "That is not the point Vicar. A promise is a promise. I will not stand down again." I was determined to give in my notice when my next quarterly cheque was due. Another Senior Curate was duly produced, a nice gentle and somewhat fragile little man in the late thirties. I was however saved from having to hand in my notice by the unexpected offer of the post of Domestic Chaplain and Secretary to the new Bishop of Ripon, Dr. T. B. Strong, late Dean of Christ Church, Oxford. Together with the offer of this interesting work went the Incumbency of the small Parish of North Stainley, outside Ripon, the Parish in which the Bishop resided. Within a few days of my acceptance of the Bishop's offer, the Vicar at some local function made a speech which was reproduced in the local papers. It was a disquisition on the many curates he had had in a long career, the two most outstanding of so many good men being the late Bishop of Suffragan of Stafford and the Rev. A. L. E. Williams now leaving to take on the very responsible work of Chaplain and Secretary to the Bishop of the Diocese!

I am afraid that there were a few cynical comments, and they were not confined to members of my household.

Another aspect of my Vicar's manœuvring which gave me food for thought was the question of my salary. How was it that he could only afford to give me £180 per annum when I was the only curate in the Parish and yet could give Clare and Buchanan salaried curacies as well? This was still before the days of Parochial Church Councils. One day the Chairman (Treasurer) of the Parish Vestry stopped me as I was walking across The Stray:

"By the by I do hope that you are pleased with your increase of salary?"

I was completely nonplussed.

"Increase of salary?"

"Yes. You were only having £180 last year and you have worked like a horse. It was the unanimous vote of the Vestry, with the exception of the Vicar, that your stipend should be raised from £180 to £250 per annum. That was over four months ago. Surely you had your increased quarterly cheque last month? The Vicar was to tell you all about it when he sent you your cheque. As a matter of fact I thought that you might perhaps have sent me a little note about it."

"I have had no increase of salary. This is absolutely the first I have heard of the whole business. The Vicar has not said a word." I am sorry to say that Mr. Jowett swore—but not at me.

Later that day I saw the Vicar and said what was on my mind. He was very suave:

"Ah yes Williams, The Vestry did vote to raise your salary four months ago, but they said nothing about *when* the increase should begin! I had thought of waiting until next year."

"Mr. Jowett said that the understanding was that I should have it at once."

"You shall, you shall."

Sometimes the Vicar was very amusing (generally unconsciously) and many were the good stories told about him by his former curates including the Rev. J. A. S. Griffiths (who married his second daughter) and the Rev. Fred Harrison, later so many years Chancellor of York Minister. I shall however confine my reminiscences to my first hand experiences.

"Williams, I am very sorry that I cannot take Baptisms this coming Sunday afternoon. I know that you have taken most Sunday afternoons lately, but I have a *most* important engagement."

"Actually I have an engagement too Vicar."

"Well I am sorry, but you must just turn up late for it and excuse yourself."

I did. My engagement was a tea-party at the beautiful home of one of our local great ladies. The other guest was the Vicar, who was very surprised and not too pleased to encounter me there, even over half an hour late. On my walk home he accompanied me, nothing abashed.

"It is quite all right, Williams, for you to know some of our 'nicer' people, but I think I can say that it is better for my curates normally to confine their attentions to the *poor* of the Parish and leave the *rich* to me."

On the Sunday before Christmas the Vicar gave out the following impassioned notice to an amused congregation: "Will you all please return your Missionary Boxes to me at the Vicarage, not later than the 31st December, as I start for my annual holiday in Switzerland on 2nd January."

He could not see it, even when it was slowly explained to him by a laughing Churchwarden in the Vestry after the Service.

Another day it was:

"At the end of this service, our Organist will be giving a short organ recital. I do beg musical members of the congregation to endeavour to remain in their seats."

This got into Punch under "Impending Apologies."

Sometimes in his preaching—for all his past academic distinction—he became curiously incapable of the operative word. One day he was well away with the Parable of Dives and Lazarus. We had had a racy description of Dives "with his Rolls Royce and his bulging bank balance". Then we got to Lazarus—"poor Lazarus lying there by the gate of that smart mansion, practically naked, with nothing to cover his—to cover his—his—(a long pause) his *features.*" (Collapse of at least half the choir.)

On one occasion my sympathies were entirely with him. It was a grilling hot Sunday morning in July. Into the Vestry after the service came a very wealthy lady, who had a large house on the Stray facing the Church. She only spent the summer there as she had a villa on the Riviera as well. The Vicar always did his best with her, thinking no doubt of her annual cheque. She was especially gracious that day as she had come to ask a favour. Would he witness her signature to various documents? I was still in the Vestry quietly changing out of my robes into my outdoor clothes, and the signing and witnessing went on amicably. The Vicar was "all over her".

"And do tell me, dear lady, how is your poor husband bearing the dreadful heat?"

There was a pause and a sudden change of atmosphere, almost one might say a fall in temperature. One could have heard a pin drop.

"Mr. Guy, you *buried* my dear husband three years ago." She gathered up her papers and departed in frigid fury. I almost loved him when he said:

"Well, that's torn it", and collapsed with a sigh into the chair she had just left.

The Vicar rather teased and bullied our saintly Verger Thomas Grainger, sweet gentle old man; but he met his match in old Tom Fausset, the Sexton: very Yorkshire and distrustful of Vicarious diplomacy and machinations. One Sunday morning the Vicar descended severely upon Tom just before Matins:

"And how was it Tom that I heard no bell ring for eight o'clock this morning?"

"Well, it were this way Vicar. I couldn't have bell rope in bed with me."

At the annual Choir outing the Vicar's teetotal instincts were frequently hurt by the crude determination of old Tom. On one occasion their coach had only been about an hour on its way to some chosen resort, when it drew up with a great flourish at a large and blatant public house.

"Tom, Tom, why are we stopping here?"

"Like enough Vicar, 'cos t'hosses are dry and so are t'men."

When he liked Douglas Guy could be very companionable. I once spent three days with him at Westgate very pleasurably. After he retired when nearing the eighties I visited him, now widowed, at Guildford and we both enjoyed our reunion and a chat about mutual friends.

The work in Harrogate and the organisations were very much the same as they had been in Kidderminster; but the whole atmosphere was quite different. Everything seemed less poignant more cheerful. No doubt this was largely because the war was over, but also partly I suppose it was due to the expansiveness and independence of the Yorkshire character. Also Kidderminster was an industrial town, Harrogate, although larger, was a pleasure resort, a Spa, and a residential centre. It would be difficult to say in which place we received more kindness.

As we had arrived in October 1918 the first Armistice celebrations were soon upon us. I was asked to preach at 11.0 a.m. on the Sunday at St. Mary's Church. I certainly felt the occasion; but was rather amused by a remark I overheard after I left the church and was finding my way through the large crowds still undispersed outside. A high pitched feminine voice was discussing the preacher and his sermon. "It was almost like being in the trenches. The tears were running down my face the whole time! That poor pale young clergyman! What suffering was written on his face! I expect that he must have been very badly wounded." Then she spotted me and rushed up to me. "I was just saying how wonderful it all was! You've obviously been through it, Padre! Were you very badly wounded?" "I am afraid not" I said "actually I was refused for military service in 1915 and considered too young for a Chaplaincy when I again made enquiries last year." "But I felt *sure* that you had been badly wounded." "Only an appendicectomy, I am afraid."

The Harrogate Churches were almost all well attended. Father Swann was still at the half built new church of St. Wilfrid and many of the visitors swelled the numbers already attending the one Anglo-Catholic church in the town. St. John's Bilton, still had magnificent old D. M. Alexander, now 94 and still working steadily and preaching impressive sermons. St. Peter's had a large congregation. Christchurch did quite well. Mr. Foot the Vicar of St. Peter's was a wealthy old gentleman of the old school, distinguished and usually to be seen with a carriage and pair progressing around the town. His appearances in church were few and in the Parish officially, rarer still. If once heard reading the Lessons he was seldom forgotten. His technique of concentrated violence of diction suited the more blood thirsty parts of the Old Testament admirably: but sounded odd in passages where the theme was love or comfort. Like Mr. Gladstone he addressed individuals as though they were large public meetings. One day in crowded James Street, which he was actually gracing with his presence on foot, he roared at me amiably. "Last winter I had cold after cold. At last I discovered the reason—no radiator in the corridor between my bedroom and my bathroom." All this was said in a tone of voice more suited to a hanging judge announcing with relish that he had had twenty men hanged after the recent Assizes. He was a very handsome old man, and did he know it! My Vicar was always "that little fellow Guy". They did not get on particularly well. Most of the other churches (as in so many health resorts) were in the hands of Low Church Trusts (St. Peter's, St. Mary's, St. Mark's, etc.). When the Evangelical Bishop Drury was succeeded by Bishop Strong, nurtured in the Oxford Movement tradition, D. S. Guy began to raise the tone of the Services at Christchurch.

One of the best features of Church life in Harrogate in the first half of the twentieth century was the large number of leading doctors who were keen and practising Christians, many of them being Churchwardens, sidesmen and (later) Parochial Church Councillors. The influence for good of a doctor who is a convinced and practising Christian can be incalculable. As Bernard Shaw has pointed out, in the Middle Ages people were greatly influenced by what the parson said: today it is what the doctor says which counts. Unfortunately it often goes further than that. Men are still as superstitious as ever. In the days of the ancient Greeks they believed the oracles: in the Middle Ages they believed the Church: today they believe the advertisements in the papers. None the less even today an alliance between the clerical and medical professions often makes all the difference to the life and character of many a town or Parish. I wish more of the younger medical men today with their fine ideals and pre-disposition to unselfish service would more often realise this. Anyway Harrogate was a happy example of this productive partnership. One of the places where it showed best was in the hospitals where there was a real recognition of the fact that human beings had souls as well as bodies. Matrons and nurses, as well as doctors, were almost uniformly friendly and helpful to the clergy in their ministrations there.

I remember one occasion when I was sent for by the Matron of the main Harrogate hospital on a winter Sunday afternoon. A charming girl of about eighteen and a member of several of our Church organisations, was dying of acute peritonitis and in terrible pain. When she telephoned, Matron said "You are the only person who can do anything for Lily Wheatley now." I went at once, and I spent about twenty minutes with the dying girl who had her Communion; Matron also kneeling with me behind the screens. "I don't mind dying" Lily said "but please ask God to take away my pain." At Evensong that night I told the congregation of about 300 people about this and we had a few minutes special silent prayer. I returned to the hospital about nine o'clock and saw Matron again on my way to Lily's bedside. The girl smiled when she saw me and whispered "No pain at all now", and Matron added, "Sister says that her pain stopped completely at exactly seven o'clock." "That" I replied "was also exactly the time at which I asked for the prayers of the whole congregation at Christchurch tonight." Lily died some five hours later but without the slightest recurrence of pain, sleeping peacefully away.

I have been to hospitals in many parts of England where I had similar help and cooperation; and I have alas, also had to minister to sick and dying people in hospitals where both doctors and nurses did not attempt to disguise the fact that they regarded the clergy as irrevelent nuisances and their ministrations mere mumbo-jumbo. These hospitals were never very happy places for the patients, nor the most efficiently run incidentally. One was the dirtiest institution I have ever seen. One dared not kneel on the floor.

If I preferred work in Harrogate to Kidderminster at all, I suppose that it was because my work in the Yorkshire Spa brought me into contact with rather more diversified types. My love of music brought me into close touch with Julian Clifford the Conductor of the Orchestra at the Royal Hall and the Hon. Mrs. Clifford and their delightful teenage son, also so musically gifted. The symphony concerts meant a lot to my mother and me, and I was always sorry that they did not receive more consistent support and feared that they might be given up. The Opera House, with its decorations by our friend Frances Darlington (who also did the panels at St. Wilfred's Church) —was a handsome little theatre and there were often excellent plays to be enjoyed. There were also occasionally good lectures and exhibitions of pictures. Altogether it was an attractive place with lovely public gardens. The beauty and interest of the surrounding country—dales, abbeys, castles and stately historic houses, added to the attraction. There was always something to do on one's "day off".

When I had had two very happy, if in some ways disillusioning years at Harrogate Bishop T. B. Strong invited me over to lunch at the Palace, just outside Ripon and offered me the post of Secretary and Domestic Chaplain. With this went the Incumbancy of the little Parish of North Stainley. Each of these two posts the Bishop thought would be a half time job. I immediately fell for his charm and humour and knew that there was a man, however eminent and brilliant, who understood young people and human nature.

Years later I contributed about two chapters to Harold Anson's book on Bishop Strong, Dean Vice-Chancellor and Bishop, my contribution describing his routine of life, his humour and his deeper and more withdrawn spiritual side. It would be impossible to give a full picture of him which would not use some of this material; but I hope that I shall be able to add some other recollections which have not yet been printed elsewhere.

The Freeman family who lived at Bilton Court on the Wetherby side of Harrogate, consisted of Mr. Walter Freeman (twice a widower and then in his middle sixties) and a family of four. There was an elder daughter, Margaret (Madge) by his first wife. By his second wife (now also dead) two sons, Hanson and Henry and another daughter Mary (Mollie), twelve years younger than Madge and the youngest of the family. Mr. Freeman was a J.P. and a generous and public spirited man, the Chairman and later Hon. Treasurer of Harrogate's great rheumatic hospital (the

Royal Bath Hospital) and much respected in the town and district. I gathered that he was considered (to put it mildly) a forceful character. He had read Law at Cambridge (Trinity Hall), but had only practised for a very short time, as, on the death of his uncle, the late Mr. Hanson Freeman, he had inherited his uncle's house and property. He had therefore devoted his life to public and philanthropic causes and to looking after his family affairs, all of which he did admirably.

Hanson had been to Harrow and Pembroke College, Cambridge: Henry to Charterhouse and then to Pembroke, as a Classical Exhibitioner. Both sons were then away serving in World War I. Henry had recently been badly wounded and after much suffering had had a leg amputated.

Mollie was an attractive girl of about 23 when we first met.

The two daughters and the father were members of Christchurch congregation and were amongst those who called on us, and visits were exchanged. We went to tea and a little later on to lunch. I was much interested in the collection of pictures at Bilton Court (several being of the French Barbizon School) and even more so in the younger daughter. She seemed so natural and unaffected and I felt sure that besides being attractive, she had a thoroughly sweet and unselfish disposition. She was very musical, played the violin extremely well and was now studying for the L.R.A.M. in piano. She and her sister were also deep in War work in Harrogate. I fancied that Mollie did not disapprove of me altogether.

One or two people in Harrogate who knew the family and us, made rather embarrassing remarks, such as—"Aren't you finding an attraction down at Bilton Court? Be careful. Old Mr. Freeman would eat anyone who tried to get hold of one of his daughters." One mutual friend a Mr. Rhodes, a Club crony of Walter Freeman's, and a man who had known me since by boyhood's days at St. Wilfrid's Church, said to me "Watch your step, Lewis. When matrimony looms on his family horizon the thunder clouds gather." Both Mollie and her elder brother found this out. The other two never married.

"My father-in-law elect summed up thus: "I don't like parsons. I don't like Irishmen. I don't like only sons, nor do I like delicate men who will die young and leave their widows with a family to cope with". Well, well! That was fifty years ago.

Ultimately on 14th June 1922, when I had been Vicar of N. Stainley for over a year, we were married at Christchurch, Harrogate, by the Bishop of Ripon, Dr. Thomas Strong, assisted

ABOVE: A group at Christchurch, Harrogate, 1921. Bishop
T. B. Strong and Rev. D. S. Guy (seated) with Rev. A. L. E.
Williams and Mr. T. Grainger (standing)
OVERLEAF: Our wedding day, 14 June, 1922

by Canon Guy who read the preface, and by my uncle Canon Ion Murray who gave (what I am told) was an eloquent and beautiful address, of which neither of us remembered one word unfortunately. My Grandmother Williams was not able to come over from Ireland for the occasion. She was now over ninety and although very much on the spot mentally could not face the long journey. We spent a sixteen day honeymoon in Paris and Fontaintheau.

When we arrived back in Harrogate my Mother met us and she and I spent the afternoon together, whilst Mollie went down to see her old home. My Mother was going over to Co. Mcath, in Ireland to stay at Ashfield near Bean Parc with my uncle Ion Murray for six to eight weeks. It would allow us to settle down together at North Stainley Vicarage. After that she was going to make her headquarters with us. My uncle had inherited this charming old house and estate from the Murray cousins in 1918.

CHAPTER IX

North Stainley And Bishop's Chaplaincy (1921-25)

FROM 9 A.M. until three or four o'clock on weekdays I was Secretary and Chaplain to Bishop Strong of Ripon. After that each day I was Vicar of North Stainley. The two posts together made quite a busy and interesting job. The Parish only contained about 350 inhabitants and as there was only one church, except for three months in the summer when we had an additional afternoon service in a charming old barn in the tiny hamlet of Sutton some three miles away, there would certainly not have been enough for a young man to do if he had only had the Parish. I mention this point because when I was first appointed the Squire of the village, Miss Rosebery Staveley asked me over to luncheon at Old Sleningford Hall. When I arrived the lady was not present but I was greeted by a charming old man, a Major Young, the only other invited guest. Whether it had been arranged so, or whether it was out of the kindness of his heart, he used the five or six minutes of our tête-à-tête to prepare me for something of an ordeal and to warn me that the old lady was extremely annoyed at the appointment which the Bishop had made (without consulting her) and that I must be prepared for a somewhat tempestuous welcome! He had got no further than this when Miss Staveley appeared, an untidy old lady with a red weather-beaten face and refractory wisps of grey hair. Her first remark was—as she held out her hand:

"I should like you to know that I am absolutely furious with the Bishop for appointing you! "

"Oh dear" I murmured, "I am very sorry to hear that."

"Oh, it's not *you* personally. Simply that I wanted a Vicar who would be *our own* and not just some young man—of whom we would have only what was left over from the Bishop's demands. We don't like having this place used to provide a stipend for the Bishop's Secretary."

"I think that the Bishop considers that there would not be a full time post here for an active man unless the Parish and Chaplaincy went together."

"I don't agree with the Bishop and that's that! Will you have a glass of sherry?" (A charming smile here.)

"Thank you very much."

This little episode was in a Wagnerian sense a sort of theme tune of what was to be expected by any Vicar of North Stainley during his Incumbency. The old lady had a peppery temper and a squirarchical complex, but was essentially nice and kind hearted. There would be the occasional little breeze; but on the whole we got on well and indeed one got to like her very much. She was absolutely sincere. The Staveleys had been there since the days of King Henry VII and she was the last. She had her birth and traditions; but there was not much money to speak of, and the house was dilapidated as well as untidy. She had a few treasures: including some old furniture and silver and a fine Romney (sold later to pay for a trip round the world). She also had a magnificent pearl necklace (often left lying anywhere) and once, when she was away, worn triumphantly by the kitchen maid at a rowdy village dance. The old lady was a very out-door type and tramped the country lanes interminably. When it was wet she still walked the two miles to the Parish Church and back as usual on Sundays, often twice. On these occasions her attire was supplemented by a pair of black riding breeches under her skirt. Sometimes portions of mysterious garments trailed behind her, not "like clouds of glory" as she came. I have seen her at an eight o'clock Communion on Sundays, with a good half yard of white calico sweeping up the chancel behind her. Her great interest was in the Church, the village and her tenants. She played the Queen in the village and the Organ at the Church and I think that this latter activity in Bishop's Strong's eyes, was one of her greatest crimes. The Bishop who was a Doctor of Music of Oxford, amongst other things had a sensitive ear. For four years every Christmas Day the Bishop used to preach for us but he never got inured. When I went to the Palace the day after my Institution and Induction, he said to me:

"Nice little church, a very good congregation; but that Organist! Why don't you sack her? She is quite awful!"

I had to explain who she was (as although they had corresponded, they had never met as yet)—the Squire, the builder of the Chancel, the landlord of all the choir members, and the heir of a dozen generations of Staveleys. Then having explained my dilemma, I added brightly, "Anyway it saves the Church money as she plays free of charge."

"Ah, but at what a cost!" commented the Bishop sadly.

There were frequently times when Miss Staveley was quite

obviously accompanying one Psalm and the choir and congregation were singing another. Often after I had given out a well known hymn and she played over the first line by way of encouragement, one thought "Oh dear, why can't we have the usual well known tune instead of something so exotic! " Then it dawned on one by the time we were half through the first verse that it *was* the usual tune or at least was meant to be. One could truly speak of her "infinite variety" at the Organ.

The people at North Stainley Hall were Major Harold Grotrian and his wife Phyllis, life long friends of ours. We played a lot of keen tennis together and all belonged to a very jolly amateur dramatic society amongst the hunting folk in the North Riding. Our company was called "The Jacobites" and included Maud Prior-Wandesford of Kirklington Hall, the Reverend Walter Fawkes of Finghall, Hudsons, Stobarts and Mackintyres. We went far afield. Incidentally we made quite a lot of money for various good causes. Phyllis Grotrian also was musical and the Sunday music was often agony to her. Once when the Psalm chant had been particularly inept and we had loyally sung the Gloria at the end of the Psalm selected three and a half times before Miss Staveley desisted, Phyllis ventured a protest at the end of the Service.

"Really, Miss Staveley, the music was not too good this morning was it! I really do think that you overtax yourself walking down all that way to Church and then having to cope with the organ! I am sure that it would be better for you if you let Miss X play on the Sunday mornings."

"How could anyone play properly with you screeching out of tune in the front pew, Sunday after Sunday! " the old lady retorted, as she shut down the organ with a resounding bang.

I was nearby, but seeing the storm clouds gathering I am afraid that I quietly retired into the Vestry and left the two ladies to it.

The other occupants of the remaining large houses in the Parish were the Artons, wealthy and kindly people from Bradford and the three Misses Yorke who came not long after us to Sleningford Grange.

The three Yorkes, May (Mary Augusta), Katharine and Ethel were three of the nicest women one could meet and all so different. They were the three unmarried daughters of the late Mr. Yorke of Halton and Bewerley Halls, Yorkshire. They represented the finest traditions of the old county family type and soon became much loved in the village, taking an interest in everything and supporting the Church most loyally. Quite candidly

I think that Miss Staveley slightly resented their presence; but to us their arrival made all the difference. Katharine was not very strong; but managed to do a great deal for other people, always sweet considerate and kind to everyone. Ethel, the youngest, was a good speaker and an indefatigable worker for the G.F.S. and other good causes. May, the eldest of a family of ten, still seemed mentally the youngest and most alert of all. She was an extremely handsome woman and in many ways her mind and sense of humour were more like those of a clever university don. How she had remained single was a mystery to everybody. She became one of my greatest friends and also the close friend of my mother and wife. When I got to know her better, I once jokingly said "Can't think why you never married! " and got the answer:

"I could have, more than once or twice. Never met anyone near enough to my own age whom I liked sufficiently. I *do* know *someone* who was born twenty-five years too late—for me."

May Yorke was my mother's age and from the time she was a little over fifty until her death at the age of ninety-two, she was the closest woman friend I have ever had. She out-lived all her brothers and sisters and retained all her faculties and interests until the very end. Her vast knowledge and experience were always at the disposal of her intimate friends and she was to me as much a comrade and confidant as any of my great men friends. When our family came along May became Robin's godmother, Ethel was godmother to Anne, our second girl.

North Stainley was a cosy little Parish. The "big houses" set a good example and the church attendance and the moral tone of the whole place were exceptionally good. Our week-night Lent Services used to bring an average of fifty people. Every organisation was well supported.

The oddest thing about the whole set up was the queer little Vicarage, which lying low near the Church and the Churchyard, had a permanent lake in its cellars! One old farmer told me how the Vicarage came to be built in such an unlikely place. "You see," he said "that bit of land was no good for ought. In summer it was a marsh. In winter it was a pond, so Old Squire (Miss Staveley's father) gave it as a site for the Vicarage. Old Squire, he thought he'd done enough when he built the Church." I remember one hot summer day I swam all round the cellars in five or six feet of water. When on advice we ultimately had the drinking water tested, we were told that the Churchyard drained that way and that we were no doubt "drinking the parishioners". However we survived; and the water in the cellar remained.

The income was about £320 a year. Most of it came from tithe and there were about 300 tithe payers, some of whom paid 6d. or 1s. a year or even less. The curious dilatory old tithe collector often had to write two or three times to some of the payers of these trifling sums, so that the money spent on collecting them often exceeded the amount due! I was Vicar for over eight months before I received one penny of income from this gold mine. A new Tithe Act soon enabled me to force compulsory redemption on all sums of tithe due, under the annual value of £1. This reduced the roll of tithe payers from about 300 to a mere 40 or 45. It also reduced the expenses of the collection proportionately. The net result to the income was a gain of about £25 a year. Of course I also had my stipend of £120 a year from the Bishop, so I felt comparatively well-to-do (after my two curacies) with a house rent free and double the income I had enjoyed even in my more opulent last six months at Christchurch, Harrogate.

We became very fond of the villagers who usually combined bluntness and friendliness with good manners. The character of the "locals" was more that of the reserved North Riding than of the expansiveness of the West, but there were many warm hearts. The clergyman was to some extent exempted from the experiences of many of the newcomers into the village and district. I remember on one occasion hearing the tail end of a furious battle of words between two old ladies, both leaning over their garden gates on opposite sides of the village street. The honours were pretty evenly divided until one (a native) got in a decisive shot: she screamed "Anyway you're nowt but a furriner! Not been here more than twenty-eight years, I reckon." There was no gainsaying that, so the other contestant retreated and banged her front door behind her. She had had it.

We had a small Church School in the village in which I taught once a week when possible. There was something very attractive about the sort of family feeling which existed in this small Parish, due partly to the matriarchal sway of Miss Staveley and the other good ladies in the large houses, and partly to the fact that a succession of Vicars knew everyone by name.

The Methodists were very friendly and their small Chapel almost adjoined the Church. Their local preacher, an elderly farm worker, attended Matins at the Parish Church almost every Sunday. So did other Methodists. This amicable arrangement had only one drawback. One Methodist farmer's wife said to me one day laughingly:

"I shall be having to give up coming to Church on Sunday

mornings I think, Vicar. You see it so often means that I get the same Sermons and the same hymns twice a Sunday! Our old Mr. Binks takes you down and gives it us again at night, with hymns complete."

I did remember before this enlightenment noticing that on two or three occasions when I passed the Chapel on a Sunday night, the small but hearty congregation were giving vent to the same hymns which we had sung in Church that morning. I was always careful to choose a hymn for after the Sermon which would rub the teaching in, and not be like the bird in the parable, which came and took the seed away.

Social life was quite gay. Many people called upon my Mother and me when we arrived in the sociable Ripon district, and after I married my wife and I got a great many invitations to tennis parties in the summer and luncheons and dinner parties in the winter. Rural North Yorkshire was very sociable in those days.

There was a story of some bachelor parson who came to some village in Wensleydale North of Ripon, who was not very versed in social techniques. He got a printed invitation from Ripon to some social function and was perplexed by the letters printed at the bottom corner, R.S.V.P. He appealed to his housekeeper for elucidation and got the ingenious suggestion, "I shouldn't wonder if it did not mean 'Ripon Society Very Pleasant'." It was incidentally.

It is amazing to think how all this sort of mild gaiety has gone out of English life since World War II came along and practically put an end to the kind of entertaining and hospitality which had formerly characterised English life at any rate in the country and country towns. What was the cause of this change? Some of it may be due to the practical disappearance of the domestic servant, some of it perhaps to greater financial stringency in a particular class. Much of it, I suspect, is however simply due to the fact that a generation has grown up which dislikes any general entertaining. People now prefer getting into little groups or coteries of their own liking. They also prefer dining out in hotels and restaurants or meeting their friends in some particular bar. Many seem to dislike nothing more than to have to entertain in their own houses. The same sort of thing has happened at dances. In the old days one danced with several people as a social duty, and if you did not know many your hostess introduced young people in need of more partners to one another. Now you take your partner or go in a little pack of four or six and never look at any one else all night. All these things make for great loneliness for newcomers to a district if they have no special introductions to key people. I remember one lady (quite young) whom I called upon when I was a Vicar in a Southern town. When I said "Can I come in and visit you?" I got an unexpected response. She burst into tears and said "Oh please excuse me; but I am so lonely! We have been here six months and you are the first person to ring our door bell except the postman and the milkman!"

Sometimes I visited alone in North Stainley village; but often when visiting the outlying farms, which meant long walks in the lanes and countryside, either my Mother or my wife would come with me. Almost everywhere one got a real Yorkshire welcome. There was no radio blasting away: no T.V. and farmers and their wives seemed to enjoy having us and had generally any amount to talk about. The meals that we had to eat were often embarrassingly gargantuan: wonderful home-cured hams, with a flavour and a fragrance which seem now to be a thing of the past: heaped up plates of Yorkshire tea cakes hot and swimming in butter and finally the rich home made plum cakes. For one to have refused anything would have been taken amiss and many a time one had to sacrifice one's digestion in the interests of the Church's good name. There was very little shyness amongst those warm direct country folk once you knew them and got through a mere surface reserve. They talked easily about the things that interested them including frequently the Church and religion. If there were grievances they usually came out quickly and without rancour. There was little artificiality or triviality. You knew exactly where you were with them.

The village ran both a cricket club and a football team. I was too careful of my reputation and prestige even to attempt to play the former, but I used to play right-half for the soccer team without disgracing myself. As an Irishman, I could never understand either the true nature of cricket or its fascination for most typical Englishmen. At School at Worcester in the summer terms I rowed and swam and so avoided the cricket fields. Football was a game which one could enjoy, even if not in the first flight; but cricket, unless one was a good batsman or bowler seemed to be excruciatingly boring.

We had many very nice young men in the village. Young farmers and agricultural workers. Of course one subscribed to the cricket club and came and watched; but the soccer was fun. Sometimes we went off in a bus to play a neighbouring village. The matches were spirited and energetic. After one match which ended with a hearty score of "nine all", a hefty grinning young man came up to me and said in broad Yorkshire "Eeh—Ah had thee down int mud three or four times. Ah'm sorry. Ah didn't know thee wast Parson." "That's all right," I said "the mud was softer than if there had been a frost like last Saturday." There were Sunday mornings when one was so stiff that kneeling and getting into the pulpit were quite something.

Perhaps the strangest episode in our four years at North Stainley was connected with our churchyard extension. Our little churchyard was almost full. I therefore got a strip of adjacent land from Miss Staveley and we raised the money to have it decently walled and nicely laid out. The Bishop came and duly consecrated it. Everyone was delighted. But what happened? Normally we had four or five funerals a year, people often being brought from distances to be buried near relatives. None the less no funerals took place in our new extension despite the flowers and shrubs with which we decked it. Nearly two years passed and there were still no interments! Worse still at least four people had died in the Parish and for one reason or another they were all buried elsewhere. One old woman was taken off to Leeds to be buried at Lawnswood. I discussed this seeming boycott of our new cemetery with May Yorke, so knowledgeable about Yorkshire and its manners and customs. "Don't you know why?" she asked with a twinkle, and when I shook my head she continued—"They are all waiting until some stranger dies here and they will bury him in our new Churchyard at night. Then all will be well." Evidently I still looked somewhat mystified. "You see the locals all think that the *first* person to be buried in a *new* graveyard will belong to the devil, his little rake off, as it were." There was evidently something in what she said, for sure enough, a few weeks later some traveller, staying at one of our little village inns died suddenly and in no time they had him in our extension. Soon there were four or five tombstones proudly raising their heads over the well cut grass and flower-beds. Old superstitions evidently die hard in some parts of the country.

The second year of our time at North Stainley saw the sudden death of my step-father in Manchester. We both went over to Manchester and saw to the funeral. It was a trying time for my Mother. It brought back the whole sad history of her tragic second marriage. In 1923 it became evident that she herself was seriously unwell. Although she had delighted in the arrival of our eldest daughter, Adelaide Edith, born on 1st May, 1923, she became increasingly breathless, faint and ill. I took her to see one of the leading heart specialists in London, on the advice of our local Ripon medico. I shall never forget the hour and a half I spent in the Harley Street waiting room whilst Mother was with the specialist having a thorough series of tests and investigations. At the end she came back into the room looking in spite of all she had been through, a good deal more cheerful than I was feeling. The specialist invited me to come into his private consulting room and there he told me that my Mother's heart was "just about as bad as it could be." I asked what that meant. He said that she was to go to bed for a month and then to get up a little "when she felt like it". He added: "She might live six months; but I doubt it". I had to go back to her, looking as cheerful as possible and tell her that she was to have a rest cure. Whether the specialist made a wrong diagnosis, or whether it was my prayers, I don't know. Anyway what seemed to be a miracle took place. Mollie and I made Mother rest and for months she lived a completely quiet life. Then we tried to get her as much outside pleasure and interest as possible and she slowly improved. She lived not six months but another twenty-four years and gradually got stronger and more active. Indeed when she was in the late seventies she was capable of enjoyable long walks and other activities which twenty years earlier would have been absolutely beyond her. If I had lost my father when I was one year old and had consequently never known him, I was at least allowel to have my Mother until I was over fifty-five and to give her every possible comfort. How much of this was due to the goodness and unselfishness of Mollie I could never express. Mother had a serene old age. She enjoyed her grandchildren and made many friends in my different parishes.

At North Stainley Vicarage was also born on 20th May, 1924, our second daughter Anne Margaret. She was as dark as Adelaide was fair, and from the time that she was six months old it was evident that she was going to be the possessor of an enormous sense of humour. Adelaide was a large and pretty blonde and Anne a small brunette; curiously enough when Anne got to fourteen years of age she began to grow rapidly and in a few years she was to become the largest and tallest of our three daughters, having the graceful long-limbed McNeill figure of my Grandmother Williams. Incidentaly Granny who did not die until April 1924, a month or so before Anne's birth had the pleasure of seeing Adelaide her first great grandchild in the summer of 1923. Adelaide was much admired by relatives in Larne and Belfast, and we were very proud to be able to show her to the family. Old Mr. Freeman thawed considerably when he became more acquainted with his two elder grand-daughters and on one occasion (Robin's christening) commented on their charms, adding as a pendent to his verdict upon them "I like the naughty looking one particularly." I suppose it cannot have been much later than this that we took the little girls to their first pantomime ("The Babes in the Wood"), at the Opera House in Harrogate. We had seats in the middle of the first row in the dress circle and the two wicked henchmen of the even more wicked uncle were disporting themselves after leaving the poor babes to die in the wood. Suddenly a shrill voice of rebuke sounded to every corner of the theatre "Stop it, you naughties". For a split second there was a complete cessation and silence even on the stage. Everyone in the stalls looked round and up. Anne was standing in the attitude of an earnest police constable, holding up the traffic, arm upraised. "No, we won't" shouted the robbers in retort. The whole theatre rocked and then the performance resumed its riotous progress.

I think when we left North Stainley after four and half happy years the two little girls were as much missed as any of us.

My work at the Palace was of course my principle job and interest. There was the double thrill of contact with one of the great personalities of that day and the first contacts with the great world of the Church as provided by the Northern Province of York and elsewhere. There was a succession of notable clerical visitors, including the Archbishop Dr. Cosmo Gordon Lang, the Bishop of Durham (Dr. Hensley Henson), the Bishop of Wakefield (Dr. Eden), the Dean of Lichfield (Dr. Savage), the President of Trinity College, Oxford (Dr. Blakiston) and Dr. Headlam (Bishop of Gloucester) the Dean of York (Dr. Foxley Norris). When these and other illustrious personages stayed for more than a night and my own Bishop was away for some hours keeping some diocesan engagement, I was sometimes commissioned to stay and take the guests for walks or to show them the sights of Ripon or Fountains Abbey.

Archbishop Lang was indeed a formidable visitor. On his first visit I was told to stay to lunch so that I should meet him. He ignored me completely until the port and cheese were on the table. A General Election was imminent and he had been talking very freely about Lloyd George and Ramsey McDonald. It would indeed have been difficult to decide of which of the two he had the poorer opinion. He then referred to something in the nature of a minor *contretemps* which had occurred that morning before he left Bishopthorpe.

"Naturally I was in a terrible temper," he said to Dr. Strong "my Chaplain caught it". Then he turned and made his one and only remark to me.

"I expect that you catch it, when your Bishop is in a temper, young man! "

"My Bishop is never in a temper, Your Grace."

"Oh, indeed, isn't he! H'mm, Hah."

He gave me a searching look and then turned to Dr. Strong once more. How marvellously he mellowed after he went to Canterbury. He certainly became quite benign and fatherly. I remember on one occasion when I had to speak at an Adult Education Meeting at Lambeth Palace, how kindly he congratulated me afterwards and put his hand on my shoulder.

Dr. Foxley Norris (Dean of York) was an artist to the fingertips and he gave me great encouragement over my oil paintings. Later he most kindly proposed me for membership of the Parson Painters Society. One day the Bishop and I were having tea with him at the Deanery in York and he began to speak of his plans for the Minster.

"At present it is almost black and colourless; too like King's Cross Railway Station! I intend to make it glow with colour again."

He went on to speak of the repainting and gilding of the innumerable carved bosses and coat of arms, of the screens and adornments of the many Chapels. He also described what could be done with the magnificent Medieval glass—the vastest collection in England. Much of it had been jumbled up during inexpert repairs in the past centuries, so that it was now a kaleidoscopic chaos. Also it was dimmed by the dust and dirt of ages. In Fred Harrison, Minor Canon and Librarian (and later Canon) he had a capable and learned colleague. So was the work begun which, in spite of another World War and a second removal of the windows to safety, has gone on triumphantly for several decades. The vast jigsaw puzzle of the windows was in due course sorted out, heads and bodies of saints and worthies, parted for years, came together again and broken stories were literally mended. York was fortunate to have two such artistic Deans as Foxley Norris and Milner White.

By far the most interesting of Bishop Strong's clerical visitors (to me) was, however, Dr. Henson, the Bishop of Durham. I used to stay for luncheon during his visits and mealtimes were a riot of fun when two of the cleverest and wittiest men in England expanded and let themselves go. Archbishop Lang and Bishop Strong had both had their portraits painted recently by Orpen. There have been many stories told of both these somewhat controversial pictures. The famous one about the Archbishops' portrait was of course Bishop Henson's comment on a complaint by Dr. Lang himself who said that someone had blamed the picture for making him look "proud, pompous and prelatical" and Dr. Henson had mischieviously asked "And to which of these epithets does Your Grace take exception?" Less well known is the other story which Bishop Henson told Dr. Strong and me at the luncheon table. The Archbishop asked the Bishop of Durham what he thought of the picture then on show at Bishopthorpe for a meeting of the Bishops of the Northern Province. Dr. Henson replied: "Well, Your Grace, I must say that I think that it is very hard luck on a life long teetotaller!" "What exactly do you mean by that?" "Well, Orpen has given Your Grace an ultra-marine nose has he not?" In due course this remark bore fruit and the artist toned the nose down to a more neutral tint.

Of Dr. Strong's portrait, Bishop Henson said "Well, when it gets to Christ Church Hall it will certainly make most of the other portraits look asleep." Dr. Strong was at the time highly amused by the fact that in the middle of painting these two portraits of the Archbishop and himself, Orpen was sent for post haste by the French Government to paint the notorious murderer Landru ("the French Bluebeard") for their famous gallery of notable criminals. I remember him saying "I am sure that the portraits of the Archbishop and myself benefited greatly from this experience of Orpen's. No doubt it enabled him to get his hand in better and bring out more of our subtler characteristics!"

Dr. Henson had a wonderful way with young men. His friendliness certainly drew me well out of my shell and his sense of fun and humour soon overcame any shyness I might have had in the presence of a man so famous for his brilliance and powers of sarcasm. I remember that on the second day of his visit after lunch he said to Bishop Strong "I am going to get your Chaplain to take me for a walk, and to give me the 'low down' on you." Actually almost the first thing he said to me as we wandered through the gardens and woods in the high ground behind the Palace, was, "I expect that you know what a wonderful privilege and education you are having, in being in daily contact with such a man as dear Tommy Strong."

I agreed with enthusiasm, and Dr. Henson went on:

"All the Bishops in the Northern Province look to him for advice at one time or another. He is the wisest of men and can take an objective view of almost any problem."

I met Bishop Henson only a very few times again in the years which followed; but after his retirement when he published his autobiography (*Retrospect of an Unimportant Life*) I wrote to him and had in reply the interesting letter which follows. As this letter has not previously been published and contains some of his views on some important questions of doctrine and Church affairs, I give the correspondence more or less in full.

From Canon A. L. E. Williams
The Vicarage,
Banbury, Oxon.
March, 14th, 1944

My dear Lord Bishop,

I hope that you will not think that I am taking too much of a liberty in writing to you to say with what intense interest and pleasure I have read the two volumes of your Retrospect. In the second volume alone there is mention of more than forty people whom I have known well or comparatively so. You may or may not remember me. I was Bishop Strong's Secretary and Chaplain, when you visited him at The Palace at Ripon, and I have never forgotten these occasions. I took you some walks all round the grounds and woods, and we discussed a wide range of subjects, all so interesting to me.

I do not know whether the two following little comments on points raised in Vol. II of your book would be of any interest to you.

On page 221 you mention my old Vicar, Canon D. S. Guy and his book—"Was Holy Communion Instituted by Jesus?" Canon Guy wrote this for his B.D. at Cambridge. He never proceeded to the D.D. degree. I remember having large chunks of the M.S. read to me. The book was not welcomed by the Knaresborough R.D. Chapter, and exception was taken to the title. The whole effort was considered to be anything but helpful. I gather that this was more or less your feeling about it.

On page 343 after noting the death of the Bishop of Ripon (Burroughs) you make some observations on his relation to the Group Movement. Arthur Burroughs was a very intimate friend of mine, although I sometimes doubted whether he was at his best as a Bishop. I am quite sure that Arthur towards the end of his life came to distrust the Group Movement.

In the spring of 1934 he spent three months on the Continent, but came home to Ripon feeling no better in health. He was very depressed and his sister was away in Canada fully immersed in the Groups. I was visiting him, and he gave vent to some very acid criticisms of the influence which Buchmanism appeared to have upon people's sense of domestic responsibility. He was not referring so much to his sister's absence in Canada, as to the vagaries of some other mutual friends whose home life had almost been eliminated by a long drawn out orgy of House Parties.

96

I hope that I have not wearied you with all this, and that you will not feel in any way bound to trouble to reply.

If however you do feel inclined to write I should be more than grateful to know what is your ultimate opinion on the situation which has developed since the final rejection of the Revised Prayer Book. This Book is now used more or less in the majority of churches, which suggests that the Church has ignored the Parliamentary vote, and perhaps that Parliament is chary of intervening and stirring up a hornet's nest. Is this gain or loss?

With apologies for such a long and meandering letter.

I remain,
Yours very truly,
Anthony L. E. Williams

The Rt. Revd.,
Bishop H. Hensley Henson, D.D.

Hyntle Place,
Hintlesham,
Ipswich.
March 16th, 1944

My dear Canon Williams,

I am greatly obliged for your very interesting letter, which I was very glad to receive. It pleases me to know that you retain a pleasant recollection of our walks and talks in the gardens of Ripon, and that you have found my "Retrospect" readable. My own position with regard to the Dominical Institution of the Holy Communion by Jesus is two-fold. I think that there is a question to be answered, partly by the critics and partly by the Church. *On critical grounds, I myself believe that the Church is right and therefore I am confident that, so long* as the authority of the Church is admitted the position of the Holy Communion in the thought and habit of Christian folk is secure, but if the critics should succeed in establishing the negative conclusion then, I think the Holy Communion would fade out from the use and wont of Christian folk. *I do not think Modernists realise sufficiently the religious effect of their own procedures.* The Christian religion has claims of its own, which Christians cannot ignore. Take for example the question which, in my opinion, goes to the very heart of the Christian discipleship—*the Sinlessness of Jesus.* If Modernists should claim to have demonstrated that Jesus was, in however slight a measure, a sinful man, it would, in my opinion, be impossible for informed and considering men to place Him in the position which, at least since the time of St. Paul, He has held *as the Object of Christian worship.* I think the question is a fair one, and I think also that it must be answered by an appeal to the New Testament for such answer as it is competent to give. There are Modernists who do not scruple to maintain the negative. I think that on critical grounds their position is untenable. If indeed, there were nothing else but the New Testament documents to reckon with, one would, of course be compelled as an honest student to accept a conclusion which annihilated one's personal discipleship, but there is the whole

97

problem of Jesus in the Church and in history to be taken into account, and these, it seems to me, do not require from history more than history alone can give, viz., *such an account of Jesus as is congruous with the faith and worship of the Church*. In this larger treatment of the subject, I am prepared to maintain that the Christian Tradition is adequately sustained by the original records. My complaint of the Modernists that they ignore elements in the great argument, which (though they lie outside the handling of the textual critics) cannot be reasonably excluded from the verdict on the main question. I am perturbed by the recklessness with which Modernists pursue their studies. The New Testament was written *by* believers, *to* believers, *for* believers, and I do not think justice can be done to its teaching except *by* believers. *This does not carry me to a blind unquestionable acceptance of tradition, but it does forbid me to exclude from my examination of the New Testament that faith in Jesus which provides the key to New Testament Exegesis.* All this is very confused and inadequate, but I think you will discern the outlines of an argument which a Modernist may fairly allow, and which a Christian may safely accept. *"In the mouth of two witnesses shall every word be established"*. It is by the combination of History (New Testament) and tradition (the creed of discipleship) that firm ground can be provided, even today.

Your account of Bishop Burroughs interests me greatly. I am glad to think that he had been led to modify his attitude towards the Group Movement. All that I have learned about it since I criticised it in my Quadrennial Charge has strengthened my conviction that Buchman was not a trustworthy spiritual guide, and that his so-called Oxford Movement was not fundamentally sound. That great mischief was done to many young men, I have good reason for knowing, and no reason at all for modifying my opinion respecting "Frank".

You ask me what is my opinion of the situation which has developed since the final rejection of the Revised Prayer-Book, and I can only answer that I think the position, so far as the Church of England is concerned, has definitely worsened, in spite of the valorous language used in the Church Assembly on the morrow of the second rejection, *the Church generally has done what I feared that it would do, viz., taken it "lying down"*. I am more than ever convinced that Disestablishment is morally requisite. This year (1944) is the Centenary of the Liberation Society, and is being commemorated as such by Nonconformists. *I have contributed a short article to the April number of the "Congregationalist Quarterly", of which Mr. Albert Peel is Editor. I think I have sufficiently explained my opinion of the situation in that article.* I do not think it is true to say that the Revised Prayer-Book is much used in the Church. *Parts of it are used by Anglo-Catholicks in order to assist their own objects, which are very generally the very objects which the Revised Prayer Book was intended by the Bishops to restrain or disallow.* I think that the first step in ecclesiastical reconstruction after the war, *ought* to be an Act of Disestablishment, and I should not despair of such an act being framed in a friendly spirit in the Church of England if the Church were to co-operate with the State in terminating a legal relationship which is demonstrably unsatisfactory, but I am not hopeful, and I do not feel much confidence in the present leaders of the Church.

Believe me,
Yours sincerely and obliged,
H. Hensley Henson
Bishop

The Vicarage,
Banbury,
March 23rd, 1944

My dear Lord Bishop,

I am most grateful to you for your extremely kind letter and acknowledgement of my note to you with reference to your most interesting book. It was very good of you to write so fully.

You may be right about Disestablishment. Logically I expect there is really no answer to your points. It may be that the Anglican Church in this Country would gain considerably in efficiency and cohesion through some measure of Disestablishment, but I feel that it might be at the cost of greatly narrowing its purview, also that such a move would as it were "unbaptise" the nation. My own hope is that some characteristically illogical working compromise may yet be found or evolve. I am aware that this sounds rather unreasonable but possibly somthing higher than reason may come to the rescue.

May I once again say how greatly I value your kindness in acknowledging my former letter and dealing so comprehensively with my questions.

I remain,
Yours sincerely and gratefully,
Anthony L. E. Williams.

At times elusive, Bishop Strong was definitely shy with women. I remember him saying to me "There are only three women in the Diocese with whom I can ever think of anything to talk about. Mrs. Owen (the wife of the Dean of Ripon), Mrs. Wyndham Beresford-Peirse (of Bedale Rectory) and your wife."

He was an adept at summing people up in a sentence, and even if the words contained criticism, the light tone and the impish smile took much of the sting out of the remarks. Of a not too energetic country incumbent of the promising name of Earley Ayre, he said "I fear that his name belies him." A highly "successful" cleric he described as "an experienced ecclesiastical brigand". A Leeds incumbent who would have liked to impress the Bishop was "One of those people who have merely got a face". An abnormally oleaginous Evangelical clergyman was dismissed as "buttered on both sides".

He was much amused when told of the reaction of a very dominating lady, the wife of a country Rector when someone tried to explain to her about the new legislation creating Parochial Church Councils. As she had ruled her husband (and his Parish) with a rod of iron for many years, she smelt treason, commenting darkly, "No one told *me* anything about all this! " "Another Athaliah! " cried the Bishop.

When I once asked Dr. Strong what a certain rather emotional northern Bishop was like he simply replied "His favourite hymn is 'Hark hark, my soul'! "

As can be imagined every day had its little delights in such company; but there was also the serious side: the enormous mental energy: the quick and acute decisions, none of them as far as I can judge, ever wrong: the clarity and adroitness with which he organised and streamlined his work. One of the best comments on his outstanding qualities as a scrupulously fair and businesslike Chairman was that of his successor as Bishop of Ripon, Arthur Burroughs, who said that his detachment from any subject was only exceeded by his complete knowledge and mastery of it. I could never express all that I learnt from Bishop Strong, both in dealing with work and people. No wonder that Oxford University requested him to do a second period as Vice-Chancellor.

One of the important pieces of work that Bishop Strong kept on, after he became Bishop of Ripon was the Chairmanship of the Joint Committee of the Royal Commissions on the Universities of Oxford and Cambridge. The additional amount of work and concentration demanded by all this was tremendous. I got to know something of the extent of it all, since as his Secretary I wrote most of his letters. The Meetings of the Joint Committee were not without their lighter moments. Before almost every session the Bishop was interviewed by the Chairman of the Cambridge Commission, the Master of Gonville and Caius College. Apparently one of the constant objectives of the heads of the other Cambridge Colleges, was to curb the influence of Trinity. That great and wealthy institution was, I gathered, very suspect in the eyes of the other Colleges, who were inclined to combine to ensure that things in that University were not unduly dominated by one institution. This phobia almost amounted to an obsession and Bishop Strong was much amused at the ingenuities and subtleties evolved by the Masters of the smaller colleges. "They are all determined that Trinity shall be a *minority* of one and not a majority of one. Thank goodness we have no such problems at Oxford." Bishop Strong conceded that one Oxford College was inclined to be a little "cagey" about divulging all its considerable sources of revenue. It was the same College which in the Civil War of the seventeenth century had been least generous financially to Charles I in his financial hour of need and was credited with having safely *buried* its silver until better times. "Curious how history can repeat itself! " commented the Bishop.

Another interesting sideline of this wonderful man was the work which he still continued to do for the Oxford University Press, after he came to Ripon. He was still one of the Delegates and used to "read" many books for them to see whether or not the volumes in "question" should be published by such an august institution. "There are three things to look for" said the Bishop, "Sheer importance of subject, originality of contribution and treatment and the style." Often I have seen him start on some voluminous manuscript at tea time. The next morning he had not only read the book, but was in such a complete position of mastery of it as to be able at the same time to criticise its whole worth and to go into the smallest details of accuracy and style. After having dealt with fundamentals he used to go on to point out all sorts of slips and inaccuracies. "The reference on page 209 is incorrect. There is a split infinitive on line 10 of page 243." Sometimes at the end of a hectic day for letters I used to come into his study with a great sheaf for him to sign. He would say: "Leave them there; I will sign them later. You have had enough of them. Now we will have some tea and then perhaps a little Brahms, so soothing for the nervous system."

Bishop Strong used to like to describe himself as "a Catholic in doctrine but something of a Cistercian in practice". Ritual and ceremonial he preferred reduced to a minimum. This at times could lead to somewhat incongruous situations, as when after a really great occasion when the chancel, etc. of a new and mag-nificent Church was dedicated with much dignity and pageantry he *read* the final Blessing off the printed service paper with a cool simplicity of technique which I have never known anyone else to equal.

His pet hatred in the way of unnecessary and clogging pomps, was the official pastoral staff of the Bishop of the Diocese of Ripon. It was a handsome silver affair, meant to look very medieval no doubt; but slightly bogus, or perhaps merely Victorian. It was cumbersome and heavy, as the Bishop's Chaplain found out, when it had to be carried on occasion in long open air processions.

"I have tried to lose it several times" complained the Bishop.

The Anglo-Catholic incumbents in Leeds often enquired anxiously as to whether the Bishop had brought it with him and received such replies as "No, I have forgotten it—fortunately."

One afternoon he and I set off in his car for some rather big occasion at All Souls Church, Leeds, and the Vicar had rung me up that morning to make a special request that I should bring the pastoral staff. The Bishop and I were sitting in the back of the car with a large fur rug over our knees. The Bishop shifted his position slightly and his foot struck the long case on the car floor.

"Ugh! " he said, "so you have brought that old nuisance of a thing, have you?"

"The Vicar made a very special request", I explained.

"Queer minds some people have", was the rejoinder.

I was all the more surprised therefore when I arrived at the Palace one morning, the day after the Bishop had (unaccompanied by me) been the previous night to a very remote dale parish to institute a new Incumbent, when I was told how useful his Crozier had proved on this occasion.

"As I was implored by the new Vicar to bring my staff, I took it with me. At last I found a real use for the thing. Apparently no Bishop had been seen in the place within living memory. The truly rural Churchwardens shied when they saw me—rather like a couple of young horses seeing a motor car for the first time! We did the usual marching round the Church, the Wardens still apparently paralysed with fright. As we processed up a side aisle we came to a doorway which led down some steps into some dark stoke hole or cellar. Imagine my surprise when one of these excellent men suddenly turned into this exit! I just had the presence of mind to say to myself 'No, you don't', and to hook him by the back of his coat collar, with my Crook. Most effective. He made no further attempts to escape, and the service really went off quite well."

All this sort of thing was amusing; but it was not all. Underneath there was great and deep devotion. A profound mind had worked out a reasoned and orthodox faith.

"Never despise tradition. There is always some reason for a tradition. Quite frequently the reason is very simple: it happens to be the truth."

This was the verdict of one of the most acute brains of the generation. I must say I found his views and his reasonings about the Christian faith, much more constructive and helpful than what is today sometimes described as the new Cambridge way of approach, or "South Bank" religion: a form of apologetic which suggests the saying "emptying the baby out with the bath water." God is IT: nor must "He" (?) be thought of as being anywhere. No doubt before long an improved version of the Lord's Prayer will be produced by these "trendy" theologians. I wonder whether many people would find it very helpful.

Bishop Strong's marvellous memory which failed him so tragically in his last few years was still quite abnormal in his Ripon days. On one occasion he required a certain quotation from Thomas Aquinas and sent me into the next room where many of his heavier tomes were housed. I was told not only the number of the volume but the page. Then he added "Each page is divided into two columns, the actual line I need is near the top of the left hand column, about ten to twelve lines down." I found it without any difficulty. It was on line eleven and lightly marked in pencil.

Afterwards I asked him when he had last looked it up; the reply was "Shortly before last Christmas". That meant about eight months previously.

After I had been Chaplain for about two years I had one rather alarming experience (although, I suppose that I should have regarded it more as an assuring one). I arrived one spring morning as usual at 9.30 a.m. having cycled from the Vicarage which was nearly three miles away. The Bishop was standing in the hall with his overcoat on. His car was at the door with the engine running and his chauffeur was just carrying out a suitcase. The Bishop said:

"I am just off to Paris. My brother has died very suddenly and I must get there as soon as possible. Open all my letters and answer all that you possibly can. Do your best with the Diocese. If it is really a case of S.O.S. ring up the Bishop of Knaresborough: but I expect that you will manage all right. I should be back in about a week, I hope."

Before I could say more than a couple of halting sentences he was gone; and I was left with the Diocese, so to speak, on my hands. Fortunately nothing untoward happened, and I did not have to appeal to dear kind old Bishop F. L. M. Bottomley-Smith at Methley. Apparently I did the right thing with about 150 letters and I think that I even managed to save the Bishop three or four tiresome interviews. When he returned about ten days later he was very sweet to me and I got a most unexpected gift of £5 worth of books with an affectionate inscription in the one at the top of the pile.

One of my more interesting activities was to act as Secretary to the Annual Meeting of the Rural Deans. This used to take place in the summer and the Rural Deans (twelve in all) were housed at the Palace, together with the Suffragan and the Archdeacons. There were some interesting personalities: including the Vicar of Leeds, B. O. F. Heywood, so charming and wise (afterwards successively Bishop of Southwell, Hull and Ely) and Canon Egerton Leigh (Rector of Richmond), a forceful and unpredictable character of whom there were many good stories. One Lent he announced his mid-week Course of Addresses as "Conversations with the Devil". Setting the scene at the first occasion, he said "I am up here in the pulpit, as you can all see. You cannot see the devil; but we will give him the front pew." There followed a dialogue of a sort of ventriloqual kind. The devil in a Punchinello voice hazarded a number of questions and criticisms which the good Canon proceeded to pulverise. It was noticed by members of the congregation that two devout spinster ladies who had been sitting uneasily in the second pew on the first occasion, had moved to the back of the Church the following week.

On another occasion the Lenten Course was on "Little Sins". The first address was on "Worrying". "This is a truly dreadful sin. Now take my Aunt for instance. . . ." This was said as he waved his hand in the direction of the old lady herself, sitting in the Rectory pew. No one knew whether it would be quite nice to listen or not. I remember that I was once asked to preach at Richmond Parish Church and to stay the night. We had an excellent supper after Service and much stimulating conversation. As the clock struck ten the Canon sprang to his feet and walking to the door of his study said "Well, I'm off to bed now. I don't know what you are going to do" and switched out the light.

Canon D. S. Guy, my former Vicar, was one of Egerton Leigh's *bête-noirs*. Whenever Guy used to address his brother Rural Deans, Egerton Leigh, stretched at full length on a sofa in a corner of the Holden Library, used to sniff and snort in this self chosen background. On one occasion Oecumenical problems and projects had been lengthily discussed and Canon Guy was expatiating on how during a recent holiday (not in Switzerland this time but in Margate) he had spent his Sundays attending (incognito in a soft collar) the Services of various non-Anglican religious bodies—everything from the Congregationalists and

Methodists to the Friends and the Christian Scientists. His eloquence was rather damped down when Egerton Leigh suddenly shouted out "Great waste of time. I move that we go on to the next business."

Bishop Strong greatly appreciated Canon Egerton Leigh and knew what a power he was for good in Swaledate despite his eccentricities. Needless to say I learnt a great deal from contacts with such men as the two Vicars of Leeds, Heywood and Thompson-Elliott, who were always so friendly, as well as some who were deeply versed on the problems and needs of the rural areas.

In the spring of 1925, Ian Alan, eighth Duke of Northumberland, offered me the Rectory of Kirkby Wiske. This was entirely unexpected and I was in a quandary as to what to do. I did not want to leave the Bishop and the Chaplaincy work of which I had now got the measure; but Kirkby Wiske was eleven miles from the Palace and too far to come daily in the winter months. We were also very happy at North Stainley and had many friends. May Yorke did not advise me to accept. Her brother-in-law Herbert Watson had been there before becoming Archdeacon of Richmond and Canon Residentiary of Ripon. There was much less social life than in the area nearer Ripon. In fact Kirkby Wiske was rather isolated. There were two churches and double the population of Stainley. It would mean relinquishing the Chaplaincy before next winter. In favour of going was the fact that a third child was expected in addition to our two little girls Adelaide and Anne, and North Stainley Vicarage was getting very small for us. The income of North Stainley was only about £330 per annum; that of Kirkby Wiske was over £800. The Rectory was a good modern house and there was a fine vegetable garden: I talked to Bishop Strong. He said he did not want me to go: but he thought perhaps that I ought not to turn the offer down. With very mixed feelings I accepted and we moved in April. Bishop Strong instituted me and Archdeacon Watson inducted me. The Bishop appointed the Rev. A. C. Brashaw, Curate of Masham as his new Chaplain. I came over to Ripon a few times and showed my successor the ropes, so to speak; but within a very few months the Bishop himself was leaving to become Bishop of Oxford. I think that he too suffered from very mixed feelings at the prospect of change. Oxford had been his life since his boyhood and he had at first been very homesick for it after he came to Ripon in 1920. He knew however that the Bishop of Oxford's work was much more outside the city and

University than inside. He had also become very happy at Ripon whilst he had gained a perfect grasp of the diocese. He was very popular with the business men of Leeds, especially at the Club there, where the leading men of the city liked and admired him immensely. He had also won the affection and regard of the clergy of the Diocese, both in the towns and the remote country areas. Now in his sixties if he had consulted his inclinations he would have preferred to stay on at Ripon for another eight to ten years and then retire. He knew the almost insoluble problems of the Oxford Diocese with its three counties and its 600 parishes.

The news of the Bishop's imminent departure made me glad that I was well settled before he left. I did not know then that I was to become a Chaplain to his Successor, and that for many months at a time during the next five years I was to be back at my old job in the vacancies between the comings and goings of three or four Domestic Chaplains. Arthur Brashaw stayed only about two to three months after Arthur Burrough's arrival and then went to a Parish in Dorset. I returned to the Palace two or three days a week. After some four or five months came Ruthven Wright who stayed about a year. It transpired that he had once volunteered for work abroad under the C.M.S. Quite unexpectedly they claimed him and the Bishop feeling that this was a prior claim let him go. Back I came this time for a longer time than before. Ultimately Harold Mulliner arrived and proved an able Chaplain, though perhaps not so much suited to the simpler folk of the Parish. His modernistic sermons on the Incarnation and Resurrection were not for them.

About the middle of this period of comings and goings Bishop Burroughs appointed me Editor of the new diocesan Magazine: "The Ripon Diocesan Messenger". I enjoyed this and managed to get a considerable number of leading Church dignitaries and laymen to contribute special articles.

In these ways, although I had left North Stainley, I kept right in the middle of the affairs of the Diocese: and although it would have been difficult to find two Anglican Bishops more different than Thomas Strong and Arthur Burroughs I was fortunate in having a deep friendship and affection for both of them. Chronologically my period of work with my new Bishop falls under my incumbency at Kirkby Wiske and I shall leave it until my next Chapter to say something of Arthur Burroughs, a lovable and brilliant person, never, in my opinion, adequately appreciated by the Diocese as a whole.

CHAPTER X

Rector Of Kirkby Wiske (1925-31)

THE PARISH was extensive, lying along the eastern bank of the river Swale into which flowed the meandering waters of its eastern tributary the more modest Wiske. Both could swiftly swell to flood in rainy weather and the Swale in particular could assume a menacing and sinister character in its muddy swirling lower reaches, with its piled up banks near to bursting. The country was flat and a great contrast to the hilly scenery of the upper part of Swaledale. The Parish, however, had many fine views of the Hambledon Hills to the east and was well wooded. Stretching for almost seven miles from north to south it lay between North-allerton and Thirsk, some eleven miles north-east of Ripon. It was bounded on the eastern side by the diocese of York. Roger Ascham (tutor to Elizabeth I) was born here and amongst past Rectors were an Archbishop of Cashel and two Bishops (Suffragan) of Richmond.

The Church was the most beautiful I have ever had. There was a lovely Norman south doorway, an Early English nave, a spacious and dignified decorated chancel and a fine stalwart early perpendicular tower. There was much fine carving in the interior, specially in the chancel, with sedilia on the south side of the sanctuary and the remains of an Easter Sepulchre on the north. The furnishing was good and modern: fine solid oak pews throughout and good choir stalls. The glass was modern and good in colour. The exception was the large east window, which though of the mid-Victorian period was at least a good specimen of a bad period. It was by Capronnier and made in Belgium. There was a reasonably good organ in a handsome case and there was seating for about three hundred people in the spacious nave. Like my Parish Church in my first curacy, its dedication was to St. John the Baptist.

Geographically it was undoubtedly an awkward, isolated and scattered Parish. It was also far from all the centres of activity in the diocese—Ripon, Harrogate and Leeds; nor was there any real centre of population near the Parish Church or anywhere else. There were three tiny villages, first Kirkby Wiske, then a good two miles away to the west near the Swale, Maunby with its little red brick church of St. Michael; then on, north of Maunby, nearly another two miles away was Newby Wiske. This third village had no Church; but across the river Wiske, less than a quarter of a mile to the east was South Otterington (in the York diocese). North of Newby Wiske the Parish ran on for nearly another two miles and there were many large and isolated farms in all directions. Some of these could only be visited with any ease either in drought or frost, as they were at other times usually surrounded by quagmires through which one could neither be sure of being able to drive a car, nor of walking on foot without sinking ankle deep in to the mud! It was not therefore a well centralised Parish in which it was easy to collect a large congregation at the Parish Church. The Maunby people naturally went to their own little Church. The first Rector of South Otterington, in my time, was an active poacher in Newby Wiske, even sending printed invitations to one of my Church wardens and to some of my Choir members to attend his Easter Day Services, and visiting constantly in that end of the Parish so close to his own. I told him that he was of course welcome to visit those of my Parishioners who chose to go to his Electoral Roll; but I had to forbid the sending of invitations to those who were not. I also ran a bus to Kirkby Wiske Church on certain Sunday evenings and for the Morning Services on Christmas and Easter days. This met with the most encouraging response of my whole time in the Parish; but I do not think that it endeared me to the Rector of South Otterington. He was an irascible little old man and far from friendly. On several occasions we met head on, so to speak, in the Newby Wiske area of the Parish. I usually tried to make some reasonably pleasant remark or pass the time of day; but my sallies were generally rebuffed. My wife and I had rather a joke about this gruff clerical neighbour. We built up a theory that he had during his Missionary career in Africa or India (I forget which) studied the lore of the witch doctors and qualified as a "rain-maker". Anyway whenever I visited the part of my Parish near to his it almost invariably poured with rain! After his sudden death and the arrival of a charming and aimiable successor, one no longer got soaked when visiting parochially in those parts!

In our Churchyard adjacent to the large east window were buried the local magnates, mostly members of the Lascelles and Pulleine families. I am afraid that our family rather disrespectfully christened this line of impressive tombstones "Nobs' Row".

There was however one curious mystery connected with it. It produced a strange effect upon our little son, Robin, born in August, 1925. For the first three years of his life from the moment when he began to take any notice of his surroundings, if ever he was taken through this part of the grave yard he invariably stared gravely at these emblems of mortality and violently snorted like a pig. Did he see something which we could not? The mystery has remained unsolved, for when questioned at a later age Robin denied all recollection of these manifestations.

The Hon. George Lascelles and Lady Louisa had lived at Sion Hill nearby where they produced a family of twenty-two children, beaten for the Parish record only by their own coachman who had twenty-three! In that large house with its bulging family there was in those good old days no water laid on upstairs. One can imagine the toiling and moiling with endless cans of "hot and cold" to supply the legion of bedroom hip-baths. After the Lascelles, came the Percy Stancliffes who bought the place for the sake of the lovely gardens and grounds, but wisely pulled down the inconvenient old house and built a most beautiful modern Queen Anne home with every possible convenience and refinement. I can see still Mrs. Stancliffe's boudoir panelled in satin wood with built-in cupboards filled with exquisite old china. The Stancliffes were wealthy brewers from Macclesfield and a very good couple. He was one of our Churchwardens and put all his business acumen at the disposal of the Church. Mrs. Stancliffe was an extremely sweet and gentle little lady and became a great friend of my Mother's. They had two grown up sons, Richard, who married a Stobart and George who never married but took up farming in Cumberland. Both died comparatively young. Mr. Stancliffe who was one of Robin's godfathers, had a long and lonely widowed old age, cheered by his grand-daughters' visits.

At Breckenborough Hall were Mr. (later Sir) Francis Samuelson and his unmarried daughter. He had lost a very beautiful wife under most tragic circumstances—burnt to death when having her hair done. A fine marble memorial in the Church displays the lady and records the fact. Although he was Jewish, Sir Francis was none the less one of our most generous subscribers to Church needs. He was extremely wealthy, having vast numbers of both indoor and outdoor staff. His war-time economy had been to reduce the indoor staff from fifteen to fourteen by not replacing the pantry boy when he enlisted. Sir Francis was the Chairman of the great engineering firm of Dorman-Long & Co. and, like Percy Stancliffe, a first rate administrator. He was also very artistic, painted well in water colours and made a choice collection of the works of such well known modern artists as Paul Nash, Hilder, Edmond Dulac and Arthur Rackham.

At Maunby Hall were Major Alan Hill-Walker, V.C. and his charming wife, Lilias. More than any of our local magnates these two were the greatest personalities in the district. The Hall was hers. She had been Lilias Walker and he Alan Hill. When they married they combined their names as well as their resources. Alan Hill had got his V.C. in South Africa. He was a very modest young man, and having heard that when he, as the conquering hero, returned home, was going to be greeted by a brass band and a civic welcome at the railway station at Northallerton, he bribed the engine driver to stop the train a couple of hundred yards short of the platform. He accordingly descended with his suitcases and went quietly home with his groom and dogcart which he had arranged to have strategically available nearby. Lilias Hill-Walker bred alsatians and the house was infested by pedigree bitches of doubtful temper and temperament. The Hill-Walkers were on a party telephone line with us and others. Occasionally one got snippets of alarming conversations, such as—

"Yes, she is expecting her family one day now, so she is very fidgety and difficult. Yesterday she bit both her sisters! "

It was from contact with this doggy world that our little daughters learnt a coarse word. One day my wife and mother were discussing some definitely adult topic at the luncheon table. I saw Adelaide (now about five) pricking up her ears and gave warning in my best dog-French.

"Pas devant les infants! " "Ah", said Adelaide "I know what proverb Daddy is thinking of: "Little *bitches* have long ears". Major Hill-Walker used kindly to read the Lessons at Maunby Church. He barked them out, irrespective of their context like a R.S.M. on the barrack square. There were times when it became almost unbearably embarrassing or incongruously comic. Our Maunby Evensongs were very friendly and informal. One Sunday evening after finishing my Sermon I gave out from the pulpit the number of the next hymn. It was not the number advertised on the hymn board (which was wrong, also unsuitable and entirely unfamiliar). My hymn was correct and from the Hymn Sheet. The following conversation ensued.

The Major (holding up his hand): "No, old boy, you've got

it wrong. It's so and so."

Myself: "Actually it is the hymn board which is wrong, Major."

The Major (saluting): "As you were! As you were! "

Nearly all the funny things seemed to happen at Maunby rather than at the Parish Church. One Sunday as I finished giving the final blessing and before the little harmonium had time to wheeze out a faint Amen, my daughter, Anne, in piercing tones addressed her Mother.

"Mummie, are we going to have those buns with pink icing on them for tea to-day?"

On another occasion I was preaching on a warm Sunday afternoon on the subject of Church attendance and ventured to ask a rhetorical question.

"Do you really believe the man who goes out fishing instead of coming to Church, when he says that he can worship God just as well on the river bank?"

A large buxom lady crimson with fury, immediately jumped up in her front pew and shouted:

"I don't see why he should pick on *my* husband! " and banged out of Church.

A definite ripple of laughter went over the whole congregation and I had some difficulty in composing my face and taking up my parable once more. Sunday Evensongs were rather a rush: Maunby Evensong, 6.0 p.m.; Kirkby Wiske, 7.0 p.m. Our nice young Organist, Winnie Appleby, used to manage by leaving everything ready for the Parish Church Evensong after Morning Service. We left Maunby in my car at precisely 6.50 p.m., did the two miles in five to six minutes, and at 6.57 she was beginning her Voluntary at the other Church. As we were only human there were certain snags. One Sunday night at the Parish Church after I had finished reading the Second Lesson there was a pause, Winnie looked round wildly from her seat at the Organ and asked me in a distracted stage whisper—

"Where are we now anyway?"

"Nunc Dimittis", I replied firmly.

At Newby Wiske we had at Solberge Mr. Benjamin Talbot, Chairman of the British Iron and Steel Federation, a kind man with a nice wife, a son and a daughter who sang and ultimately married Sir Thomas Nussey. When my musical friend Tom Bye was with us he was in great demand to accompany Viva Talbot. I remember one night when we all four dined at Solberge (my Mother, Mollie and I and Tom). Poor Tom had to work very hard after a more than ample soporific dinner. Twice she sang the Erl King after a whole series of Schubert Lieder. When she finished she was still as fresh as paint. Tom was almost in a state of collapse after the two excursions through the tempestuous accompaniment, when all he had wanted to do was to go to sleep.

At Newby Wiske Hall (the old home of the Smithsons and Percys) were Mr. and Mrs. Ernest Doxford of the Sunderland shipping firm: very rich and very kind to us. This little country Parish had some of the wealthiest people in the North of England resident in it. They were all extremely good to us. Few people know that the little county town of the North Riding of Yorkshire, Northallerton, with its environs, was considered by the income tax authorities as one of the richest areas in England, in proportion to population.

Our visits, specially to the more remote farms were amazingly welcome, and as at North Stainley, we had often to put away immense "high teas". One devout Roman Catholic family (the only one in the Parish in those days) actually wrote and asked me to call, which I did quite regularly once I knew that there would be a welcome. They became most friendly and took our Parish Magazine and Church Kalandar every year. At some of these isolated farms one seemed to jump a century back. In one of them there lived an old man and his three sisters (one a widow). Their outlook was quite eighteenth century. The brother whose rule was absolute, went to market once a week. Two of the sisters went perhaps once a quarter. The eldest sister had not been out to market for years. I think that she had probably taken in that Queen Victoria was dead: but I never saw a newspaper in that house and I think that the only news that the sisters got of the outside world was what their brother chose to tell them after market days. There was no radio in those days. They used to come to Church three times a year, Christmas, Easter and Harvest, and were extremely kind and hospitable folk. The only trouble there was that we had always to be entertained in the "best parlour" and even if a fire was lit in our honour the room (which had been shut up for months) was still as cold as the tomb; and to recline on the settee or in one of the large armchairs was like collapsing into a snow drift. Many an hour have we sat and shivered in that best parlour, whilst the eldest sister wandered around the house preparing a feast, and talking to herself nineteen to the dozen—relapsing when words failed her in curious cadenzas of "Hums and Hahs". Each re-entry into the room to lay the table or to bring in some vast ham, or huge plum cake was thus musically accompanied. At times we nearly became hysterical.

There were several "characters" in Kirkby Wiske Village. The farmer at the Glebe Farm, our tenant, a mild enough man as a rule and in complete subjection to a shrill voiced wife, had a life-long enemy across the road in a certain smallholder. Many were the wordy warfares bandied across the street of a summer evening as each leant on his front gate. The finale never varied; old Humphreys always got the last word by shouting:

"Well, I'm off to get my gun" and dashed into his cottage.

Humphreys had an exceedingly ancient cow who was just about as much of a character as he was. Every year he used to drive her to Northallerton to sell her at the market; but he never succeeded in getting her there. At a certain spot not far from the town the resourceful old animal invariably gave him the slip and cantered off reaching home an hour or so before him. We were there some six years and during our time she must have been taken at least five times; but when we left in 1931 she was still triumphantly resident in the village.

Another of our locals was a strange wild looking woman who took in "boarded out" children. She was the grubbiest creature I have ever seen and her house was unspeakable. (We called it "The Creepers".) How the court authorities ever permitted her to take the children we could never fathom. However she had several very nice little girls and they always seemed healthy and happy enough. Miss R. was the best advertisement I have ever come across for the Group Movement. Somehow and somewhere they got hold of her and she was so fundamentally "changed" that she became quite clean and tidy, as did her house.

Many of the people who worked for us at our thirty-roomed Rectory were definitely "characters". Teddy Lofthouse, our gardener, was an unusual young man. Aged about twenty-four he was the despair of all the village maidens. His only love was the three-acre garden at the Rectory, which he tended with the utmost devotion. Expected to arrive at 8.0 p.m. he usually appeared about 7.15. With the help of a small boy in the autumn, when the yew hedges (dating from Queen Anne's reign) had their annual trimming, he kept that large and lovely garden immaculate. Occasionally I mowed the tennis lawn. I also took over the rock garden; but otherwise everything depended on Teddy.

"There were five lovely tomatoes coming on in the glass house yesterday. There are only two to-day!" commented Teddy severely one day.

I and my two small daughters maintained a guilty silence. Dick Priestman, despite his name and the fact that he was Sexton-Verger of the Church, was essentially a secular person. Although I never had proof positive I was frequently made aware of the fact that he took with him to Church on a Sunday, "the Sporting Pink". He was an undoubted expert on racing form. As he worked the hand blower of the church organ in the discreet shadows of the North Aisle, he allegedly assimilated his knowledge of those things, enjoying especially the leisure offered by the Sunday Sermons. Most of the families in the village had lived there for generations and there were several feuds of long standing. Our cook (the Sexton-Verger's wife) Mrs. Priestman knew all the histories. Her home was the other side of the Churchyard from the Rectory; but she would never go through the grave yard in the dark. The only annual exception was on the 5th of November. Once some of the naughty boys had thrown a large Chinese cracker under her skirts as she went home round by the village street. After that, once a year, she preferred to face the spooky terrors of the Churchyard. She had as her immediate neighbours a curious and slightly mentally sub-normal family who hated her with all the intensity of which they were capable. They always alluded to our Mrs. Priestman as "Her". One day I was visiting this family and tried to encourage them to come to church. It was however no use. How could they come to church—

"With *Her* with that mouth on Her, going there every Sunday?"

On one occasion their resentment took a more positive form of expression. As she passed their door one cold winter's evening Mr. and Mrs. S. who had been waiting for her, rushed out and each threw a bucket of icy water over her.

We liked "Nanny Peesum" as our children called her, although we were not unaware of the fact that she had her little ways and was not everybody's cup of tea in the village. She was very loyal to us according to her lights and liked her post at the Rectory. She had also liked our predecessors (Prebendary Cook and his daughter Dorothy). Their great merits in her eyes had been that they "did not bother too much about the house", and bought endless joints of meat. One could see why these facts were considered as virtues. "Nanny Peesum" used to bring a large *empty* basket with her every morning to the Rectory. Her conversation was very amusing and full of local information. A thumb nail sketch of anyone in the Parish was always available at a moment's notice. One could always add a little pinch of salt. Sometimes her "warnings" could be very valuable. As we had a house parlour maid, a tweeny, a Nanny, a laundress and a gardener as well, she did not mind the considerable amount of entertaining which we liked to do. On one occasion there were many chauffeurs awaiting their employers and "Nanny Peesum" entertained them handsomely in the kitchen. One chauffeur ventured the remark—

"Pretty smart place this for a Vicarage! "

"T'aint a Vicarage" came the crushing reply.

"Oh, well what is it then?"

"It's a Rectory."

"Same thing isn't it?"

"No, it's 'igher."

Our son Robin must have had the same idea, for when later on I was leaving Kirkby Wiske Rectory to go to Banbury, he burst into floods of tears when told that his father would no longer be a Rector but a Vicar instead.

News travelled fast round the village as none of our staff "slept in" except the children's nurse and the tweeny. One summer evening I left the house immediately after dinner to keep an appointment at a neighbouring farm house. On my way out of the Village I passed a row of cottages all with their front doors wide open because of the heat. One could not help hearing snippets of conversation here and there. As I passed the last house in the row I heard the following item of news.

"I hear they had jugged hare for dinner at the Rectory tonight."

Where upon a second voice chimed in—

"*And* redcurrant jelly."

A curious sensation of insecurity and living in a glasshouse overwhelmed me. How careful one must be!

Like my predecessor, the good Prebendary Cook, we ran a Men's Club in the roomy basement of the Rectory. This Club had a billiard room, a general reading and writing room and a modest little accommodation for the provision of cups of tea or coffee. I think that it was much appreciated and it was certainly well patronised. It also gave me a better opportunity to get to know some of our men who worked long hours on the land and were not often to be found at home.

My life was quite full and busy and although the Parish had only some eight hundred inhabitants, the distances were long. I was the editor of the new diocesan magazine *The Diocesan Messenger,* and I usually spent two days a week on the average at the Palace at Ripon helping Bishop Arthur Burroughs who was, as often as not, without a Resident Chaplain for some years.

There were many things waiting to be done in the Parish. There was no proper school playground and the sharp corner of the road into the village round the Churchyard was a real danger to the children. I got a nicely laid out and fenced playground. I also built sorely needed and decent lavatory accommodation. We were fortunate in having as our headmaster John Sanderson, a fine and attractive young man with his work at heart and plenty of ability and energy. He was a Lay Reader and his influence and my frequent presence in the Schools ensured that we had practically all the Day School pupils in our Sunday Schools also.

We also succeeded in restoring the Church Tower and some portions of the Chancel which needed attention, as well as the much weathered exterior of the North Aisle of the Nave. Our three bells were in a poor condition. One was badly cracked, the other two were out of tune. Consequently it was not considered safe to attempt to ring them. Our gardener's father, old Tom Lofthouse used to chime them in a fashion and the result was not very attractive. We had the cracked bell recast, the other two tuned and turned, and we added three more, having the whole ring of six put into a new steel frame, which took up much less room in the ringing chamber and actually lightened the weight on the tower. The result was great enthusiasm for bell ringing and before long we had two teams of keen young adolescent ringers, six boys and six girls, vying with each other for the greater proficiency. Altogether we raised about £5,000 during our six years at Kirkby Wiske and left both Church and Church School in much better condition than we had found them. The only person who was not pleased about the bells was poor old Tom Lofthouse, who refused to learn any new tricks and become a ringer instead of a chimer of bells. To signalise his disapproval of any change he also resigned from the Choir of which he had been a unique member for about sixty years. His uniqueness consisted in the fact that he was "illiterate" and despite his long and faithful service as a chorister, he had never learned to read. It might well be asked how then did he manage to function? and the answer is—far better than one might imagine. He had a good ear to begin with, and he knew the Canticles by heart, also at least twenty or thirty hymns. When it came to the Psalms or to less familiar hymns he refused to be defeated and made up his own words to the music as he went along. It was not I who discovered this; but my wife, who occasionally played the Organ when Winnie Appleby was away. One day she leant over to hear what verse in a particular Psalm had been reached. The nearest chorister was old Tom; but what she heard did not give her the information which she desired. Tom was happily singing away "Puss, puss, puss, puss, puss—bow-wow, wow, wow, wow, wow, wow." Perhaps from a sense of solidarity none of the other choirmen had ever told us of this: but they all knew and were completely accustomed to these variations and not in any way disconcerted by them.

We had six very happy years at Kirkby Wiske. I think that the congregations and collections increased. The Church and School were in much better condition and we had made many friends. When we were leaving one of our young farmer sidesmen with a certain grim sense of humour said to me:

"Well, Rector, there is one thing you have succeeded in doing in your six years here. You've got two of the three Dissenting Chapels in the Parish closed."

I refused all responsibility for this feat, and also to regard such closures as necessarily a good thing. We had had very friendly relations with the Methodists and I had preached in two of the said three Chapels more than once.

While I was at Kirkby Wiske I was one of Bishop Arthur Burrough's Chaplains and often for months at a time I went to the Palace at Ripon about twice a week to help with his more important correspondence and arrangements. He had also a lady secretary who attended to the more routine affairs. In time the Bishop and I got very close to one another. He was utterly different from Dr. Strong whose long experience had made him stand so firmly on his feet and able to grapple with practically any situation with immediate wisdom. Arthur Burroughs was highly strung and sensitive. His enthusiasm and conscientiousness made him worry more than he should have. Also his health was far from robust and he had long and trying bouts of sleeplessness. He was splendid with young people; but not so good with those older than himself. However as time went on things improved, and I am sure that if he had not died so young he would have made a fine Bishop in time. He had first rate brains and the kindest of hearts. He was full of charm and fun. He also had excellent artistic taste. I have still got several of the records of classical music which he gave me. Sometimes solemn and serious people considered him tactless. Sometimes his very quick Irish sense of humour was misunderstood.

One illustration of all this is provided by the story of his part in the dedication and opening of the new residential Hostel which the Mirfield Community of the Resurrection built at Leeds

University. Arthur had compiled with great care an entirely tactful and suitable address and I had taken it down and typed it out for him. Unfortunately at the actual ceremony on the spur of the moment he had inserted a would-be humorous remark which was not in the text. He prefaced his oration with saying that he was very glad to see that Leeds University was going to have at last a residential hostel of this kind. He had just come back from Oxford—ah, that was indeed a *real* University—and these newer places would become more like the great universities the more residential they became. This sally did not please Yorkshire's pride in its very promising and thriving University, recently refreshed with several generous gifts and endowments. There were adverse comments and angry letters in *The Yorkshire Post*: even a rather critical leader. Resentful letters poured in at the Palace, deploring such depreciation of Leeds' young University. Poor Arthur was very upset. He had only meant it as a joke.

Actually one good witticism came out of it all. Canon R. H. Malden, the Vicar of Headingley, was being shown round the new Hostel a few days later, whilst the angry reactions to the Bishop's *faux pas* were still reverberating in Leeds. He looked at the two niches on the building, one with a figure in it and the other still empty. His guide pointed to one niche and said:

"That niche contains the statue of Dr. Frere, the Superior of Mirfield, who laid the first stone."

Like lightning came the rejoinder.

"Ah, and I suppose that the empty niche awaits the statue of Arthur, our Bishop, who dropped the last brick!" In spite of his critics however Bishop Burroughs did an immense amount of good during his all too short episcopate at Ripon. He understood young people and he had a whole series of inspiring gatherings and conferences for Youth. The Palace was always full of young men and they were invariably full of enthusiasm for the Bishop. Former pupils of his from Oxford constantly turned up and one and all, each in his own fashion, commented on the way in which Arthur seemed so easily to appreciate their problems and points of view. Arthur actually had a very strong element of youthfulness and power of enjoyment in himself, another Irish quality. When he was in good form and not weighed down with some special worry, he and I had some extremely jolly times at the Palace and peals of laughter could often have been heard from his study as we were working over his correspondence or discussing some lighter diocesan happening.

In his letters, articles and preaching he could be quite brilliant and one was reminded that here was a former Head Boy of Harrow and one of Balliol's most distinguished scholars.

He tried hard to keep me in the diocese when the offer of Banbury came from Bishop Strong, offering me Horsforth or Wetherby and promising more; but much as I cared for him I felt that Bishop Strong's claim on me was paramount, whilst the prospects of getting back to the neighbourhood of Oxford was altogether alluring.

We had by this time quite a family. Adelaide had been born in 1923 at North Stainley, Anne a year later in 1924. Robin arrived in August 1925, some four months after we came to Kirkby Wiske. Cynthia (Mima) was also born there, but not until 1929.

Between 1920 and 1931 I had worked in four parishes: but one special parishioner had remained constant. Mrs. Louisa McMahon, widow of Archdeacon McMahon of Madagascar. She had become a great friend of my Mother and me, when I was a Curate at Christchurch, Harrogate. When we moved to North Stainley, she took rooms at the Staveley Arms, in the village, and later at The Cross Keys. Four years later when we left she moved to the Post Office at Kirkby Wiske in our wake. When six years later again we left the North for Banbury "Granny Mac" took up residence in the Horse Fair, just opposite our new Vicarage. She was a darling old lady, a reincarnation of pious Anna who haunted the Temple Courts of Jerusalem two thousand years ago: the most hundred per cent Christian I have ever known, though she never failed to call a spade a spade. She loved us all and we all loved her.

One looks back to those days in the North Riding of Yorkshire as very gay. In the summer we used to go once (or twice) a week sometimes to wonderful tennis parties at many of the lovely country houses round about. In the winter there always seemed to be at least one dinner party each week. We thought nothing of motoring ten or twenty miles to these various festivities. Kirkby Wiske was only about ten miles from North Stainley, so without losing our old friends in our former Parish we made a host of new ones also in the Thirsk and Northallerton areas. Looking back I can never remember more sociability than we experienced in that North Riding countryside—from Masham to Kirkby Moorside—except during the six years of my episcopate in gay little Bermuda. In Banbury we were too busy for social activities outside the Parish, even if there had been much scope. Then came World War II and the practical end of any real social life in England apparently.

It was in the April of 1931 that my father-in-law, Walter Freeman of Bilton Court, died quite suddenly.

Madge and Henry Freeman, the two unmarried members of the family continued to live on at Bilton Court for about another six or seven years, finding increasing difficulty in getting adequate staff. Finally the whole place was sold up.

It was in the August of 1931 that we left Yorkshire with much sadness as we thought of all our good friends there; but we looked forward to the challenge and interest of one of the great centres of Church life in the Diocese of Oxford and to having Dr. Strong once more as our Bishop.

CHAPTER XI

Vicar Of Banbury (1931-46)

I WAS thirty-nine when I was offered Banbury by Bishop Strong who in his letter suggested that I should come and visit him and talk it all over. He considered Banbury one of the "Key Parishes" of the Oxford Diocese and the work there arduous and responsible. "It is a real centre of Church worship and life" was the way he summed it all up. He advised me to go and have a talk with the former Vicar, Canon A. J. Jones, a Welshman as the name suggests, who had recently become Vicar of Bray. The old gentleman received me with great dignity. He answered my questions briefly and I felt that he probably had someone else in view for the post. The only thing that he told me with any enthusiasm was that his first impression was that I was "far too young for such a Parish". I told him that I was about two years older than he had been when *he* had gone to Banbury. His final comment was that Bishop Strong knew nothing about the place and would have been well advised to have discussed the matter with him or at any rate with Bishop Shaw (at that time the Assistant Bishop for the Oxford Archdeaconry). It was evident to me that the good Canon did not know much about Bishop Strong if he imagined that the Bishop did not at least know all that was essential about any subject in which he was interested. Bishop Strong happened also to know that Bishop Shaw had his own candidate for Banbury and had already told me so.

When I went to Banbury I had a very nice welcome from the people at large, although one or two ladies whose devotion to Canon Jones was particularly intense were not at first very friendly. One professional man's wife, who came to call (curiously enough under the circumstances) hissed at me as she pushed away my hand when I tried to shake hands with her, that she had had to "force" herself to come and call, as she could scarcely bear to see anyone else daring to occupy the post and the house which that wonderful man had graced for so long. Another lady said to me: "Well, you are a brave young man to try and follow a man like the dear Canon". I am afraid that I was rather pert in my reply to her when I said: "Oh, but I am not sure that I *am* going to *follow* him. I think each of us should take his *own* line". Incidentally she became later a great friend and worker. Canon Jones had been a very popular Vicar and deservedly so no doubt.

One rather amusing little incident occurred in my first few weeks at Banbury. I attended some clergy conference at Hertford College, Oxford. At luncheon in the Hall, knowing nobody I sat down in the one empty seat left at a long table. Around me were a lot of elderly clerics who all evidently knew one another very well. The subject under discussion was not that of our Conference: but the way in which important livings in the Diocese were being filled by "outsiders". Two parishes and their new incumbents were mentioned. Then someone said: "And now it is the same story at Banbury! Why did the Bishop have to bring someone all the way down from his old Diocese in Yorkshire? Aren't there plenty of good men here?"

"What's the man like? Do you know anything about him?"

"No. I don't. Some quite junior man: Some pet of the Bishop's I gather."

Although no one at the table had said a word to me during the whole of lunch time, I felt that perhaps I should, in fairness, now join in. Naturally I should dearly have loved to hear more about myself; "Actually *I* am the Bishop's p— the new Vicar of Banbury," I interjected. Collapse of the whole outfit; and a moment of silence and perspiration! Then one of the old gentlemen said rather breathlessly and with a painful smile: "Oh, an admirable appointment I am sure". I had to giggle. After lunch the dear old man asked me to go for a walk with him and we became very good friends and remained so until his death several years later.

People who, like myself, have been accustomed to warm hearted Irish people and forthright Yorkshire folk, may at first think Midlanders rather unfriendly; but one learns in time how fundamentally nice they can be and that once they take to you, they are friends for life.

The Parish of Banbury was about the size of St. John's, Kidderminster, or Christchurch, Harrogate, having in the 1930s a population of over 10,000; but it was an ancient parish. The old Gothic church, one of the largest and finest in that part of England, had suffered the same fate as Banbury's castle and its ancient gates and walls. It had been demolished in the eighteenth century. Parts of the huge Vicarage dated from the early days of the sixteenth century and the general effect was of a pleasing

Tudor mansion built of the golden brown Hornton stone. The income which went with this important Parish and palatial residence was £376 per annum. In the Middle Ages Banbury had been a wealthy living, as with the Parish had gone a Residentiary Canonry at Lincoln Cathedral. However during the Reformation period when the Diocese of Oxford was formed and Oxfordshire was no longer in the Lincoln Diocese, the endowments of this post were split, two-thirds going to the Lincoln Canonry whilst the Rector of Banbury became a Vicar instead and had to be content with only one-third of the former income.

Canon Jones as a bachelor had just been able to manage. His two predecessors, Mr. Back and Canon Porter had had no children and rich wives, the former having lived in considerable style and having sported a smart carriage and pair.

It was lucky for us that, with four children to educate, we were not dependant upon the riches of the benefice, and as we ran two cars for some years, we were of course credited with vast wealth.

The late Classical Church of the Seventeen nineties, though rather shapeless in its massiveness outside, had a real grandeur within. In seating accommodation it was one of the largest Parish Churches in England. It was also one of the best buildings for sound that I have ever known. Its acoustics enhanced the excellent choir which was to continue to hold the Oxford Diocesan competitive Choir Shield during the whole period of my incumbency.

Banbury Parish Church was very fortunate in its Organist. Charles Palmer was also Music Master of what is now the Grammar School and used his opportunities to get musical boys with good voices from this ample source of recruitment. He not only took immense pains in training his choir, but also a real interest in their general welfare and future. Many a young man later doing well in after life has owed his initial advancement to the efforts of Charles and Clare Palmer.

Charles Palmer was a great character and many are the good stories about him. Banbury became accustomed to the bracing entry form for boy choristers at the Parish Church. Parents had to sign this document which included a consent for the Organist to cane any boy should he consider such treatment desirable! (This clause later caused great shock amongst the fond parents of the little pets who joined St. Peter's Choir in Bournemouth, and who often arrived in large limousines if the weather was wet or doubtful.) Charles had his own sense of humour and could tell a good tale: but sometimes other people's jokes did not strike him so forcibly. One of these occasions was an important funeral (fully musical) at St. Mary's. Some of the family and friends were coming from London and the time of starting the Service was rather delayed. The person who was being buried was one of the leading butchers in the town. The Choir and clergy, all robed, were sitting waiting in their stalls. Charley Palmer had played all his usual suitable "funeral music" over and over again. Then he had an inspiration—a little Bach. He played it and clergy and choir all smiled. "Sheep may safely graze." However it took quite a lot of explaining to him afterwards.

When I went to Banbury in 1931 there was besides the Parish Church a daughter church on the Warwick Road, St. Paul's. This served the growing areas on the north west side of the town. At the south end of the town also there was in the Easington **area a large new** population growing up. There was neither church, church hall nor Sunday school except for what the Methodists were doing to try to meet the situation. Also, although the population of the Parish was growing steadily there was already a tendency (seen in most growing places today) for people, especially the more well-to-do, to move into the outskirts or even into the country and surrounding villages. More and more of the beautiful old houses in the centre of the town were being turned into offices and shops. The whole place was bristling with problems and I soon realised there were four main efforts which I must make.

There was first of all a considerable need for a thorough visitation of the whole place so as to draw more people into the sphere and service of the Church. Then secondly, as soon as possible there should be the raising of funds to build a Church Hall in a central site (already obtained) amongst the three thousand residents in Easington so that there could be a church, a Sunday school and a suitable meeting place for Church folk and their activities. Thirdly, there was a good deal to do to the Parish Church itself, the organ needed considerable attention and indeed completion; whilst the decorations of the large eastern apse had been so decayed and defaced by the gas fumes of a huge chandelier, only recently electrified, that their subject had become more like the markings on a mouldy cheese. The fourth problem was that of the Church Schools. Educational reform was in the air. Our present St. Mary's Church Schools catered for three departments: infants (mixed), boys and girls. The teaching was good, the staff efficient, but the buildings were tending to become sub-standard. What was needed was to let these buildings become a Junior School only, after a complete overhaul; and to get a site on the nearby Southam Road and build a new Church Senior School there.

My predecessor's two Colleagues, the Rev. J. A. Hultgren experienced and shrewd, and the Rev. W. Windsor-Cundell, a popular young man with charm and enthusiasm, both accepted my invitation to stay on for the present. They proved most loyal and willing assistants.

The Parish was peculiar in having not two but *three* Church-wardens at St. Mary's as well as two deputy Wardens at St. Paul's. All these were good men. At St. Mary's I was fortunate in having a most delightful gentleman-farmer as Vicar's Warden, Mr. W. I. R. Lidsey of Hardwicke; whilst another substantial farmer from the opposite end of the Parish, Mr. Arthur Hemmings, and Mr. John Collingridge a first class businessman and former Mayor, were the People's Wardens. One of Banbury's ablest and most outstanding citizens, also its leading archæologist and the Editor of the *Banbury Guardian,* Mr. William Potts, was with us as Vice-chairman and leading spirit on the large Parochial Church Council. He could always be counted on for wisdom, tact and courtesy. We were fortunate also in having about forty good sidesmen and a really large band of ladies ready to help in raising funds for all Parish needs. When we had our Annual Bazaar (mainly for the Curate's Fund) we could proudly print the names of some one hundred and fifty helpers on the programme; and each year saw a rise in the amount made. My first Bazaar (1931) was an increase on former days and reached a total of about £380. Our last effort, fourteen years later, produced the all time record of £987.

In my first year I managed to pay personally just under 2,000 visits. Few people avowed religious or doctrinal difficulties as reasons for non-attendance at Church. Apathy, not hostility, seemed to account for loss of contact with the Church in almost every case. Without appearing too stereotyped or professional we had a definite set of questions in mind when visiting: which included the question of Churchgoing (if not, why not). If there were children questions of Sunday School or Confirmation came up. If there were invalids, they got on to someone's lists. One's reception was invariably friendly. There were of course amusing incidents. One comfortable old couple who entertained me in the "back room", insisted that before leaving I should be conducted to the "best room" to see their "three piece suite" (a magnifical affair in red plush). I admired it, as expected, and the episode ended with the comment: "I don't suppose a poor parson like you often sees a set-up like that".

"No indeed," I replied.

Some of the reasons for having given up Church going were strange. "Nobody has ever visited us before, so we have never visited you!" "One of the curates promised us milk tickets for the baby; but we never got them; so that finished us with the Church." The strangest was: "We used to come and always sat under the pulpit; but Canon Porter's false teeth fitted very badly, so we went to Christchurch". I assured them that my teeth were all my own, and they came back—after thirty years! One good lady said that she had given up Church because she found it "so depressing". Further enquiry revealed the fact that the only services she was in the habit of attending were *funerals*! I suggested a course of Festival Evensongs at Christmas, Easter and Harvest Thanksgiving as the thin edge of the wedge for the evolution of a more cheerful view of organised Church services. I discovered later that this particular character divided her loyalty between the Anglican and Roman Churches as regards the various charities available. When she had exhausted the possibilities of the Anglican charities over Christmas she started a campaign at the Roman Catholic Church. I think that in time both Father Wall and I got her summed up, and we used to warn one another about her recent activities and practise rather more economy where she was concerned. "I'm a good Catholic, Father", meant that she had temporarily exhausted the financial possibilities of local Anglicanism. "I'm a good Churchwoman, Vicar" meant that she had got all she could from Rome for the time being. A very broadminded woman.

To ensure that the whole Parish could be covered, without neglecting other duties, I soon got a third Curate, the Rev. T. H. South of Queen's College, Oxford and Cuddesdon: an attractive and capable person, with some years of banking experience behind him.

Our first effort at Easington was to obtain the use of the Territorials' Drill Hall on Sunday afternoons and to announce in the papers the forthcoming opening of a Sunday School. I remember so well the first occasion. My wife and I arrived a quarter of an hour before the time advertised, taking with us in our car a small portable harmonium and fifty hymn books and expecting perhaps forty or fifty youngsters. The number of children who turned up was one hundred and sixty. Two nice girls whom I had got to come and help took over those of from six to nine; my wife played the hymns, whilst I had a mixed class of ninety boys and girls of from ten to fourteen years of age. Armed with this proof of the real needs of the district, I then launched an Appeal for £2,000 and with the additional help of a Diocesan grant the money was soon forthcoming. Bishop Shaw (now very friendly) laid the Foundation Stone of St. Hugh's Church Hall in 1932; and a year later Bishop Strong came and dedicated the completed building which was packed to capacity. It was quite an attractive little place and all the fittings were good. The Chancel could be completely shut off, and what was the nave on Sundays, was a Social Hall during the week. The two cloakrooms became on Sundays the Infant Sunday School Classrooms. There was also a useful kitchen at the back of the east end on one side and a Vestry on the other. Tommy South became the first Curate-in-charge, and when Jack Hultgren (who was older than I) left to become Vicar of Colnbrook, William Cundall took over St. Paul's and the Rev. Norman Wilkinson joined my staff at St. Mary's. Norman Wilkinson had been at Peterhouse, Cambridge and taken Honours in Science but had followed this with a graduate course at the University of Jena in Germany. He was a very gifted young man and was not only an exceptionally good preacher but an excellent pianist. He could be most amusing. How well I remember one meeting of the District Visitors (for the annual distribution of Christmas Charities), when one earnest lady exclaimed with rebuke in her voice: "But Mr. Wilkinson, don't you remember Mrs. Huggins and Mrs. Buggins? Can't you *try* to remember them from year to year?"

"No, no," he replied, "*I try* to *forget* them!" This silenced the lady, but the remark made history in these meetings. Incidentally these numerous little charities were becoming a farce. Many of them were of the character of "four yards of calico or red flannel for twenty god-fearing widows who attend church regularly". Did "god-fearing" mean Church-going? What was wrong with spinsters? What was "regularly"? Anyway who wanted calico or red flannel in those days (if they ever did in the days of long ago, which I rather doubted)? I took great pleasure in getting all these problems straightened out after a most complicated correspondence with the Charity Commissioners; and before long we had all these ridiculous conditions abolished and gave straightforward tickets of credit at one of the local grocery stores. The change was much appreciated by the recipients whether god-fearing widows, regular church-goers, or not. There was a good deal of poverty in certain districts. There was also a good deal of begging. One woman in particular was a well known practitioner of this art and could be seen coming jauntily up the Vicarage drive. By the time the door was opened to her however the tears were coursing down her cheeks. She was known all over the town as "Blubbing Emma". In spite of being nearly inarticulate with sobs and groans, she could produce some original gambits.

"My daughter tried to throw herself out of the train coming back from Leamington last night and I tore her coat something awful saving her life."

Another day when my wife answered the door it was:

"My husband's been in a temper and threw my only 'at into the fire. What am I to do?"

As we lived on a busy main road we got a lot of would be travellers, mostly Scotsmen, who merely wanted their fares to Glasgow, Edinburgh or even Dundee. One day we found a young man apparently in a half fainting condition by our hall door. He had a bloodstained bandage round his head. He was "nicely spoken". Could he come in and rest for a short time? He had had a motor-cycle smash. In a few minutes my wife and mother were doing the ministering angels, although he refused to have his bandage removed and his head bathed. His great trouble was that his mother was expecting him home in Southampton that night; but he had no money for a railway fare. As he had given us the name and address we offered to telephone; but he explained that his mother was an invalid with a weak heart. If she heard that he had had an accident she might have a heart attack! So urged on by my compassionate ladies I gave him one pound and he wrote me a receipt with a very shaky hand and said I would have the money back by return of post. We took him down to the station in our car. After a week I wrote to the name and address he had given and enquired for his health and said that I would be glad to be repaid. Ultimately my letter was returned by the Post Office marked "No such Address: Return to Sender". He had really done the job quite thoroughly as he had stopped some motorists outside Banbury, begged a lift from them and given such a graphic account of his accident that they also had "lent" him a pound and called at a local Garage on his behalf. The Garage man had promptly sent out his break-down lorry to the exact spot, only to find that there was no motor bicycle. I knew the garage proprietor quite well and we compared notes and found fairly speedily that his villain and mine were one and the same. History repeats itself, we are told. A few weeks later a young man, bloodstained bandage and all, came to a Vicar in Nuneaton with the same sad story about the smash and the invalid mother in Southampton. All went well until the Vicar took him to the station and unfortunately purchased the ticket to Southampton himself, despite the young man's protests that he really need not bother. With suspicions aroused, the Vicar hid round the corner and heard and saw the young man, back at the ticket office saying:

"Look here, I find that I cannot travel on this ticket this evening after all. Could you please refund the money?"

It was thus that he became the guest of His Majesty. I forget how many other cases were taken into consideration; but he had specialised in the clergy of the Midlands.

Having got our Church Hall going nicely at Easington ("St. Hugh's" after St. Hugh, Bishop of Lincoln, who had property in Banbury), I turned to the needs of the Parish Church. We raised some two thousand pounds for the Organ and not only completed the stops required, but built the handsome oak case on the North East wall and had all the pipes both there and in the Chancel gilded to match with the general scheme of the Church. Before that the pipes in the Chancel had been a very disturbing shade of blue with a faded pattern which suggested that the instrument had at some time suffered from a severe rash. I discovered about this time something which had apparently been forgotten for well over fifty years. There had once been a modest one thousand pounds endowment for a Chancel Repair Fund. This had been quietly accumulating and when I dug it out again after all those years there was something in the region of four thousand pounds. Some of this I used for the restoration of the paintings in the Apse which had become so indecipherable.

The greatest work of my pre-War period at Banbury was of course the scheme for a new Church Senior School. The considerable negotiations and work for this covered the years 1935-9. All went well. An adequate and suitable site was obtained on the west side of the Southam Road under a quarter of a mile out of the town and beyond our existing schools. There was ample space for playgrounds and recreation fields. Some sixty thousand pounds was either collected or promised. The plans came back fully approved from the Board of Education; but the very next week Hitler started World War II and that was the end.

I think that in the midst of all our national troubles and anxieties which resulted, this was the biggest disappointment of my ministerial career. When the War was over and I had left Banbury, my successor Dick Carpenter had to abandon a scheme which now seemed likely to cost at least three times as much as the original estimate.

It was about this period of my ministry that I took up an old interest again. When at North Stainley and Kirkby Wiske I had written two little Nativity Plays which had been published and had some success and been fairly widely used ("The Christmas Vision" and "The Holy Family"). They had been acted not only in the Ripon Diocese in several rural Parishes as well as in Harrogate and Leeds, but in London and Brighton. I now launched into a much bigger and more elaborate effort and wrote a Missionary Pageant Play in six episodes and entitled "The Two Ways". This was published by the Society for Promoting Christian Knowledge for the Society for the Propagation of the Gospel and ran through two or three editions. The general idea was to show that there were wrong as well as right ways of trying to "spread the Gospel". There were scenes in The First Crusade (France, 1096, A.D.). The Spanish Inquisition (Spain, 1560, A.D.). The Founding of the first Missionary Society of the Anglican Church (The S.P.G.) (England, 1701, A.D.). The Church in Action in the Moslem World (India c. 1925, A.D.). Finally, the Jerusalem Conference (Palestine, 1928, A.D.). This was written with the encouragement of Bishop Kenneth Kirk of Oxford for the Oxford Diocesan Missionary Festival (1938) and was performed in Banbury, Aylesbury, Maidenhead and Oxford during the Festival period. It was also later performed in London, South Africa and several other places, and finally was broadcast by the B.B.C.

After this the S.P.G. asked me to write more for them and suggested a Missionary Play with a message given through the medium of comedy, in contrast to the many consistently evincing a more serious strain. In response I wrote "The Happy Heathen".

In spite of the exigencies of the War years the Oxford Diocese celebrated its Fourth Centenary in 1942. One of the features was to be a series of short episodic historical plays covering periods in the history of the Church in this area. Again I was asked to contribute to this effort. There were some really distinguished people amongst the others who consented to help. Seven plays or episodes were written in all. Nevill Coghill (then a Fellow of Exeter College, Oxford, and well known as a Chaucer authority) wrote Episode I, "The Coming of Birinus". Episode III which dealt with the appointment of St. Hugh as Bishop of Lincoln, was written by B. C. Boulter. Episode IV, dealing with Robert King, first Bishop of Oxford, was written by the authoress, Elizabeth Goudge. The Rev. C. A. M. Adams (of St. John's College) wrote on Archbishop Laud. I wrote Episode II (Frideswide: Saintly Intercessor—dealing with the foundation of what is now Christ Church Cathedral); Episode VI (Robert Skinner, Bishop of Oxford under Puritan persecution); and Episode VII Samuel Wilberforce, Bishop of Oxford. These plays, either as a whole or separately, were acted all over the Diocese. I think that my most vivid memory is of that performance of Episode VI about Bishop Skinner and his secret seminary for Ordinands at Launton Rectory, being given there on a perfect summer afternoon in that lovely old Rectory garden, with Bishop Kirk in the audience. He congratulated me very nicely afterwards.

Another activity of Banbury days was my work with and for the Venerable Order of St. John of Jerusalem (the St. John Ambulance Association and Brigade). The organisation was very active in Banbury. Dr. Clive Gardiner-Hill and Sister Winifred Ellis (later Matron of the Horton Hospital, Banbury) were particularly energetic. I was happy to be drawn into it all. When the new Banbury Headquarters were dedicated and opened I officiated. Being unable to procure any official form of Service I composed what I hoped might be a suitable one and had it nicely printed and set out with the St. John Cross on the front page. A Knight of St. John, came down from Headquarters at Clerkenwell to officiate.

"I have never come across this official form of Service before," he said, "but I like it very much. May I take a dozen copies away with me for future use?"

"You may, indeed," I replied, "but I am afraid that it is not 'official'. In fact I put it together myself, not being able to get hold of any official form."

"You can take it from me, padre, it will be official all right."

Shortly after that I was appointed an Assistant Chaplain of the Order (Serving Brother), and a few years later, as my work for the Order in Oxford County increased, I became a full Chaplain (Commander), finally reaching the height of my ambition and hopes in this direction by becoming a Sub-Prelate in 1956, on my appointment as Bishop of Bermuda. Through St. John, apart from much interesting and worthwhile work I came into touch with many charming and interesting people including Lady Bicester, formerly Lady Sybil Smith (née Macdonnel), a member of the Antrim family, to which family in the long ago my great-great-grandfather (George Hill of Hillmount) and my great-grandfather (George McNeill) as well as my great-uncle William McNeill had all been Agents and legal advisers. I also met on several occasions Lord Wakehurst, who when Governor-General of Northern Ireland, cleverly managed also to continue as Prior of the Order by flying over from Belfast for all the Meetings at St. John's Gate. Always very friendly and knowing of my Mother's family's friendship with a former Irish Lord Lieutenant (Earl Spencer) he once asked my wife and me to visit them at Government House at Hillsborough, County Down. He was in all his many capacities and important posts one of the most charming and tactful of men and administrators. It was through St. John also I got to know that wonderful woman Countess Mountbatten. At one time I was on three different committees with her and on several occasions we were asked to those notable summer parties at Broadlands. (This was when I was Vicar of Bournemouth.) Lady Mountbatten was one of the first people to write and congratulate me when I was appointed Bishop of Bermuda. She invited me to lunch in London to talk over St. John plans for those Islands. She was even then contemplating that remarkable tour which she made a year or so later to the West Indies and Bermuda. Indeed it was in Bermuda that we last met. In Bermuda she made a tremendous impression. I believe that she was the first woman ever to address the Bermuda (Hamilton) Rotary Club amongst other things.

"She may be the first woman to address our luncheon Club," said one of Bermuda's leading citizens to me at the end of her speech, which was a masterpiece and made without a single note —"but she is the best speaker we have ever had at Rotary here."

She was working terribly hard and had had a tight packed programme of some weeks in the Carribean before coming to Bermuda. She was staying at Government House with Sir John and Lady Woodall and I saw her three or four times. Our only regret was that she just had not time to visit us at Bishop's Lodge. I thought her looking tired and strained: not that she would own up to it. She was telling me of what she had been doing in the West Indies.

"Anyway," she said, "my next trip will be an even bigger one in the *East* Indies, just for a change! "

"Not, I hope, until you have had a good rest," I ventured.

"A good rest! I hate resting! There is so much to get done. I shall just stay in England long enough to get a look at my family and re-organise my kit; then off I go."

She laughed when I asked her if she really thought it wise. Glittering in a marvellous iridescent gown and wearing a flashing tiara, she looked the personification of feminine elegance, intelligence and energy; but I felt somehow uneasy. I could only say—

"Well, I admire your zest; but if I may say so, I doubt the wisdom of it all—without a real rest, much as you may dislike the idea."

Only as it seemed a week or two later there came the sad news of her very sudden death, in her sleep.

This digression has taken me far from Banbury days.

Into our life at Banbury there came when we had been there about four years a great new friendship. On the retirement of Bishop Shaw as Assistant Bishop and Archdeacon of Oxford, Dr. Strong, now beginning to fail in health and memory himself, appointed as Bishop Shaw's successor, Gerald Allen, at that time Suffragan Bishop of Sherborne in the Salisbury Diocese. From being "+ Gerald Sherborne", he became "+ Gerald Allen, Bp." (and Archdeacon of Oxford). It was not until a year or so later that Bishop Kirk succeeded in getting a third Official Suffragan See for the Oxford Diocese and Gerald became Bishop of Dorchester. One of Gerald's very first engagements in the Oxford Diocese to which he now returned was a preachment at Banbury Parish Church on a Sunday evening. The great Church was packed. Later he told me that he had never seen such a congregation in an ordinary Parish Church. He and his wonderful stepmother, Dora, came to supper with us that night and then and there there began one of the great friendships of my life. Gerald's open and affectionate disposition made an immediate appeal, and he soon became much loved from one end of Oxfordshire to the other. He was frequently called "*Our* Bishop". I remember Kenneth Kirk once commenting upon this to me, somewhat wryly. He was as good as gold, a typical "once born"; but this did not mean that he had not a useful streak of clinical discrimination. He could recognise wickedness, ulterior motives, humbug and superficiality in a flash, however carefully disguised. Gentle and peaceable he could be very firm and even devastating when occasions really demanded it. I shall never forget once when an angry (and somewhat inebriated) local V.I.P. in the Banbury rural area rang him up at our Vicarage. I was going to get out of earshot, but he signed me to stay. Beyond gathering that the conversation from the other end was very rude and noisy and also somewhat incoherent, I got little of its detail, but enough of the general import. Gerald's replies were like a fall of icy water on a crackling bonfire.

"Does Major X understand that he is speaking to the *Bishop of Dorchester*?"

"I do not at all agree with what you say, still less do I like the way you put it."

"I thought that you were supposed to be an educated man and more or less of a gentleman."

Finally:

"I suggest that you ring up again when you are sober." Two days later he got a handsome letter of apology, so he told me!

The departure and decline of Bishop Strong was to me a deep sorrow; since, much as I came to admire the brilliant qualities of his gifted successor, Kenneth Kirk, I realised that I was exchanging a Bishop whom I had known and loved for nearly twenty years for a stranger who knew not Joseph.

Actually Bishop Kirk was nearly always very friendly and kind. He encouraged me to write plays, he made me Chairman of the Diocesan Union of Benefices Committee and after he had been with us two or three years he made me an Honorary Canon of Christ Church. Indeed I was much the youngest of the Honorary Canons when he kindly gave me this honour. I always felt about him that something (probably his almost continuous ill health) made him rather unpredictable. When I had been ten and again twelve years at Banbury I told Bishop Kirk that I thought that both I and the Parish might well benefit from a change. Three times I received absolutely out of the blue and entirely unsolicited, offers of other posts in the Church outside the Diocese. One offer was of a most important living in London. Another was an offer from a Duke (not Northumberland, my former Patron): two glorious churches, a most lovely Tudor Rectory and a dream garden; also a workable income. With this came a letter from the Bishop of the diocese concerned, pressing me to take it and saying that he visualised me as jumping right into the centre of the work of the diocese! The third offer had equal attractions. I did not want to stay at Banbury until I got stale. Each time I went straight to Bishop Kirk and said that I would not like to leave without his blessing and approval. Each time I got the same answer.

"You are *not* to go! I have reasons for saying this."

So I stayed where I was and in the days of World War II took on more and more work. I had been Rural Dean since 1935. Refused for an Active Service Army Chaplaincy in 1939 (because I was now forty-seven) I was appointed an Honorary Chaplain to the Forces. I also had now the Chaplaincy of the Horton General Hospital, Banbury; quite a heavy job and one which increased enormously during the War years.

With the outbreak of the War in the September of 1939 a new phase of work in Banbury began. The work also naturally increased whilst all sorts of things that one had planned and fostered just died on one. Nothing could be done about the Schools and our Church House, the centre and hub of all our Parish activities, was commandeered (as an ammunition store). The Vicarage became perforce our centre for all meetings and activities, and we took in three or four Wartime billetees. Troops poured into the town and district. Together with the excellent Senior Methodist Minister and a few of our leading laymen, we started a Soldiers' Club in a part of the Marlborough Road Methodist Sunday School buildings. We got together a billiard room and games room, a small writing room and a canteen. We visited regularly and we asked to the Vicarage innumerable officers for lunch or supper and as many non-commissioned private soldiers to tea or for the evenings. My wife also helped to run a Service Canteen at the Railway Station. On top of the Parish, with more claims upon us than ever, a whole new set of responsibilities and activities grew up in a matter of weeks. In addition to everything else my wife and I became Air Raid Wardens and were often clambering over the vast roof of the Parish Church at 2.00 or 3.00 a.m. in the complete darkness of "black-out" on a moonless night. When Coventry was so cruelly blitzed and every building in Banbury all those miles away, shook and shuddered as the heavy bombs came down, we could see the whole sky to the north of us glowing red in that awful holocaust from our vantage point above our great Church.

Banbury was lucky in the days of the air raids compared with many other places. The large aluminium works, so cleverly camouflaged, remained unscathed. Bombs dropped on the town fell either into open spaces or harmlessly into the canal. Only once, when an oil bomb fell at the station, were there any casualties. Within an hour I saw them up at the Hospital. Poor fellows, except for their boots, they had every stitch of clothing blown off them by the blast, and they were completely coated in black oil and blood from their abrasions. Three were killed, the others recovered.

It was very thrilling and hush-hush when I and a few other people in the district were called together by some Government V.I.P.s and entrusted with some extremely secret (not to say startling) instructions and responsibilities. There were actually thought to be some possible future German Gauleiters in our midst, ready to take over if the Nazis landed. How amazingly quickly the War mixed people up together and how many friends one made and was enabled to help, whom one would never have met otherwise. Banbury had several thousand evacuees from East London mostly children within the first week of the War. The first contingent of troops whom we had for any considerable time in Banbury were a lot of young fellows just drafted from Worcestershire into the Worcestershire Regiment. There were several from my old Parish in Kidderminster and three or four of these youths came round to the Vicarage with notes from their parents whom I had known or married in the days of my first curacy. They were living hard, sleeping (with one or two thin blankets each) on the bare floors of the Territorial Drill Hall (where we had only a few years before started our Easington Sunday School). Many of these lads had never been away from home before in the whole of their lives. I think they liked the atmosphere of our old house with its warm fires and comfortable chairs; and the fact that I knew their parents and home town.

"I am afraid we'll be back here a lot, Vicar," they said, "You'll have to throw us out when you have had enough of us!"

Two of them spoke of another Kidderminster boy whose family I had known, and who although invited that night had not turned up. I asked about him and young Ernest Waldron had to go into explanations.

"He said that he was not fit for company. He was too miserable."

Then he added:

"He is a sensitive sort of chap, quite clever: never been away from home before and taking it all very hard." I asked him to bring this boy round another time if he could persuade him. His name was Cyril Talbot.

The following Tuesday night I went round to spend an hour or so at the newly started Soldiers' Club. Often I put on a soft collar and club tie, so as not to overawe any of those young creatures and appear too official. I went into the Games Room where there was a Draught's Competition in full swing. I was immediately greeted by one or two young soldiers who knew me and I was challenged to play the winner. Quite a little crowd gathered round and I think that my victory was quite popular. Afterwards they all moved off to watch some table tennis, all that is except one youth who came up to me and asked if he might talk to me. He was the kind of person who could hardly escape notice. Not only had he a mass of the most unusual dark red hair, but his clear cut features and look of real intelligence marked him out.

He then poured out his woes, pausing every now and then to say:

"Somehow I feel sure that you will understand." He was obviously a different type from the others. It came out that he wrote poetry, read good literature, loved beauty and the countryside and was devoted to his mother and his home life. He spoke at once so sincerely and with such a command of language that I was surprised when he told me that he had left school at fourteen. It was also clear that he was a fish out of water there, although he spoke nicely of the others. When the time came for me to go he asked if he might walk with me and only then did he ask me where I lived and who I was. When I told him he was as much surprised as pleased.

"Why—then it was *your* invitation that I refused for last Sunday! We were evidently meant to meet! My name is Cyril Talbot."

I said that I had guessed as much already. We became friends that night and have been so for well over thirty years now. I suppose that every week since they left Banbury one of us has written to the other and the return letter has followed the next week. Time and place have not made any break. His letters have come from Canada, the U.S.A., Arabia and China, mine have gone from England, Ireland, Bermuda or Portugal and when we have met again time and distance have not seemed so important.

Another great local friend was Allan Campden, the third of the four red-headed sons of a red-headed Mr. and Mrs. Campden. The father was high up in the local railway hierarchy and a convinced Conservative. They were a gifted and delightful family. Two of these boys have become clever electrical engineers, the two others gifted artists. Allan began as a choir boy at St. Mary's and I got to know him well only when he most unaccountably failed his entry to the Banbury Grammar School. It was more than strange as he was one of the most intelligent boys at St. Mary's School—apart from being quite the nicest and most reliable. I used my position as a Governor to remedy this situation and of course Allan did extremely well at School both in work and play. After this I think he came to regard me as a sort of fairy godfather. When we left Banbury he must have been about fifteen and he was quite upset. We remedied this as far as possible by having him to stay at Bournemouth and managing little trips to London to the theatre. After leaving school he did very well in the R.A.F. taking up electrical engineering. When he had finished his National Service he got a good post in "English Electric" at Rugby and has continued to progress. He married very wisely and has two fine little boys (both red-heads of course), whom I baptised as well as having married the parents. It would indeed be hard to find a more satisfactory young man than Allan.

Owing to the ill health of the Vicar of Christchurch, Banbury, I had taken on the Chaplaincy of the Horton General Hospital after I had been about six years in Banbury. With the outbreak of the War this became a much bigger responsibility. Some three of four large new wards were added and later on many American soldiers were treated there also. I got together a small committee to try to do something to make those young soldiers' hospital time rather more interesting. One of our efforts was a weekly series of talks, debates or a form of "Twenty Questions" on reasonably topical problems and occasionally on religious subjects. We got some excellent speakers from the Universities of Oxford and Birmingham and Sir Miles Thomas, at that time resident in Adderbury, was a great help to us, as was the scientific inventor, Mr. Bell-Walker of Banbury. He was a charming and gentle individual with a vast amount of scientific knowledge which he had the ability to put across attractively. Often about four or five of us would sit at a table and then invite questions from the soldiers. It was curious how often—after we had the American troops with us—that the "colour question" came up. Debates on this tremendous subject almost invariably followed the same pattern. The Americans, skating over their own domestic problems extremely cheerfully, tended ultimately to talk about India's "agony" under "British oppression". Even such adjectives as "satanic" were produced. We, British people, often wondered where these people (mostly Middle Westerners, or Bostonians, if they were very critical) got their ideas of British India. Looking back now I think that much of it must have come from definite German propaganda in the early days of the War. In retaliation some of our British patriots cited instances of more than callous segregation in the States—churches with notices of "no coloured admitted", pavements in towns such as St. Louis, where no negro might walk. After a time we found it wisest to make this heat-producing subject taboo; and all remained peace and love.

The first American troops we had, especially during the earlier period of the American "invasion", were a delightful lot, both officers and men. They came almost exclusively from Virginia and a very high proportion of them were Anglicans (Protestant Episcopal Church of America). The first time that they had a Church Parade at the Parish Church they came over six hundred strong and a very large number of them gave dollar notes (or if they had English money) half crowns in the collection, much to the benefit of our Church funds! I was much amused the next morning by a comment made to me by an excitable and economical local tradesman's wife.

"Oh, Vicar," she cried, "I was so upset yesterday in Church when I saw so many of those poor young men putting all those paper dollars into the Collection! I nearly ran out into the aisle and shouted 'Don't give so much'! "

Laughingly I replied:

"If you had, I should have come out into the aisle also and shouted you down. Remember, they are very much better paid than our chaps."

We made great friends with several of the officers of whom I remember best Colonel Thornton Mullins and Captain Dick O'Shea; both, alas killed in the D-Day landings. I shall never forget some of Thornton's American "funny stories", which could be safely trusted to take a minimum of fifteen minutes to narrate. Years later (1957) when my wife and I were staying in Washington D.C. at the Jefferson Hotel, for the first of our three visits there, we motored over to Richmond, Virginia for a hectic day of sightseeing. The temperature that June day was a hundred and four degrees and we soon got tired of walking from one place of interest to another, so we took a taxi. We got a charming, knowledgeable and educated man as our driver. He turned out to be Thornton Mullins' greatest school friend! He was as much thrilled as we were to be able to talk of our delightful mutual friend now dead so many years.

I used to get invited to luncheons at the American Officers' Mess at Banbury quite frequently. In those Wartime days in contrast to our rationing their meals assumed the character of a Belshazzar's Feast. I remember the first occasion when after turtle soup, roast duck and very creamy strawberry shortcake, all washed down with copious draughts of very black coffee, the terrible indigestion I had to endure at a large Children's Service at which I was the preacher that same Sunday afternoon. On a later occasion after another such luncheon we were all sitting smoking in the Officers' Mess recovering from a more than ample meal. There was a loud knock on the door.

"Come in!" shouted the Colonel.

A bright and on-coming young private soldier appeared and without any beating about the bush, said—

"Say, Colonel. Were you thinking of using your car this afternoon?"

"No, I guess, I was not," admitted the Colonel.

"Then may I take it?"

"Why yes."

"Thanks a lot, Colonel."

The young man was gone. Then the Colonel said with a smile:

"Now that's what I call 'discipline'! He *asked* if he could have my car. He didn't just take it!"

I suppose I must have looked somewhat surprised, so the Major leant over and whispered to me:

"That boy's father is one of the richest men in 'Frisco. I reckon the Colonel is hoping for a good job in that family's firm, when all this is over!"

Everybody seemed to regard the incident as a mild joke. I could not help wondering what a German or for that matter even an English Colonel would have done in similar circumstances, if similar circumstances could be imagined!

The Americans certainly livened up Banbury. I remember one friend of ours having an amusing experience. Their shabby old open car had a leaky radiator, so it was their custom to carry a discarded gin bottle filled with water on the front seat. One day he returned to his car after doing some shopping. What was his surprise to note that his bottle of water was gone and its place taken by a five dollar bill. On a small scrap of paper attached was scrawled in pencil:

"Thanks a lot for the gin. G.I."

He always said he would have liked to have seen that G.I.'s face a little later on, when he had his first swig.

One habit of these young Americans in our public houses rather shocked us in Banbury. Many of them used to buy a drink, take it outside and put it into a bottle, then return inside and repeat the process ad lib. After the final refill, they did not go back to the bar, but merely threw the glass down in the street. I have seen the pavements littered with broken glasses.

Much valuable old engraved and cut glass was destroyed in this way and many houses became quite short of anything to drink from. The publicans had to insist that all drinks should be consumed on the premises. Not until I went to Bermuda years later (where there were two American Service Bases) have I seen so much broken glass as I saw in the streets of Banbury during the period of the "American occupation" in those War years.

With one exception all my assistant clergy during my fifteen years in Banbury were loyal and able men.

Some of my other clerical friends should be mentioned. It was nice to have Basil Buchanan (my colleague and "best man" from Christchurch, Harrogate days) as a near neighbour, first as Rector of Broughton and then as Vicar of Bloxham. Six years after our wedding I had married him to Elene Cubitt, one of the most charming and sensible of women.

Walter Mervyn Grogan, Vicar of Sibford was another close friend and we had many interests (such as philately) in common. After I left for Bournemouth he was a most faithful correspondent and one of those who kept us in touch with doings in the Deddington Deanery. His sudden and comparatively early death was a sad blow.

Another friend was Harold Pickles, Rector of Woodstock and then of East Hendred. We really saw more of each other outside the Oxford Diocese than in it, as we were contemporaries in Church Assembly and Convocation, and Harold became a member of my club, the Athenaeum. He and I together with Gerald Allen (Bishop of Dorchester) were more or less a trio when in London for the various meetings of these bodies. Harold was one of those genial friendly people who knew everybody. I was so glad that when I left the Oxford Diocese he received the Honorary Canonry which I relinquished at Christ Church.

About the end of the first year of the War (autumn 1940) the well known preacher and broadcaster, the Rev. W. H. Elliott, then Vicar of St. Michael's, Chester Square, London, had a bad breakdown and his doctors sent him to the comparative quiet and serenity of a North Buckinghamshire village. Unfortunately he was miserable and lonely there. No one (not even the Incumbent, whose Church he regularly attended) took any notice of them and he and his wife came over two to three times to Banbury to see us. As his health and nervous system improved he began to hope that he might perhaps work again. I encouraged him to preach for us one Sunday morning, and this proved a fresh start. To make a short story of it, he suggested that he should come to me as a sort of honorary assistant. I got him and his wife and family suitable accommodation in the town and he was soon preaching three or four times a month and taking occasional late Communion Services. His eloquence and wide spread fame on the **radio brought large additional numbers** to St. Mary's Church, including many Nonconformists. We became very attached to one another, although he was in no way an easy man. He literally tortured himself and seemed incapable of the serenity which he so often preached to enthralled congregations. The sudden death in a cycling accident at Christmas time of their second son, Robin, brought fresh anguish to both him and his wife. It also produced one of his best books (*Rendezvous*). Up to a point I think that I was able to help him and he always said that I understood him better than any of his other clerical friends. After about eighteen months with us he was well enough to attempt another post on his own. After a partial restoration to health he tried two other posts. For some four years he was Sub-Dean of H.M. Chapels Royal, with the attendant interesting duties which brought him into close touch with King George VI and Queen Elizabeth. Very soon after he took up this post, some new Priests-in-Ordinary had to be appointed, and I was invited to be a Deputy Priest-in-Ordinary. I held this post from 1945-56, i.e. during my last year at Banbury and during the whole of my time at Bournemouth. That meant long after Elliott himself was gone and Foxell had succeeded. Naturally I much appreciated an honour which brought me to some extent into touch with their Majesties, and gave one the occasional pleasure of attending such interesting and beautiful functions as the Maundy Services and the Installation of Knights of the Bath at Westminster Abbey. Until after the restoration of St. James Palace Chapel, when Foxell relegated the Priests-in-Ordinary to a separate robing room, one had also the pleasure of meeting in the Chapel Vestry many old friends amongst the Bishops and Royal Chaplains who came to preach.

Poor Elliott's last days were tragic as his mind gradually failed. He was in a hospital at Virginia Water and he used to write me pathetic letters. I sent him books and also visited him when possible. He developed a sort of persecution mania. Convinced that while in his room he was continually spied upon, he would only talk if we walked in the grounds and even then he viewed every tree and shrub with suspicion. It was strange that one of his favourite sermon topics had been the sinfulness of worrying. I suppose that it was just another illustration of the old saying that the best preachers are those who preach to themselves. It was a sad thought that he who had comforted so many others could not himself find that which he gave so abundantly.

Another good friend whom I made through Church Assembly and Convocation was John Rawlinson, Bishop of Derby. For some reason he was always absolutely charming to me and we often used to go for walks together in London. His brilliance and wit were a delight. I remember him saying one day, as he looked at me very solemnly—

"You have great qualities—you take that excellent Church paper The Guardian and you only rarely speak in Church Assembly, and then only when you have something to say, O si sic omnes!"

Some of his comments on other members of these Church bodies who loved the sound of their own voices were extremely droll. There were indeed some clerics little known or heard of in their diocese (or even, dare one say it—in their own parishes) who came out in Convocation and Church Assembly like butterflies flashing in the sunlight.

Canon Wallace of Lichfield Cathedral was another very valued friend, gentle and scholarly with a happy turn of phrase and sense of humour. He also belonged to the Athenaeum.

In 1940 our eldest daughter Adelaide, left Headington School, Oxford, at the age of sixteen, much against the wishes of the Headmistress who thought that she was good enough to win a Scholarship to the University. She took up War work at the Ministry of Aircraft Production in Banbury. In 1942 at the early age of eighteen (January 1942) she married a young kilted Army officer of twenty-one. He was then Lieutenant Temple Primrose Blair Nimmo of the Queens Own Cameron Highlanders and ended up as a Major in the Gordon Highlanders after coming safely through the invasion of Italy (Anzio Beaches) and the closing stages of the War in Europe. After the War Temple returned to a junior partnership in his step-father's "export" business in the City, and soon they were living in Brighton. A year later our second daughter Anne followed a somewhat similar path. After doing well at school she too left rather young and went to the Ministry of Aircraft Production for her War work. She actually met her fate even younger than Adelaide. When she was still a schoolgirl of sixteen and before Adelaide had met her future husband we had a call from a nice looking and pleasant young Army Officer in the Cameron Highlanders. Actually he was the Reverend Lieutenant Geoffrey Milroy. He had gone from Magdalen College, Oxford, to Cuddesden Theological College and been ordained to a London Curacy by Dr. Geoffrey Fisher, then Bishop of London. He had been active for some years in the Territorials and was a member of the Honourable Artillery Company. So he went to see his Bishop when the War began and explained that he had had his "calling up" papers. What was he to do? As usual Dr. Fisher was kind, wise and to the point.

"What do you want to do?"

"I want to go, my Lord—as a combatant."

"I gathered as much," said the Bishop. "Well, as you are only in Deacon's Orders I think I can allow you to do so."

Geoffrey had a long diaconate, as he went all through the War before being priested. His entry in Crockford's Clerical Directory reads "Deacon. London 1939. Priest. Winchester 1946". It was at my suggestion that he had inserted in that revealing volume "serving with the army 1939-1946". It was not desirable that anyone should imagine that it had taken him seven years to pass his Priest's examination!

I shall have more to say about our children and their marriages later on. Suffice it to say now just two things.

Firstly, we ourselves had suffered so much from opposition and interference when we fell in love, that we knew what it meant to have to fight for what we wanted. We had long decided therefore not to interfere with our children when their turn came, unless we knew of something definitely wrong. So we just ignored the head-shakings of certain wise-acres who said on each occasion—

"Oh, don't you think that your daughter is far too young?"

Secondly, we happened to like and to trust the two young men who won our daughters' affections; and subsequent events have proved that our first impressions were right. Both young men were Christians and Churchmen and had gentlemanly instincts and outlooks. We have never regretted these early marriages.

When World War II ended my wife and I were fairly if not completely exhausted, and my dear Mother, now nearly eighty, was losing her memory, although still looking wonderful and able to enjoy getting out and about. I had been fifteen years at Banbury and a whole series of new problems were coming up on the horizon. I had been very happy there and I loved the people; but I just felt that the time had come when I should go elsewhere and Banbury should have a "new broom". I was now fifty-three.

We had a whole series of evacuees in our Vicarage during the War and we began the week that the War began. First we had three women from the East End: a Russian Orthodox Jewess, a school teacher and her sister. Mrs. Lipsky was usually rather silent, but occasionally came out with some surprising or well-considered remark.

"Well, you watch Russia! One of these days she will surprise the whole world." (How right she was.)

We tried hard to meet her rigid dietary requirements as a strict practising Jew. Once however my wife slipped up badly and we had pork and beans. Mrs. Lipsky dined well and said at the end:

"Well," (all her remarks began with that word) "I do not know what I have just eaten but it was real good; the best meal I have had since I left my own home."

Mollie thought it better not to enlighten her.

My father's old first cousin Alice Williams joined us about the time our East End trio departed for other quarters: Mrs. Lipsky to rejoin her Polish husband over his Fish and Chip Shop in Limehouse where he was apparently still doing a roaring trade; Mrs. Green (a nice woman) and her sister also returned to London.

Alice Williams, one of my Kinsale great-uncle's large family had after her father's death earned her living as a Governess and had spent twenty years with a titled Austrian family in their Vienna and Prague homes, and at an amazing medieval castle in the mountainous wilds of Transylvania. She had gone as Governess to the eldest daughter and stayed until the youngest of the family was grown up. She spoke German like a native and had seen Society and the world. Unfortunately she had invested her life's saving entirely in British Railway Stock which meant, alas, when she retired that she only had an income of about one-third of what she had hoped for. Living in lodgings alone; but near her neice Stella (Williams) she enjoyed London until the bombing started in the second year of the War. At this very time she developed what was then known as pernicious anaemia. She was well on in the seventies and she was told to rest. Under the circumstances she found herself spending night after night in cellars and shelters. When we heard of her plight we invited her to come to us "for the duration". Her doctor was not encouraging. He wrote privately. "You will have a funeral within six months". However one of our good doctors in Banbury took her in hand and she made an amazing recovery and lived for another sixteen years to the ripe age of ninety-three. She enjoyed her new life, surrounded by our family, plunged right into the midst of all the Parish and family doings and with her vivacity and humour made a great number of new friends. She and my Mother were great company to one another. As the War years went by and my Mother's memory deteriorated Alice did a lot to cheer her.

Alice stayed with us until the end of the War. Adelaide's and Anne's weddings were two occasions which highlighted her visit to us.

After our East Enders left us, we had many other evacuees. One was a middle aged lady, whom I met wandering distractedly around the Church. She was a Miss Horatia Seymour and she had just succeeded in getting her ninety-year old Mother, Lady Seymour, into a local Nursing Home. After that achievement she had spent two whole days in trying to get some place for herself, but without success.

"Perhaps we could take you," I said, "Come and see my wife."

"But you know nothing about me. I might walk off with the silver."

"Highly improbable, I should say."

She gave massively impressive references:

"My sisters Lady Mersey and Lady Cheetham and of course Winston and Clementine Churchill. I was one of her bridesmaids."

Her father had been Mr. Gladstone's personal Private Secretary (Sir Horace Seymour) and she knew "all the crowned heads of Europe". While she was with us she frequently went off for the weekend to some Duke or Earl or one or other of the Rothschilds. The menus which she recited, especially after a visit to the Rothschilds, had a disturbing effect upon us in those days of rationing. Actually she was an interesting and well read woman. It was she who had first interested Sir Winston in the novels of Anthony Trollope which he took as his bedtime reading during his afternoon rests in the War years. One amusing incident came about in this connection. Lunch was sharp at one o'clock every day at the Vicarage and no-one was ever late. At precisely twelve-fifty-five one day the telephone rang in the hall. Our tall and impressive looking elderly Irish cook, Mrs. Bovingdon, answered it.

"This is Banbury Vicarage."

"This is Number 10 Downing Street, and I am speaking on behalf of the Prime Minister."

"Splendid. Queen Mary at this end," retorted "Mrs. Bov", thinking that someone was pulling her leg.

"Do not be so ridiculous! " came the angry rebuke, "The Prime Minister understands that Miss Seymour is staying at

Banbury Vicarage and wishes a word with her."

Even "Mrs. Bov" almost collapsed at that; but fortunately at that moment Horatia came in at the front door and was breathlessly appraised of the situation. Sir Winston wanted an elusive Trollope *Is he Popinjoy?*, unobtainable in London. Could she find a copy in Oxford? She did.

Then early in 1946 came a letter from Mervyn Haigh, Bishop of Winchester (whom I had never met). Would I care to be considered for the post of Vicar of St. Peter's, Bournemouth (i.e. to be in effect the Vicar of Bournemouth) and with it Rural Dean of a Deanery with some sixty clergy in it? Anyway would I come and stay with him for a night and talk it over? He was not the Patron of the living; but Sir George Meyrick would like him to find somebody suitable.

I immediately rang up Bishop Kirk and without saying anything about this letter got an appointment to see him two days later in Oxford. In the meantime I wrote to Bishop Haigh and accepted his invitation to come and see him.

My interview with Bishop Kirk was not happy. He reminded me that he had said more than once that I was not to leave the Oxford Diocese.

"I have told you that I do not wish you to leave the diocese. Why only a few weeks ago the Bishop of —————" (he mentioned an attractive Northern Diocese) "wrote to me and told me that he wished to warn me that he was proposing to write to you and offer you a Residentiary Canonry at his Cathedral, together with the Senior Archdeaconry of the Diocese."

He paused for a moment and I said nothing, waiting for a full revelation.

"I wrote and told him that he was to leave my diocesan clergy alone and I forbade him to write to you."

"I should at least have liked to have had the opportunity of considering the offer myself."

"Well, now you see that I am determined that you shall not leave the diocese. Now I want you to write to Bishop Haigh and tell him that you have thought further and decided not to come and see him."

"I am afraid that I cannot do that."

This was practically the end of the interview.

Looking through Kenneth Oxon's letters to me I am conscious of their kindness of tone and I should not like to end my references to him in the somewhat sour strain of our final meeting. There was certainly one instance in which he had proved most understanding and helpful. In the early days of the Second World War I noted the regular and devout attendance at Communion of a sad tired looking man of early middle age at the Parish Church. At last I overcame his evasiveness and got to know him. He was obviously a gentleman and his work was rough and heavy, nor was it what one would have expected even as "War work". We asked him and his charming wife in to a meal. He refused to come until I had heard his story.

Some three years previously he had had a serious illness (which had had its mental manifestations). While only convalescent he had run away with another woman (the nurse who had brought him gradually back to health). This had ended in a suicide pact in which the woman had died, but he had been saved. His Diocesan Bishop, ignoring what a noted London specialist had to say in mitigation, had sacked and black-listed him, although his wife had taken him back, nursed and forgiven him.

I took the case in due course to Kenneth Kirk and he was wonderful. This poor broken priest was duly licensed to me and allowed to resume his priestly functions gradually. After a year he was allowed to take charge of a small Parish of which I was nominally in charge. He did an excellent work there and won the love and respect of the whole place. Later he held two successive country Parishes, completely rehabilitated. It was a very happy story in the end and Kenneth Oxon's sympathetic attitude was quite splendid. He fought down the unforgiving old Bishop's opposition with the most complete pleasure and success.

Actually it was a great wrench leaving Banbury. I spent probably the best years of my life there, I suppose. Our family had been all together and unbroken there; including my Mother, who had many many friends and during the War years had also enjoyed the lively presence of my old cousin Alice Williams and our variety of evacuees. Our children had grown up there. Adelaide and Anne had both had their courtship and wedding in Banbury. Fifteen years is a large slice of one's life, whatever age one is. Of the seventeen homes which I have lived in (Ireland, England and Bermuda) I have lived longer at Banbury Vicarage than anywhere else, although the twelve years which Mother and I spent in Harrogate always seems the longest spell: I suppose because the older one becomes the faster the years roll by. There is a great difference between being thirty-nine and being fifty-four, although Bishop Haigh thought that I was not fifty when I went to see him. When we departed our Banbury friends said some kind things about us and gave us some nice presentations and presents. An even greater sadness was that our doctors in Banbury now warned us that my Mother would now need two nurses if she was going to live in a large strange town. So very unwillingly we got her into a Nursing Home in Salisbury where we could go and visit her. I do not think that with her failing memory she really quite knew where she was. We used to go over regularly and take her out for a picnic tea and a country drive, which she always enjoyed.

She died very suddenly of heart failure one night some months after we had settled in Bournemouth. The date was 13th February, 1947 and she was in her eighty-first year. It was nearly twenty-four years after the heart specialist in Harley Street had given her a maximum of six months to live.

The Funeral Service was at St. Peter's, Bournemouth and was just what she would have liked, with two of her favourite Easter hymns and Bach's "Jesus, Joy of man's desiring". Our son-in-law Geoffrey Milroy took part and my two colleagues Keith Parkinson and John Coutts also kindly assisted. Charles Palmer played and the Choir turned up in good numbers. Anne and Cynthia were there. I know that I was very fortunate indeed to have my Mother until I was fifty-five years of age, and more than fortunate in having such a Mother. Mollie and I went over to Northern Ireland and Mother's ashes were buried in Ballymena Cemetery beside my Father (dead fifty-four years before her). It is a beautiful spot. A wide vista of the green rolling Antrim countryside stretches away to the north. Above it looms the blue mass of Slemish, which had presided in the background over her girlhood's days and her ideally happy years with my Father.

CHAPTER XII

Bournemouth St. Peter's (1946-56)

BISHOP MERVYN HAIGH gave me a very good description of the character of my new post: it would be a life of continuous rush. Indeed I was to find it rather like living on a series of moving staircases, a question of keeping one's balance, of keeping on one's feet. As Rural Dean one would have in one's Chapter more clergy than many Bishops in their dioceses—about seventy. I found all this to be true and that the resident congregation was scattered all over the enormous areas and distances of both Bournemouth and Poole. I had several regular private Communions in parts of Poole and Branksome where it took over half an hour sometimes (because of the traffic) to negotiate the journey each way. By the time I had been six years in Bournemouth I was on forty-eight Committees (in Bournemouth, Winchester and London). This included one or two Convocation and Church Assembly Committees. When at length there was a dissolution of Parliament, I ceased to be a Proctor for the Oxford Diocese, but was duly re-elected for Winchester (in 1950). A very important Committee was in the Bournemouth County Borough Education Department which was bringing out a new Syllabus of Religious Education.

The two Churches in the Parish, St. Peter's and St. Swithin's had very different atmospheres. St. Swithin's had a higher proportion of residents (and winter residents), St. Peter's was par excellence The Visitors' Church. In the summer up to two-thirds of the huge congregations were holiday makers. In the winter season (roughly November until Easter) the number of visitors was considerably less. On the other hand a higher percentage of winter visitors were Church attenders so we always did well. Christmas and Easter Communicants numbered about 1600-1700 each. I always considered that it would take a very clever man to empty St. Peter's although I gathered that it had almost been done once or twice! My immediate predecessors had been first Hedley Burrows, a son of the first Bishop of Sheffield, a man of great kindliness, at that time Archdeacon of Winchester, and later Dean of Hereford: and Norman Boyd, formerly Rector of

Hendon and Prebendary of St. Paul's. He died very suddenly when he had only been in his new Parish a year. He was not Rural Dean and had hardly had time to get to know a very wide circle in the town. Amongst one's predecessors of whom one heard much was the Rev. A. E. Daldy, a fine personality apparently who had in his day dominated the Church life of the town in a remarkable manner. He later became Archdeacon of Winchester. The really great man however was the Rev. Alexander Morden Bennett, the first Vicar (1845-80), who not only was instrumental in building St. Peter's Church with G. E. Street as the architect, but who was the driving force behind the building of several other churches in the rapidly growing resort: St. Swithin's Church at the east end of his own Parish (1876): St. Ambrose, Westbourne (which duly became a separate Parish): St. John's, Moordown, and St. Michael's. He also did much towards the equipment of the National Sanatorium, with its subsequent extensions and its Chapel of St. Luke the Physician. In 1871 he opened St. Mary's Home (a Convalescent Home for ladies of limited means). It was the wisdom and energy of Mr. Bennett that built up the Church life of the fast growing seaside town on such sound foundations. He poured into his work for the Church all his resources, both spiritual and material. No doubt he now has his reward. He got however no recognition from the powers-that-were in the Winchester Diocese: not even an Honorary Canonry. I have been given to understand by old Bournemouth residents that St. Peter's Church, being from the first connected with the Oxford Movement and being the Church where Keble and later Gladstone worshipped, was not favoured by contemporary Evangelicals, at that time firmly entrenched in Winchester and Farnham Castle. That terrible label "High Church" (given with a pained whisper) was in those days of acrimonious partisanship in Church affairs, what is now called "a smear".

St. Peter's is undoubtedly a fine Church and much money has been spent on its sumptuous furnishings. Indeed the interior gives to some rather the feeling of an over decorated and crowded nineteenth century drawing-room. Almost every-inch of the walls is painted and frescoed. Seven silver sanctuary lamps hang in the Chancel and in every direction there is gilding and colouring and a variety of polished marble pillars. Those who like Victoriana will admire it. Many do not. I remember once seeing Dr. Perkins, for so many years Minor Canon of Westminster Abbey, at our Sung Eucharist. After Service he stuck his head round the Clergy Vestry door while I was disrobing and remarked "Glorious Service: hideous Church! good luck and good-bye! " For sheer beauty St. Peter's could not compete with St. Stephen's, Bournemouth (Bennett Memorial Church): but it gave out a sense of warmth and welcome. It suffered also from much bad Victorian glass, including the twelve Apostles in the north nave aisle; hideous in colour and face. These windows are some of the worst I have ever seen anywhere. I am afraid that I christened them "the twelve Borstal boys". They looked full of potential wickedness! On the other hand the richness of the High Altar and the alabaster reredos gave a good central focus and the length of the crowded nave was impressive. We got to love the Church. It always felt used and prayed in.

The work was interesting and at the same time tantalising. One had to be Vicar of Bournemouth (I was Mayor's Chaplain six years out of my ten). In this capacity I attended the Council meetings. One was indeed continually attending the chairing Meetings. Winchester Meetings (with about three hours driving) spoilt whole days nearly every week. The resident congregation, though less than that at Banbury needed systematic visiting. They scarcely knew each other by sight (except for the nucleus who were official in one or other on the Parish Councils or Committees). They came from every part of Bournemouth and many parts of Poole and lived in different social circles and circumstances. Mrs. X and Mrs. Y were both on the Parochial Church Council. To Mrs. X (widow of a General) I said:
"You know Mrs. Y of course."
"I do not."
"But you must surely! You are both on the P.P.C. and have been for ten or twelve years! "
"Oh! I know whom you *mean* of course! "
Both were charming women; but that was the kind of thing that one was up against at times in this Communion of Saints. We tried to emphasise the social side and possibilities of our Churchmanship in bazaars, meetings, and entertainments, as well as by the various Parish parties (Christmas time, St. Peter's time, Harvest, etc.). I tried in such ways to get rather more of a sense of community and fellowship; but nearly all the local circumstances militated against any kind of amalgam. The distances in a huge spread out town were a real factor to be reckoned with. Also Bournemouth was essentially a place of coming and going. By that I do not merely mean the summer visitors in their tens of thousands here today and gone tomorrow: nor the thousands

of semi-resident "winter visitors" who came year after year in November and disappeared after Easter. Each spring the hotels got them out by raising their terms and preparing for the next lot of summer visitors and holiday-makers. Further in the words of my predecessor Dean Hedley Burrows, Bournemouth was a place where death had to be continually reckoned with. The typical newcomers were the retired couples of sixty plus to whom the passage of ten or twelve years made a great difference, if it did not literally see them out. Bournemouth has one of the highest death rates in England because it is a retired people's Mecca. For 1964 the Bournemouth death rate is given in Whitaker's Almanac at 18.0 per thousand as compared with that of a great city such as Liverpool where it is only 12.0. It can also be in spite of its places of entertainment, its gay big stores, its parks and gardens, a city of loneliness. You see the retired couples in their sixties strolling around the gardens together, or sitting in the cafes or the shelters, and then you see (much more often) the lonely old men, and more often still, the lonely old women of seventy odd by themselves. Bournemouth is also a place of "genteel poverty". There are a lot of people who put up a brave front and are very proud. I can see in my mind's eye to-day a certain elderly widow, not untypical. She had a fur coat and a gay little hat and seemed to be in the swim of things; but most of her twenty-four hour day was spent in a tiny fourth or fifth floor back bedroom, with a gas stove (which devoured shillings).

She had neither the room nor the money to entertain. She was a charming and gay clergyman's widow (no family or relations) and lived like this for about twelve or fifteen years. After she had paid for her rooms she had exactly 10/- a week for food and clothing. It was nice to be able to get her the occasional grant or warm coat in good condition. She always looked smart and had beautiful white hair. She was always up-to-date in current events (thanks to the public reading-rooms or libraries) and she tried not to appear too pathetically grateful for a luncheon invitation. She was a devout and practising Christian, always doing little kindnesses for other people. One day she was found dead in her one armchair all dressed and ready to go out: a fine and courageous woman. There was an inquest of course; heart failure with some malnutrition was noted—death from "natural causes".

With so many elderly folk, Bournemouth was full of Nursing Homes (for those who could afford them) and I, like all the other clergy, had a vast number of regular invalid visitations. Some of these people were unspeakably lonely. Many had outlived all their relations and friends. One old lady I remember especially. For the last three years of her life apart from the doctor's monthly visit and the routine attentions of the staff, I was the only person who ever came to see her. She was over eighty and bedridden. Incidentally, she was extremely witty and absolutely charming. She was a bachelor woman and I remember so well the twinkle in her eye when I asked her the first or second time I came to see her, what her job had been.

"I give you three guesses! " she replied.

"Oh. I don't know at all! On the stage?"

"No."

"Newspaper correspondent?"

"No."

"Manageress of some hotel?"

"No. Matron of an Inebriates' Home! "

We both simply screamed with laughter. Then she added—

"It required a certain amount of tact, not only with the patients and staff but with the relations! I could quite easily have gone mad, if I had not been able to see the funny side of it all."

Naturally we became great friends, and we both looked forward to our regular monthly dates—Holy Communion, then a cup of coffee and a chat. I often think of a remark made to me by two good people who have dealt with large numbers of people, Bishop Bernard Heywood and Mr. Billy Graham. "My best work has been done with individuals." In spite of the huge congregations one has ministered to and preached to, I think that I could endorse the statement of the great Vicar of Leeds and that great Missioner from my own experiences. Numbers are not everything.

There was one curious old lady amongst my "regulars" in Bournemouth. She was a Miss B., known by me and my colleagues as "the old Bag", and she had been confined to her bedroom, if not to her bed, for many years. She had been a "Lady's Companion" herself and had inherited a house and an income from her former employer. Now she was getting her own back. She had had a series of companions and the current one, a nice rather nervous little woman, was much in awe of her. She always mentioned her with (literally) bated breath. Miss B. had several rules and regulations. One was that the Vicar was considered the most suitable person to give her her monthly Communions. When the Vicar was on his annual holiday, she sometimes preferred to miss her monthly celebration to descending to the assistant clergy's ministrations. Another regulation was: no talking for ten minutes before her communion or after it. So if one went to see her it had to be on a separate occasion. The companion was expected to kneel in her bedroom from before my arrival until well after my departure. Nothing made her more furious than if after an interval of three or four minutes the companion came downstairs to speak to me about anything. The bedroom bell would ring angrily and Miss X would have to rush upstairs to explain that she had been obliged to speak to the Vicar about some problem. Normally I let myself in by the unlatched front door and went out again without a single word being said except what the Service itself prescribed. Miss B. was the only person whom I have ever encountered who literally kept the Church's "Liturgical Colours" *herself*. She also sternly disapproved of women appearing in Church without hats.

"I should drive them out of my Church if I were a Priest! " she used to shout.

So when the Church came to her she applied the same principle. Her head was invariably covered. She had knitted for herself a set of large woollen caps or head-dresses: white for Christmas and Easter, purple for Lent and Advent, red for Martyr Saints and Whitsuntide and of course green for ferial occasions. I particularly remember the green headgear. It was that curiously dreary shade of green, favoured by certain Victorians, which I have always thought of as "boiled cabbage green" (and rather overboiled at that): a dirty browny-green. One day I met the current companion in one of Bournemouth's leafy roads and we walked together. The poor lady, freed from her prison atmosphere and surroundings, let herself go on the subject of her dominating employer. She was going to leave after her next pay day. She could not face telling Miss B. but she would leave a note with the daily woman. She did not describe Miss B. as an angel, quite the reverse. She finally screwed up her courage and departed. Then the whole process started all over again. Conversation with Miss B. was always rather like reading a parody of the *Church Times* aloud. It was strictly confined to ecclesiastical subjects. People such as the gloomy Dean of St. Paul or the modernist Dr. Major were sternly condemned. Vacant Bishoprics and possible candidates were discussed as keenly as members of the Jockey Club would have debated the possibilities for the next Derby or The Cheltenham Gold Cup. The generality of the clergy were summarily dismissed as "poor creatures"; "compromisers" or "not pulling their weight"; more rarely as "sound men" and more rarely still as "a first-rate Priest". Of these last her own father had remained the ideal.

"They do not make men like that these days." I hope that perhaps that "they" will not make many more women like that either.

I trust that this is not too unkind; but religiosity without Christianity always seems to me most repulsive.

The work as Rural Dean, with such a large Chapter and Conference was interesting, at times indeed inspiring. The clergy of Bournemouth were on the whole a fine lot. Bishop Mervyn Haigh and I often agreed, when discussing them, that they were as good as any group of clergy in the country. In Chapter I found the clergy both courteous and co-operative. There were no rebels; no people who rejoiced in being rude or perpetually in opposition like one curious old man whom I had had to endure for many years while in Banbury (Deddington Deanery). I particularly appreciated the loyalty and support which those of the clergy who were older than I was, gave me from the very first. I became Rural Dean from the day of my Institution as Vicar.

With a large R.D. Conference one could venture to invite all sorts of outstanding and well known people to come and speak at our Meetings.

We also had some interesting people amongst our lay members of Conference, conspicous amongst them was Lord Quickswood (formerly Lord Hugh Cecil, a son of the famous Victorian Prime Minister the Marquis of Salisbury) himself a famous Oxford don and M.P. "Quickie", as so many of us called him, was a most brilliant old man. Once he had been Chairman of the House of Laity in the Church Assembly and had been the terror of all rash speakers who did not trouble to verify their references. Absolutely charming, he could at a meeting be disconcerting at times. Twice I have known him kill discussion after a very able or a very earnest speech by someone brought to talk to us from the outside world. I remember a most impassioned speech on behalf of Church Sunday Schools from an extremely holy and dedicated woman, a Diocesan Sunday School Visitor. She had, I think, succeeded in firing her audience to a real enthusiasm and desire to crusade for larger and better Sunday Schools. When she had sat down and had received quite an ovation of applause, I asked for contributions to a discussion which I hoped would be stimulating and fruitful. Up jumped Lord Quickswood and in that rather flat Cecil voice he said with slow precision

—(no R's to speak of):

"I have never been to a Sunday School in my life and I seem to have managed all right. From what I have heard the teaching given in many cases is extremely unintelligent. Far better for children to go to Church with their parents."

No doubt it is possible to establish a case for this point of view, but the meeting never recovered from this cold douche and the devout lady nearly dissolved in tears beside me on the platform.

On another occasion our Organist, Charles Palmer (whom I had brought from Banbury to St. Peter's) read a really brilliant paper on "The Place of Music in Worship". It must have taken much careful thought and preparation and it deservedly received enthusiastic acclamation. Again dear old Lord Quickswood administered the immediate coup-de-grace. Standing up in the front row and turning to the well filled hall, he said in a voice which suggested italics:

"I have always understood that the two things which empty a Church quicker than anything else are bad preaching and *good music.*"

In the account of the proceedings the local paper next day entirely omitted any reference to Charles Palmer's brilliant and thoughtful contribution and merely headlined and reported Lord Quickswood's bon mot.

I used greatly to enjoy visiting him and he was a delightful host in his own house. He was full of anecdotes about notable personages of the Victorian and Edwardian eras, some of which may not be generally known.

One day he mentioned the fifth Earl and Countess Spencer who had been so friendly to my Grandfather, Dean Murray, who had been the Earl's Chaplain when he was for the second time Lord Lieutenant of Ireland (1882-85). He spoke of the Countess and her beauty and charm. In his later days the Earl had suffered from the effects of a stroke. There were times when he could not get the word—generally the operative word—which he wanted. His subconscious however invariably filled the gaps —not however with the right word, but always with the same wrong one. The word was "pheasants". One gathered that the Earl had always been extremely interested in the preservation of his game. Perhaps this was the explanation of his affliction! When Lord Hugh Cecil was, as a boy, staying with his parents and brothers in Rome, they were taken to tea with the Spencers, also residing there at that time. The day was hot and as Lord Spencer tired in his description of a recent visit to the Vatican the pheasants cropped up all over the place. The Cecil children became hysterical and Lady Salisbury had to take them away before their suppressed amusement became too noticeable. I understand that some reference was made to the entourage of His Holiness, Cardinals and Swiss Guard—all became pheasants!

On another occasion round about Christmas time, Lady Salisbury, taking some of her children, went with Mrs. Gladstone and some or her family to a Girls Orphanage, where there was to be a children's party. When they all arrived the Matron met them at the front entrance and warned them that they had just diagnosed two or three cases of scarlatina in the establishment.

"Oh that will be quite all right," said Mrs. Gladstone cheerfully. "We must not spoil the party! We will come in! "

Lady Salisbury, however, was of a different opinion. Her family had not had this particular complaint just mentioned. With difficulty she managed to persuade Mrs. Gladstone also to refrain, but only on certain conditions. The Orphanage children must not be entirely disappointed. Was there a piano in the large room with the big window looking out on to the lawn? Very well, would they produce someone to play dance music, gather the girls together and open the window, so that she could hear the music and dance to it on the lawn for the delectation of all concerned? and she did!

Sometimes Lord Quickswood used to discuss the Church Assembly of the Church of England, of which he had been such an active and prominent member for so many years. One soon realised that he deplored some of the ways in which the Assembly's policy had developed: also that he did not think that Consecration invariably endued all Bishops with unerring wisdom. He had at least one or two bêtes-noirs whom it would not do to mention here.

One very special feature of Bournemouth with its large population of elderly and reasonably leisured residents gathered in this "English Riviera" from all the less clement parts of the British Isles, as the number of societies or clubs. As well as the usual Scottish or Burns Society which patriotically devoured their horrible haggises and exchanged their good stories at set times, there were such clubs as the Welsh, the "Loyal" Irish, the Lancashire, the Yorkshire, and the Lakeland (or Cumbrian) Societies. No doubt there were many others of which I never heard. My particular trouble was that I was continually being rung up by intense Welshmen (sometimes hailing me in the Welsh language) and asking all manner of details about the venue, etc., of the Bournemouth Welsh Society. The conversation invariably approximated to the following:

(In a very excited Welsh voice.) "You are Canon Lewis Williams, I suppose?"

"Yes, indeed." I would reply, involuntarily imitating the infectious intonations and inflections.

"Where does the Welsh society meet, and when?"

"I am afraid I do not know."

"You *do not know*—whatever! You do not speak good Welsh perhaps? You come from *South* Wales?" (This, if he was a Northern—) or— "You come from *North* Wales?" (If he came from the South).

"Well you see, I am *not* Welsh."

"But you *must* be—yes—I suppose indeed, 'Lewis Williams'. You must be Welsh, look you! "

"No. Actually I am partly Irish, partly Scottish with a dash of English and French. In fact a complete fraud."

Some exclamation of incredulity or regret (polite or otherwise) would follow. If I got time before they rang off in a huff, I would try, "If it had been the Irish Society or the Yorkshire Club (My wife is a Yorkshire woman) I could have helped. I am so sorry! "

This must have happened ten or twelve times. Ultimately I learnt to refer them to the local Information Bureau, if they had not already rung off in disgust with such a bogus personality.

One never knew who was going to turn up in the Sunday Congregations at St. Peter's. One Sunday immediately under the nose of the Preacher in the pulpit I saw the Bishop and Dean of Gloucester (Drs. Woodward and Costley White). Even Archbishops occurred at times. Many foreign visitors, mostly French, came to us, thinking, when they saw our flood-lit alabaster Altar that this was Rome. They sometimes stayed through the whole of a Sung Eucharist still under this impression—accounting for any difference by reasoning that the British are always a little strange and different. The more perspicacious however usually rushed out after five or ten minutes. Occasionally they both realised and stayed, even coming to me or whoever the celebrant was, afterwards and saying how much they had liked the Service.

My very dear friend May Yorke used sometimes to come and stay with us. One time she went on to friends in some great country residence in Cumberland on leaving us. Arriving down in the drawing room dressed for dinner before any of the other guests or her host and hostess, she picked up the first paper she saw on a well stocked table. It was the St. Peter's Bournemouth Parish Magazine. It is surprising the number of people one meets who tell you that they have worshipped at St. Peter's at one time or other.

At St. Peter's and St. Swithin's I was fortunate again in my assistant clergy. Keith Parkinson who had been with me at Banbury, rejoined my staff. John Coutts had accepted my invitation to come with me. Then there was a delightful retired parson on the staff in an honorary capacity, the Rev. Claud Beckwith. After Keith went to be Vicar of St. Augustin's, Bournemouth, I had at St. Swithin's Peter Chandler (later Archdeacon of Cyprus). When John Coutts went to the Parish of Holybourne, near Alton, as Incumbent, I had Canon G. F. Helm, an Hon. Canon of Gloucester and former D. Assistant Chaplain General and Chaplain to the King, just retired from the Incumbency of Dursley, Gloucestershire. He was some years older than I but full of spirit, and energy. His wife had been M.U. Diocesan President in the Gloucester Diocese.

As at Banbury we had many splendid workers at both Churches, outstanding were Colonel Palmer as Church warden at St. Peter's and Colonel Stenhouse. George Head was a splendid and hard working Churchwarden at St. Swithin's for so many years. Outstanding also were Laurence Bell, a most lovable and wise man, and Thomas Ringrose, a wealthy Lancashire business man, who devoted his great business abilities and generosity to the service of St. Peter's. He was a wonderful Christian and business man. Alas that death took him from us so soon and so suddenly. Other great "stand-bys" were Leonard South, our Verger at St. Peter's and Arthur Davis the somewhat temperamentally unpredictable but invariably devoted and efficient Leader of our Servers and Bellringers, as well as an excellent producer of the many Nativity and Passion Plays which I encouraged in the Parish. Many too were the devoted ladies who served the Church, its various Guilds and Societies.

About the middle of my time at Bournemouth the Ruridecanal Chapter and Conference desired to have a Mission in the whole of the town and Deanery. We worked for well over a year in various forms of preparation and had many outstanding speakers in our preparatory stages, including several bishops and well known missioners as well as some outstanding laymen and women. I personally was never quite sure that Bournemouth was the best sort of place for a Mission (as generally understood): a place where a third of the population changed every few months.

I therefore persuaded my Committees not to try and throw the net too wide; but to make it more of an appeal to local nominal Christians, or as some of us called them "the fringe people", to come in and to take their religion more seriously. In this way it was mainly an appeal to the residents, although we were naturally glad to welcome visitors who came in casually during the preparatory period or attended the actual Mission itself. We had some good general posters and a series of regular articles in the local newspapers and Parish Magazines. Naturally anyone who knew Bournemouth really well realised how difficult it was to keep anything constantly before a town of such a size with its shifting thousands and seasonal visitors. However sympathetic the local press was it was apt occasionally to forget a long drawn out programme as all the seasonal preoccupations came in turn to the fore and competed. Each Parish had its local conditions and problems and chose their own missioners and methods. Some naturally did very much better than others. One Archdeacon (not our own) more or less criticised us and our whole technique for not being more blatant and noisy. I think that he had visions of half a dozen Billy Grahams daily on the sands and conversions by the thousand. I replied that our aim was to turn more of our nominal Christian Church folk into real Christians and real Church folk. Who can ever say of any spritual venture that it was "a success" or not? To those of us on the spot there were results which were inspiring, and also a lack of results which was disappointing. Assessment is futile. There were many parishes which experienced a great tonic and sense of renewal—there were two or three which scarcely experienced anything. There were probably at last three reasons for these varying results: the personal leadership or lack of it in the parish concerned, the thoroughness or otherwise of the local preparations, and finally the suitability or not of the particular Missioners. We at St. Peter's had Canon Roger Lloyd of Winchester, who was at his best with young educated people: Sixth formers and under-graduate types. One thing however did seem to indicate a real reaction. Practically every Parish registered a considerable increase in the number of regular communicants. Four or five years later I remember three of the Incumbents talking to me and each of them said that this new strength was still with them in their respective parishes. Their Parishes were of quite different types. One was a Visitor's Parish full of hotels and guest houses, a second was residential and rich, the third was working class and full of the people who worked for and with the visitors. Well, there is no limit to the possible influence of a converted landlady or hotelier.

That brings me to the subject of the "hotels" generally. Far more than they themselves realised the hoteliers could have a power for good or the reverse, upon the visitors who came to them. This was of course especially so where there were "winter residents"—people living in a hotel from say, October to April. There were some fine proprietors who really gave out spiritual and moral help to their clients, simply by being good Christians —genuine but unobtrusive. Alas, I know one or two hotels where the whole atmosphere was bedevilled by the cynical materialism or heartlessness of the proprietors. In one many starred hotel a very charming lady lost her husband after nearly fifty years of happy married life, in which they had had their sorrows, losing two sons in World War II and having a sadly handicapped daughter. This couple had lived for at least four years in this hotel and the Manager had changed about the middle of their period of residence. About a week after her husband's death this good woman was asked by the Manager to come into his office after lunch one day. What was her grievous surprise when she was addressed as follows:

"Do you know, Mrs. So and So, I think that it is quite time that you stopped going about with such a long face. It is not good for my hotel: my visitors don't like a 'Mrs. Mona Lott'." Then with a bright and brassy smile he added: "We must try and find you a new boy friend."!

This is a true story: the lady concerned told me herself. She left that hotel the next morning.

Another and very different picture is that of a dear old soul who lived to be a hundred and one years old who had lost all her family. She spent many years in a hotel with rather fewer stars than that mentioned above. Her three sisters, her personal maid, even her beloved nephew had all died. The last time I visited her she said of the proprietress: "She treats me as though she were my daughter. She could not be kinder."

We used to have at St. Peter's our annual "Hoteliers Service" (very well attended), and I never tired of reminding these people that they had in their hands the happiness and even at times the spiritual well-being or otherwise of many other people. On the whole they did a very good job in my opinion.

As a Diocese I never enjoyed Winchester as much as I had enjoyed Ripon or Oxford. That was probably partly because of the local "diocesan geography" which was very difficult from the point of view of Bournemouth. This great resort was right in the furthest corner of the Diocese and it was in many ways (including the financial) the most important place in the whole set up. Southampton was licking its wounds and recovering slowly from its frightful war damage. From the point of view of the Diocesan finances, Bournemouth was the goose that laid the golden eggs. I considered that this was the principal angle from which Bournemouth received much attention from a certain clique in Winchester. The Bournemouth clergy were apt to be thought of, at any rate by some of their brethren in other parts of the Diocese, as tumbling over one another in their over-staffed parishes, and living a life of relaxation in endless sunshine, in cushy jobs and with everything made easy. Personally I doubt if any parochial clergy in England have as much sick-visiting to do or more organizations with which to cope. In my time St. Peter's *Parish* alone paid a larger Diocesan Quota than several of the *Deaneries* in the Diocese. Attendance at meetings of Diocesan Committees, all held in Winchester, cost Bournemouth members much time and money. A very good case could have been made out for a Diocese of Bournemouth including the Bournemouth and Christchurch Deaneries, with Poole and perhaps a slice from the Dorset hinterland; but of course, neither Winchester nor Salisbury Diocese would have agreed. Where would their revenues have come from without that coastal strip and Bournemouth and Poole, the golden geese?

Bishop Mervyn Haigh, in so many ways able and attractive, was in physical decline during my time in the Diocese; but bravely fighting a losing battle with increasing ill health. Curiously enough we drew personally closer together after we had both left the Diocese. After his retirement we started a regular and delightful correspondence of real warmth and understanding and this deepened and developed during my time as Bishop of Bermuda. His last letter to me reached me in those Islands only three days before I was to read in the newspapers of his death.

We were indeed fortunate in his successor when Dr. Alwyn Williams formerly Headmaster of Winchester, Dean of Christ Church and Bishop of Durham, came to Winchester as our new Diocesan. I had known him a little when he was at Christ Church. He and his Highland Scottish (Macdonald) wife were two of the most delightful people imaginable. For all his massive scholarship and many abilities Dr. Alwyn Williams had the simplicity of the really great, and a heart of gold. Two more human and hospitable people could not be easily found and a visit to Wolvesey was always a joy.

In the early spring of 1956 I attended a Conference in Southampton and was told that the Archbishop (Dr. Fisher) wanted to meet me. Owing to intervening circumstances it was however only possible for us to meet very briefly. Soon after that I got a message that if I was likely to be attending the Exeter College Gaudy at Oxford, the Archbishop would like to talk to me, My friend Canon Harold Pickles' amusing comment on this was: "H'mm. That means either a ticking off or the offer of a Bishopric!" I hoped at least the first of those alternative suggestions would prove mistaken! Before the Gaudy Dinner, I got a verbal message from the Archbishop. Would I walk with him in the Fellows' Garden after coffee? We duly started out; but before we had gone twenty yards there was a sudden heavy shower and Dr. Fisher suggested we should try the College Hall, now deserted. We went there but could not find the electric light switches.

"I expect that you can hear in the dark?" said the Archbishop. So we sat down in the dimmest of twilights at the High Table. He immediately made the offer of the Bishopric of Bermuda, adding that he would not expect any answer until I had had time to look into it all.

"I would rather have liked you to have had a chat with the recently retired Bishop, Dr. Jagoe; but he lives now in Ireland."

"Actually we are going to Ireland on holiday very shortly," I said.

"Providence, my dear man" said His Grace. He added, "Do not think that because Bermuda is a small Diocese that it is necessarily an easy job nor an unimportant one. The Diocese includes the Portuguese Azores (over 2,000 miles away), and Bermuda itself bristles with problems. No Diocese could more easily be made a mess of, in spite of its undoubted charm and attractions."

My visit to Bishop Jagoe reminded me strangely of my visit to Canon A. J. Jones, at Bray, before I went to Banbury. The two large heavy men were strangely similar in both appearance and personality. Again I got very little information. Bishop Jagoe's reaction to most of my questions amounted to a little more than "Wait and see". I gathered (although not from him) that his own time in those lovely islands had not been without storms, at any rate in the earlier part of his six years' reign. However I got much useful information a little later from Bishop Stopford (then of Peterborough recently back from Bermuda) and from the then Archdeacon of Bermuda, the Ven. John Stow, who wrote me some very full letters. After an uneasy month of weighing up the "Pros and Cons" of the situation I wrote to Archbishop Fisher to say that I would be willing to accept the offer if made and confirmed, and to try and do my best. Everything then had to be kept secret until the Crown duly made the announcement some six or seven weeks later. In the meantime I had to refuse two offers of high Masonic honours without being in a position to give any reason for my non-acceptance. Bishop Jagoe had told me that if I accepted the nomination to the Diocese, I would then probably find that the Bermuda Diocesan Synod would take (as it had done in *his* case) some five or six months to consider whether or not to endorse the appointment. He had been elected by the Synod, even after such a lengthy delay by the bare majority, legally specified. However I was more fortunate and in less than three weeks I was officially informed that I had been elected unanimously.

As soon as my appointment was published (9th August) in *The Times* and other papers, I became the recipient of an almost embarrassing number of letters of congratulations and good wishes. I know that I answered personally over three hundred. The Bournemouth clergy were extremely kind and gave from the Chapter a handsome Prayer Book with illuminated inscriptions and a leather attache case. The R.D. Conference gave me book tokens and the Parish gave me a beautiful ebony and silver pastoral staff and a very generous cheque. Mollie received a handsome chiming carriage clock and many other gifts from the Diocesan, Deanery and Parochial Mothers' Union organisations as well as from the G.F.S. Hostel and Club. It was a terrible wrench leaving a Parish where we had been so happy for ten years, and we went through the same tensions that we had experienced on leaving Banbury. We both felt however that we had got to an age when a complete change of environment and of work and responsibility would definitely do us good. I was now sixty-four and although I was not conscious of feeling any older than when I had come to Bournemouth ten years previously, I knew that if I was to do any good in a new post it would be a case of the sooner the better, if not of now or never.

The Archbishop was kindness itself over my Consecration. I told him how much I hoped that it would be at Westminster Abbey, and it was. He also allowed me to choose the Preacher and I asked my old school friend, Seiriol Evans, Dean of Gloucester. It was nice also to have a companion in the Consecration Service in the person of the Rev. J. T. Hughes designated as Bishop Suffragan of Croydon. The night before the actual day (21st September, St. Matthew's Day) Mollie and I stayed with the Archbishop and Mrs. Fisher at Lambeth Palace, and I slept in the famous bed about which so many amusing jokes and stories are told.

At the actual Service I was presented to the Archbishop by the Bishops of Winchester and Peterborough (Drs. A. T. P. Williams and R. W. Stopford). I had hoped originally that Bishop Wand of London might be able to be one of those to present his old pupil; but he had another engagement. I was so grateful to Bishop Stopford for so kindly consenting to act. This was singularly appropriate, as he had only recently visited Bermuda and both he and Mrs. Stopford had been immensely helpful and informative to me and Mollie, both as to the special diocesan problems and the living conditions of those Islands. Eight other Bishops also took part in the Consecration, including the Bishop of Jamaica, who happily chanced to be in England at the time and had only recently preached for us at St. Peter's, Bournemouth. Some thirty clerical friends attended and the papers said that the congregation numbered over seven hundred. The combined choirs of the Abbey and the Chapel Royal (where I had been a Deputy Priest-in-Ordinary for so many years) sang the Service. I shall never forget the beauty of the music and the solemnity of the whole Service and setting. All our children and grandchildren (except the Flemings) were present. How I wished that my dear Mother could have been with us—but perhaps she was.

My Consecration as a Bishop automatically vacated the living of St. Peter's; but at the request of the Churchwardens I carried on with the work for another seven weeks.

Those weeks were some of the busiest and most exciting of my life. I was in all sorts of ways getting into contact with Bermuda and Bermudians and at the same time winding up the work of one of the busiest Parishes in the South of England. I wanted to leave no loose ends and spent much time in leaving full notes about everything in the Parish for my successor.

It was a great joy to us to find that we could take with us my orange cat Nicholas (now six years old and so affectionate and companionable) also our two dachshunds Gretel and her son Jeremy. They would all do much to make us feel at home in our new residence three thousand miles away from our family and friends.

There had been a great many happenings in our family circle of late years. Mollie had lost both her brothers. Hanson had died very suddenly in January 1949, having survived his wife by over ten years. He was fifty-seven. As his only child, Anne, was then still under age, Mollie had been appointed one of her guardians. Six years later in September 1955 Henry died also, aged sixty-two. He left very generous legacies to our children.

Shortly after we came to Bournemouth our youngest daughter Mima (Cynthia) after some training in London had taken up journalism and made a very promising start on the staff of the local Bournemouth paper. When she got engaged to be married at the age of nineteen the Editor wrote rather humorously to me and said that I should never have permitted it and that he was being deprived of one of his best reporters. She had been used considerably for interviewing V.I.P.s who came down to Bournemouth on more or less public occasions. It was in this way that she met amongst others the famous actress Flora Robson, who was so charmed with her that she insisted on her spending the whole day of her visit with her. She was also considered a star turn as a reporter of weddings and in this capacity she had some amusing experiences.

Her own engagement and wedding were indeed something in the nature of a whirlwind. We knew of course that she had been corresponding for about a year with an Irish Canadian R.A.F. Officer, Wing Commander J. B. Acton Fleming. Acton was a young man in his early thirties, and, as he was at that time an Attache to the Air Officer Commanding Middle East, he was stationed in Bagdad. One day we got a letter from him in which he said that he was coming on leave and had "some business" in Bournemouth to attend to. Might he come and see us? We had a shrewd suspicion as to what the "business" was and we invited him to stay. He came and he and Mima announced their engagement. They also said that they wanted to get married during his leave and that in two weeks Acton would have to fly back to Bagdad! A prospective father-in-law who was a Surrogate for Marriage Licences proved to be a boon. Within the two weeks the young couple were engaged and married with a week's honeymoon (in the New Forest) thrown in. Then Acton flew back to Bagdad and the bride followed him by air some weeks later. Acton has always been a great favourite with us. He has all the ready friendliness of the American side of the world and is a delightful host and a first rate mixer. He comes of a distinguished Canadian family on his Mother's side and there is a statue of his Baldwin great-grandfather near the Parliament Buildings in Ottawa. He was one of the makers of the Constitution of Canada. On his father's side he is connected with the Elphinstone family.

In Bagdad they had an interesting year, living in what had been the German Embassy and doing their share of the official entertaining of visiting V.I.P.s There was one amusing incident. On a certain occasion there came to dine with them an archaeologist and his lively grey-haired wife. After dinner the ladies withdrew to the drawing room and Mima asked the lady how she put her time in, whilst her husband was digging in the site of ancient Babylon.

"Oh, I am quite busy I assure you" said the lady. "I get local colour for another of my books."

"Really? I am afraid I do not know any of your books—travel, I suppose," ventured Mima.

"No: thrillers! "

"How exciting! But I don't think I have ever come across a book by you, Mrs. Mallowen."

"Ah well, you see I don't write as 'Mrs. Mallowen'. I write always as Agatha Christie."

Making the best recovery that she could Mima gasped as brightly as possible.

"Oh, of course! My father has read every book you have ever written and is a great fan"

On the Flemings return from Iraq their first child, Hugh, was born at our Vicarage in Bournemouth in December 1949. Rowena was born in 1952, Charles in 1958 and Meriel in 1964.

During our first years at Bournemouth Anne and Geoffrey Milroy had the four or five rooms at the top of our large Vicarage, whilst Geoffrey, at last out of the Army and ordained Priest, had a Curacy at All Saints, Southbourne. There Patrick was born in 1946 and later Anthony in 1949. It was delightful to have them all there; but in 1950 Geoffrey left to become Succentor of Exeter Cathedral and Vicar of Bramford Speke (famous in the days of Victorian religious quarrels for "The Gorham Case"). At that beautiful Devonshire Vicarage, with its wonderful views of the Exe Valley, their third child and our second grand-daughter, Diana, was born in 1953.

In the meantime Adelaide and Temple Nimmo had settled in Brighton. Temple also demobilised, had become a junior partner in his step-father's export business in the City of London. Their two boys Martin and Richard were born in 1947 and 1950 respectively.

Robin on coming out of the Royal Navy about a year after the end of the War found his scholastic career sadly disrupted. He had left Shrewsbury and joined up during the War on his eighteenth birthday. Instead of seeking to enter Exeter College, Oxford, he first of all tried engineering and went to work in a large engineering firm. He was far from happy either in his lodgings or his work. In the Navy where he had never sought promotion his fate had been to be to live amongst a bunch of Clydeside Reds, who had it in for him from the first because he had been to an English public school! In his engineering works once again he found himself surrounded by people of aggressive communist views: and when he avowed Tory opinions he soon found himself persecuted. After an unpleasant few months he left and we got him into the National Provincial Bank, where if not finally achieving his metier in life he spent rather a better time, coming home from Alresford and later from Reading at the weekends. It was not however until some years later that he got a post in which he could really settle happily. Through the kind offices of my old friend Canon Harold Pickles he got in 1952 an Accountant's position with the Radiators Branch of Morris Motors, in Oxford. When we knew a little later that we were going to leave England for Bermuda we were definitely worried about Robin, who, it seemed, would be left very lonely, without his weekends at home with us. The only one of his sisters who would be near would be Mima, who had recently bought a house at Broadway in Worcestershire, some thirty-five miles from Oxford. We were therefore quite relieved when Robin got engaged to a quiet and pretty girl in Oxford, Joan Westby, the only child of an electrical enginer who had worked with Morris (later Lord Nuffield) from the very beginning of his wonderful career. A week before we sailed for Bermuda, I married Robin and Joan in the delightful little Norman Church of North Hinksey, just outside Oxford, and we could think of them settling into their first little home nearby; when we set sail on our eleven days' voyage to Bermuda on the Reina del Pacifico.

The journey gave us a much needed rest and was uneventful except for the fact that we spent a day en route in La Rochelle, Santander and Corunna. My cat Nicholas made a good traveller and happily shared our first class cabin with us, also the menus of lunch and dinner. Gretel and Jerry, not so lucky, had to travel with the other dogs on board in the kennels provided. We left England on 22nd November, the country being enveloped in a white frost. We arrived in Bermuda on 4th December in a damp warmth of over 80 degrees, and began a melting process which, as far as I was concerned, lasted for the next six years.

CHAPTER XIII

Bishop Of Bermuda (1956-62)

WE WERE due to arrive in Bermuda about 9.0 a.m. on the 4th December so there was not much sleep after five o'clock that morning. About six o'clock we looked out of our cabin porthole and saw the first signs of land since we had left the mountains of the north coasts of Spain. The lamp of a lighthouse (on St. David's Island) shone brightly. Westwards on a long low grey-blue shadow twinkled innumerable little lights, white, red and green, mostly at the Airport and around the old town of St. George's at the east end of St. George's Island. Our ship's speed was now reduced to the minimum as we were about to negotiate the narrow entrance of the reefs at the extreme eastern end of the chain of islands. This dangerous ring of partially submerged rocks surrounds Bermuda almost completely. Soon we were inside and steaming slowly along westwards between the reefs and the North Shore, first of St. George's Island and then of the Mainland. Bermuda in shape is the nearest thing to the definition of a line, "length without breadth". From one end to the other this chain of islands is twenty-eight miles long and nowhere is there a breadth between the North and South Coasts of more than two miles. All the principal islands are connected by bridges. There are no mountains. The highest hills are probably Gibbs' Hill (two hundred and forty feet) crowned by its lighthouse with a powerful revolving light, and Prospect Hill, where the British Garrison used to live and where now in the refurbished buildings are a large school and the abode of the Police Force. As daylight came with an orange dawn we could now see the Mainland Island quite plainly only half a mile away. In the strange golden light it looked rather brown and was flecked all over with white and pastel coloured houses, with their white-washed roofs. Here and there were larger splashes of white where were lime-washed water-cachements on the sides of some of the hills. Bermuda depends for its water supply upon the rains collected on these cachements and roofs. There are no rivers or streams, and the few ponds are brackish. This first view was rather disappointing, as the grass looked dry and dead, whilst the whole landscape seemed covered with houses. However as we finally rounded the north-west end of the Mainland at Spanish Points, with Ireland Island a few miles to the west, we entered the calmer waters of Hamilton Harbour. Now full daylight had come and everything took on an amazing brilliance. The water was vivid with streaks of emerald green, turquoise and purple, the villas shone in the sunlight and the Fairyland area was pleasantly undulating and had a wealth of flowering shrubs and foliage. The sky was almost unbelievably blue. Although it was December it looked to us like high summer. Later we were to discover however that the really magical time of day in Bermuda was the half hour before the setting of the sun, when an almost unearthly beauty transfigured the whole landscape. The skies flamed, the sea glittered jade green and hills and houses could turn red-gold. Even the dead cedar trees turned every shade from rose and gold to tenderest mauve. We were to find the climate generally very pleasant from November until June. The summers were too damp and hot for our Northern taste. Many of the wealthier Bermudians left home from July to September when heat and humidity were both at their worst.

The Governor, Sir John Woodall, sent out the Government launch to meet us and the new Colonial Secretary, Mr. Joseph Sykes who with his family, was also on board. Sir John and Lady Woodall had most kindly asked us to stay with them at Government House for our first few days. This was a great pleasure and incidentally meant that our cases and baggage were exempt from Customs! Sir John's father, Colonel Frederic Woodall, had been an old friend of my Mother's in her girlhood's days, and as Sir John's last post before coming to Bermuda had been that of G.O.C. Northern Ireland, we had many friends and acquaintances in common. Nothing could have exceeded the kindness and friendliness of both Sir John and Lady Woodall during our time together in Bermuda. Their kindness was only equalled by their tact and wisdom. I always felt that while they were at Government House I had a completely reliable ally. We were indeed fortunate to have them for the first three of our six years.

From the moment we landed in the city of Hamilton life became hectic. Sir John Cox, the wise and friendly Speaker of the Parliament, had most kindly come on the launch to meet us, together with Archdeacon John Stow and Canon William Manning of the Cathedral. On landing we were taken up to the Cathedral where at the South Porch we met practically all the clergy of the Diocese and their wives. The Archdeacon read a formal Message of Welcome, which he presented to me afterwards. This was beautifully inscribed on a roll of parchment and tied up with a purple silk ribbon. Everybody seemed most friendly and after I had made a suitable reply, there was time to have a word with each of the clergy present. We then went and looked at Bishop's Lodge, an early nineteenth century house, lying just beneath the rising ground on which the west end of the Cathedral stood. The good Church folk had most kindly furnished the house for us; and also re-decorated and painted it. This last attention to the house the Archdeacon had advised them to leave until after our arrival, in case we did not find the house suitable; and how wise he was! The position of this house on the corner of two of the noisiest and most trafficky roads in the city we soon realised to be impossible. Except from about 2.0 a.m. until 5.30 a.m. during the night the noises never stopped. So after six months of broken nights we moved up on to the hills at Campden North to a delightful bungalow with nearly three acres of gardens and a lovely view towards the Southern ocean.

Before I go on to narrate any further impressions or events, I think that a very short history of Bermuda and a brief description of the general situation there should be given. Bermudians are fond of saying to newcomers—"Bermuda is different"; and how right they are!

It is not only different from Britain, Canada and the U.S.A., it is also different from the West Indies, of which Bermudians never tire of telling you their islands are *not* a part. Certainly the problems of Bermuda are utterly different from those of the Carribean. The West Indies are poor; and Bermuda is rich. In the West Indies some ninety-eight per cent of the population is coloured; in Bermuda (with the resident American garrisons, etc.) the population is roughly fifty per cent white and fifty per cent coloured. From the West Indies emigration is considerable, from Bermuda there is practically no emigration, except of a few of the more highly educated younger coloured people, who see more possibility of advancement elsewhere.

The beginnings of history, at any rate as far as a resident human population in Bermuda was concerned, were extraordinarily casual. They were not as occasionally described by some of the most enthusiastic coloured racialists from the U.S.A. The following incident illustrates this point. A young coloured woman in domestic service returned from Evening Service at one of the A.M.E. (African Methodist Episcopal) Churches full of the wonderful sermon just delivered by a young American negro pastor. He had spoken of the ideally virtuous indigenous coloured population of Bermuda in days of old.

"Your lovely island was a paradise of peace and prosperity until those wicked white people came here, stole your island and enslaved you!"

She would hardly believe it when her mistress informed her that when the first settlers from England arrived in the Bermudas by accident and by shipwreck, in 1609, the *only* inhabitants were the wild pigs! These were the descendants of some swine thoughtfully left there a hundred years previously by some Spanish adventurers who had discovered the islands and remained for only a short period.

The wreck on St. George's Island of the Sea Venture, with Sir George Somers on board and in command, occurred in a hurricane in 1609. Their ship with two or three others was actually bound for Virginia. Some of those thus brought there by fate decided to stay and the others eventually went on to North America. The story recorded in a letter is said ultimately to have reached the Earl of Southampton who was amongst those in England financially interested in the colonisation of Virginia. It is thought by many that Shakespeare now ailing and aging and on the verge of leaving London for his native Stratford, probably heard of this occurrence and with Southampton's encouragement, wrote his last great play "The Tempest" as a romantic dramatisation of it all.

Slaves were not imported until some years later into Bermuda. A few Africans, some North American Indians and some unfortunate Irish political prisoners were the progenitors of Bermuda's original slave and coloured population. From this mixed origin come the attractive and often beautiful coloured people of modern Bermuda. Many of these are tall and long limbed with handsome aquiline features and, in St. David's Island in particular, fair or even red hair is occasionally to be seen.

In the following years more immigrants came from the British Isles, then seething with the political and religious troubles of the first half of the seventeenth century. So a thriving population of white and British origin gradually grew up. The history of the next two hundred years was one of continuous development, with a good deal of squabbling in both Church and State; the growing pains of an independent and energetic people. Wars (such as the Napoleonic and the American Civil Wars) have usually only brought the islanders more prosperity and trade.

Early in the nineteenth century the capital and seat of Government was moved from St. George's in the eastern-most island of the same name to the new and thriving port of Hamilton near the centre of the Mainland. St. George's is now a museum town with its quaint old buildings, its ancient stocks and its three hundred and fifty years of history: a great attraction to tourists.

Today Hamilton is a very busy place with its Government buildings, its shops, restaurants and hotels. The fine modern Anglican Cathedral in its Gothic style dominates the town from its central hilltop. The rather Victorian looking Parliament Building is the next largest and most prominent landmark; but the magnificent modern City hall and the gracious Georgian Colonial Secretariat are much more pleasing. The life and prosperity of Bermuda centre in Hamilton and daily thousands commute from the whole of the rest of the islands. Traffic jams are the usual thing from 8.0-9.0 a.m. and from 5.0-6.0 p.m. The motor cars, prohibited until the advent of the American Air Force about 1939, have multiplied until they have given this little chain of islands quite a traffic problem. The first roundabout was made at a busy intersection of roads at the head of Hamilton Harbour during my episcopate. At first this innovation was rather criticised; but in time its usefulness became apparent and others have since been made elsewhere. Bermuda has a speed limit of twenty miles an hour upon its roads. To people accustomed to the great roads and distances of Canada and the U.S.A. or the dual carriage-ways of Great Britain these restrictions may seem excessive; but a closer knowledge of the narrow, twisting and often rock-edged roads of these islands soon convinces one that here is another illustration of the wise way in which Bermudians run their little country. Many other illustrations of their practical wisdom could be given, such as the ways in which their houses are constructed to meet the particular vagaries of their climate and conditions, so prone to sudden storms and heavy rains; and the non-existence of suitable water supplies from lakes or rivers.

The white Bermudians by their practical down-to-earth commonsense have made this little rocky chain of islands not only inhabitable but comfortable, convenient and prosperous. There is usually some very good reason behind what may seem to newcomers some of the strange little differences in their regulation of the conditions of life.

Bermuda, with about sixty thousand inhabitants, is one of the most thickly populated countries in the world. Its population is very mixed, almost cosmopolitan. Roughly there are about fifteen thousand white Bermudians and twenty-five thousand coloured

Bishop of Bermuda, 1956

Bermuda Cathedral, 1957

Bermudians. In addition there are perhaps some two thousand British people resident in one kind of post or another. There are also about twelve hundred Portuguese Azoreans and some thousands of American Servicemen (and their families) at the Air Base (Kindley) and "N.O.B." (their Naval Operational Base). The former occupies most of St. David's Island, once the quaintest part of Bermuda. The Naval Base occupies an enlarged peninsular at the North West end of Mainland Island. In addition there are a certain number of Americans and Canadians who have houses and businesses in Bermuda. Each year sees the coming and going of some two hundred thousand visitors (mainly from the U.S.A., but some from Canada). It is therefore no wonder that the islands are crowded and that the truly rural parts are shrinking visibly as large new hotels and more and more pastel coloured villas spring up in all directions. Kindley Field includes the fine Civil Airport as well as the American Air Base. The Canadian Atlantic Fleet as well as the British West Indies Squadron of the Royal Navy now use the old Naval Base in Ireland Island at the extreme west end of the archepelago. Bermuda has indeed been likened to Gibraltar, Malta and Aden in strategic importance to our Commonwealth. It is also "Britain's little shop window" in the New World. Its importance is therefore immeasurably greater than its small size and population would suggest. There Europe and America (and Africa too perhaps) meet. It has also become a favourite place for Conferences of world importance. What happens in this microcosm is of interest not only to the peoples of the N.A.T.O. countries, but to such countries as Ghana and Nigeria and the new countries of East Africa. Articles dealing with the colour problem in the Bermuda Press can find their way into African newspapers and vice versa.

The colour problem though not as shrill as in many parts of the world is definitely there. Today a coloured population, prosperous and educated naturally wants a larger influence upon affairs. There are many quite wealthy professional people and young people with University degrees amongst these forward looking coloured folk. When we went to Bermuda in 1956 the property qualification then enforced, limited the coloured vote. New legislation now gives many more the franchise. There are perhaps however not a few coloured people who realise that their white compatriots have not done such a bad job in many ways in the running of their little country. Of course the coloureds have their grievances, but these are rapidly disappearing during the last few years.

Until recently the more expensive hotels and restaurants and the more costly seats in the cinemas have been closed to coloured people. These restrictions have now been removed; but during our time the most expensive hotels still did not let their bedrooms to coloured people and in some of the churches (where it was still legal to rent pews) the front or best seats were denied to them. At the Cathedral I found that there were two surpliced choirs: one (white) sang at Matins, the other (coloured) sang at Evensong. After a few years I united these two choirs. I received a certain number of abusive letters from some of the die-hard segregationist white members of our congregation. One old gentleman, a member of our Cathedral Vestry and a wealthy leading citizen, wrote me a furious letter in which, after accusing me of ignorance and many other things, vowed that he would never enter the Cathedral again. I briefly acknowledged this thunderbolt by saying that I would hope to see him back in due course. In six weeks he returned. Curiously enough I got into trouble with some Bostonian "do-gooders" who attended the Cathedral shortly after I had actually integrated our Choirs. These visitors (a man and his wife) wrote that they had been "horrified at the cruel segregation" which I imposed on the poor coloured choristers, making them wear *purple* cassocks whilst the white members wore blue ones! As these people gave their address I replied to their righteous but unnecessary indignation and informed them that the coloured choristers chose their cassock colour themselves and refused blue as less becoming to their complexions! I could not help adding that friends of mine who had recently visited the States had, in my opinion, much more real causes for disquiet. One couple had noted that in Sarasota, Florida, the beaches were plastered with notices forbidding coloured people to use them before dark. Another couple had seen negroes pushed off the footpaths in St. Louis, Missouri. I said that I considered that these were much more hurtful things than allowing my coloured choristers to wear the coloured cassocks of their own choice! On the whole the white folk of Bermuda are coming to accept the inevitability of integration.

Obviously a delicate tact is one of the great needs in these days of transition.

I have always tried to avoid being like some of those caricature English people who go to all manner of places abroad and immediately tell the locals how they *should* do things. Such people deserve the unpopularity they invariably provoke amongst reasonable colonial populations, just as do some Bostonians who go to other cities and parts of the U.S.A. and try to impart their greater light to their less illuminated fellow citizens. Whilst on the subject of Boston and some of its rather aggressive do-gooders, I remember the experience of a Canadian Bishop, who did a great deal of religious broadcasting in North America. He said to me:

"Every time I broadcast I get dozens of grateful letters from all over Canada and the Northern parts of the U.S.A. Occasionally, of course, one gets the odd critical or abusive letter. These last almost invariably bear the Boston postmark."

People in Philadelphia and Washington, to my knowledge, have many amusing stories about virtuous Bostonians and their sense of mission to the other American cities; but I am straying from Bermuda.

Each of the different groups who inhabit Bermuda have their special characteristics. The typical white Bermudian is a first rate business man. Bermuda, like Aberdeen, has few Jews. When Bermudians quarrel (with each other) they do not usually allow "the sun to set upon their wrath". After all they mostly meet each other every day.

"How can one do business with a man with whom one is not on speaking terms?"

Sometimes it is:

"How can one really quarrel with a man who is not only a business contact but a relative or an 'in-law'?"

In such a comparatively small community nearly everyone is related to or connected with everyone else. One of the first things a wise outsider should learn when settling in Bermuda is not to venture unfavourable opinions on one Bermudian to another. I remember one occasion there was a great and resounding quarrel between the two Church wardens in a particular parish. The Rector appealed to me and I promised to come along in two or three days' time and be the dove of peace. The next morning however I found that this particular visit would be unnecessary, as I met the two men in question walking down Front Street (Hamilton) arm in arm, discussing some business deal no doubt. I do not think that most Bermudians are greatly interested in cultural projects or pursuits. There are very few dramatic enterprises or concerts and there is little "heavy" reading. On the other hand there is a very live Art Society, many of the modern buildings erected in recent years are good and sometimes in quite excellent taste (e.g. the fine new City Hall of Hamilton).

For the past century and more Bermuda has been cleverly and efficiently run by the leading business men, often spoken of facetiously as "the Forty Thieves", or merely as "Front Street" (where the largest and most luscious emporia are situated). It has indeed been suggested at one of the famous Somerset Island "skit" revues that the country's motto should have been changed from "Quo fata ferunt" (which I suppose describes the providential survival of all aboard the wrecked Sea Venture in 1609) to "Quo fata Front Street".

Thanks to its powerful and astute business clique Bermuda is to-day in the forefront of Western affluence. Like Macmillan's England they have "never had it so good". Tourism is of course the greatest industry to-day. Not all the Americans in Bermuda however are millionaires escaping from their own rigorous winters to palatial villas in the sun. We had many friends amongst the Americans we met. Some were the equivalent of the very best "county" peoples in the British Isles; some were young marrieds with financial problems. Almost all were genuine and friendly. Of course the little differences of outlook and deportment of the British and the Americans provoke much mutual amusement. Sometimes one gets to know an extrovert American intimately in twenty minutes (a knowledge which may tend to diminish the longer one knows them):

"Call me Elmer! "

Socially this is a hot bath, in comparison to the chill and apathy which have fallen upon what used to be called "social life" in England. One can only take people as one finds them. We have always found Americans and Canadians wonderfully kind and warm hearted and definitely interested in other people. They just do not understand the Englishman's fundamental desire to "keep himself to himself" and to despise as mere curiosity those feelings which prompt our transatlantic cousins to take an interest in their neighbours.

One other element of Bermuda's population must be mentioned —the Azorean Portuguese who for the past twenty or thirty years have been brought in (in limited numbers) to work mainly on the land, and occasionally on other energetic manual employments which do not make much appeal to either white or coloured Bermudians. The Azores (of which I will say more anon) are poor and over populated. To these tough and willing young men Bermudian wages are vast riches compared with what they can earn at home. So they come and work hard (often taking on extra jobs in the evenings) and save their money. Many have left wives and children at home and send back money to keep the family they will not see perhaps for years. Some return as "rich men" to their own Islands after eight or ten years with, say a thousand pounds, which will set them up in a smallholding. It must often have been very hard for these young fellows to be separated from their families for long; wives and families not often being allowed to accompany them. Of recent years this situation has been somewhat alleviated and some wives and families have been permitted to come to Bermuda. This has been when men have put in a stretch of years of good work and conduct and wish to settle permanently in Bermuda. I worked behind the scenes in this cause and one of Bermuda's leading citizens and business men (M. A. Gibbons) worked hard and persistently in Parliament to the same end. It proved a difficult task since there was over against what fairness and humanity demanded the realistic argument about Bermuda's population increasing at such an alarming rate. Was there justification for letting in scores of immigrant families? These young Azorean men came for the good money and knowing that it meant leaving wives and families for anything up to ten years. Incidentally the Azorean families seem to make very good citizens. Perhaps the wives do not learn much English; but the children learn quickly. An intelligent and naturally industrious and vigorous new element is beneficial to any community.

Is Bermuda, from the religious angle, better or worse than the British Isles? My own opinion is that the general situation is much as it is here. Church attendance is possibly a little better in Bermuda, although as in the U.S.A. evening Church-going is on the way out, excepting on special occasions such as Confirmations and the various Guild Services. Bermuda is certainly not "under-churched". There must be any way forty places of worship for about fifty to sixty thousand people. Of those the Anglican Church owns some twenty. Roughly half the population belongs at least nominally to "the Church of England as established in Bermuda". This means about twenty to twenty-five thousand Anglicans. The next most numerous body is the African Methodist Episcopal Church. This group is usually spoken of as the A.M.E. Next in numbers come the Romans with their resident Bishop, claiming perhaps three thousand, followed by the Presbyterians and Methodists. There are several smaller sects mostly originating from the United States and liberally financed from that country. Some of these have rather meteoric careers. A large church grows with mushroom speed: a Minister with a gift for oratory and finance crowds it. A few years later the building may be taken over by some other body or become a storehouse or a set of offices. Christian Science, without many adherents numerically, draws vast wealth from Boston and buys the largest periods on radio and television. Of recent years the Seventh Day Adventist have built some large churches.

We were all very friendly during my time and we built up a very worth while Anglican and Free Church Council of Clergy and Ministers. There we read papers to one another, had some excellent discussions, concerted joint projects of various kinds and generally got to know and to appreciate one another better. The Roman Catholic Bishop also I always found very friendly and co-operative. When I was leaving Bermuda in 1962 I was much touched by a Presentation and Address presented to me by the Free Church Ministers Association on the very morning of the day on which we sailed for home.

The Anglican Church has divided the Island into nine "Parishes"—St. George's (containing St. Peter's Church, dating from the early days of the seventeenth century, also Wellington and St. David's Chapel-of-Ease): Hamilton Parish (to be distinguished from the City of Hamilton, the present capital, which lies in Pembroke Parish), Smith's Parish: Devonshire: Paget: Warwick; Southampton and Sandys. These names recall some of the prominent Elizabethans and Jacobeans who financed England's colonising ventures at the beginning of the seventeenth century. Most of these Parishes have more than one Anglican place of worship, e.g. Pembroke, with the largest population has three daughter churches, St. George's, Sandys, Southampton, Devonshire and Smith's parishes two. The Cathedral in the centre of Hamilton City has no Parish, but had the largest morning congregations on a Sunday in my time in Bermuda, whilst Pembroke had the largest Sunday Schools. The various "coloured" Guilds with their special services and social intercourse generated considerable enthusiasm and fellowship. On the whole Youth Clubs tended to have rather disappointing and short careers, their vitality usually depending upon some one magnetic leader of genius here to-day and gone to-morrow. The difficulties confronting the work of the Anglican Church (and no doubt most of the other religious bodies) can be summarised as follows.

The young Bermudians, like the young Americans, grow up rather more quickly than the young people of the British Isles. Many were (or thought they were) "going steady" at fifteen or sixteen years of age, consequently preferring their freedom to go to cinemas or dances with their boy or girl friend, rather than to attend some regular Youth Club. The young people also felt the pressure of the continual holiday atmosphere of Bermuda with its hordes of half-clothed holiday makers swarming all over the Islands for nine or ten months of each year: people cycling, sun-bathing, boating, dancing, sight-seeing, and so on, and after dark crowding into the restaurants, cinemas and night clubs. Another situation which affected children and young teenagers was the large number of married women who went out to work. The high cost of living and the high wages also attainable tempted many mothers to go out to lucrative daily jobs. Children who went to school often arrived home an hour or so before either parent. Small children were left to the care of elder brothers or sisters or of coloured maids. A little imagination will show how this sort of situation could sometimes work out, with elder brothers or sisters of comparatively tender age trying to keep order, or even not trying.

There is no doubt also that the colour question often complicated many good works and activities. It was for instance hard to get white and coloured St. John Ambulance Classes integrated. The same thing provided problems with Scouting and Guiding at times as well as with Youth Clubs. It was also not easy to get Bermudians to take very much interest in the outside world or missionary problems. This was understandable. Bermuda had so much that it was a microcosm of modern success and achievement and the rest of the world was so far away. After all it was only the few who could dash off to New York or elsewhere for the matter of a few score pounds or dollars and in an incredibly short time. It is hardly an exaggeration to say that the Bermuda "image" to some less travelled Bermudians was that it was the centre of the earth and everywhere else had a slightly unsubstantial and probably less successful existence.

There was also a trace of anti-clericalism in the average Bermudian mind. I fancy that the origin of this was historical. No doubt Bermuda has had some fine clergy and ministers during the past three hundred and fifty years of its existence as an inhabited country; but it has also had some highly eccentric and odd clerics especially in its earlier times. Many of the first divines to come there were heretical or political refugees from England, flying from the disciplines of the Bishops of London and others; men if not with a price on their heads, at least very suspect in matters of doctrine and so on. Too few of Bermuda's clergy have been Bermudians bred and born. Perhaps some of the British bred clergy and ministers (or even those in more recent times from the New World) have been a trifle tactless, or have given the impression that they were God's gift to the natives of those remote islands: (a fault by no means confined to the clergy; but to be found also amongst many officials and administrators *and their wives*). The accounts which can be read of various squabbles in the past, both in matters to do with Church affairs as well as more purely secular problems, certainly suggest that there must have been faults on both sides. Bermudians have often had good cause to take a long look at these immigrants; both clerics and officials. Certainly they have evolved efficient means of getting rid of undesirables and no one who has not obtained the status of Bermudian Citizenship, however apparently securely entrenched in wealth and position, can presume that their residence is necessarily permanent or unassailable.

The sectionalism and cosmopolitan qualities of Bermuda's dense population give the Church (and other organised activities) furiously to think at times. Teachers from elsewhere will always do best in Bermuda if they have the tact and sense also to show themselves as learners. One well known Bermudian once made a gloriously candid and revealing remark to me on this subject. He said:

"On the whole I prefer British teachers to Burmudians." What a broad-minded man, I thought! He added:

"You see if he or she is British, you can sack them and there are no bones broken, or repercussions felt. On the other hand if you sack a Bermudian, you may have to reckon on trouble with a whole host of influential Bermudian relatives and friends."

The problems for a Bishop were, as I saw them, manifold. The clergy had to face many difficulties in their work and environment. There were never more than seventeen in number in my time. I felt sure that to regard the local Ministry *as a family* was the wise and Christian way. I wished the clergy to come to look to me as their natural ally and protector, and not as a mere official or as someone who might be swayed, by considerations of the wealth or importance of any lay magnates into taking part against them. I remember on one occasion how a certain highly intelligent clergyman roused the wrath of some wealthy and established Bermudians by certain opinions which he expressed in a newspaper article. One irate old patriarch rang me up in explosive fury and demanded that I should "have the fellow out of the Island within twenty-four hours! "

I pointed out that only the Immigration Board could do that, adding that incidentally I felt that in a free country people were entitled to an opinion of their own, provided that it was neither dangerous nor subversive. The old gentleman's apopletic rejoinder was:

"Well, if you won't get him out, I shall take steps to get *you* out in a week."

I am afraid that I replied:

"Then you had better get on with it, as I am not going to make any move in the matter," and rang off.

Nothing more happened and about a week later my former adversary invited us to lunch at the Yacht Club, and all was love and peace. It did not do to take too much notice of every little squall which passed over the Bermuda scene.

Other aims of mine, as Bishop, were to hold a Visitation of the Parishes and to get a really complete list of Church property. There was nothing of this sort available, although some of the Parishes had magnificent and valuable Church plate (as at St. George's) and others alas had had regrettable incidents in their past when, in ignorance, priceless and irreplaceable silver had been sold or even lost. Church property and even Glebe land had also been sold and muddled away for a tenth part of what would have been their present value. There was no headquarters list of Church charities. Strange stories of bygone impulsiveness and irresponsibility came to one's knowledge—such as the tale of some Church-wardens who had disliked some of their Church's furnishings (including the font) and cheerfully thrown it into the sea! That of course had been in "the good old days" and not recently. With the efficient help of Archdeacon Stow I got out a form of Enquiry which had over forty questions (with sub-sections) which we circulated in triplicate to all Church-wardens. On the whole our activities were well and courteously received and full and satisfactory information given. Only in one Parish were the Church-wardens reported as likely to revolt or resist, and to have said:

"What does it matter to the Bishop or the Archdeacon what property our Church has? That is our business." However, when it came to the day of our arrival in the Parish all went well. At another Church when we were examining the contents of a not very safe "safe", I enquired about the contents of a solid square box for which there was no key. I was informed that the key could not be found. Anyway the box, though heavy was empty, because it did not rattle when shaken. Indeed they had meant to throw it away as it took up too much room. Tiresomely I insisted that it should be opened and the resourceful Archdeacon produced two bunches of keys. About the tenth effort succeeded.

The case was opened and a very fine William and Mary period silver chalice and paten were brought to light.

Enquiry into material resources having been duly completed I went on to more spiritual matters and after about eighteen months' preparation, which included visits from Bishop Kenneth Evans (Bishop of Ontario), the Chairman of the Evangelistic Committee or Council of the Anglican Church of Canada, and of Father Genders, the Principal of Codrington College, Barbados, we launched an eight-day Mission upon the Islands. Every Parish took part in this, with the exception of the large and populous Parish of Pembroke, which, though sympathetic and helpful, preferred to have its own Mission about a year later. Bermuda with its well managed structure and economy was no less in the grip of Mammon than any other part of the world in which I have lived; but on the whole the idea of a Mission was welcomed by the Church population and by the press. The white people rather tended to think that it would be good for their coloured fellow citizens and the coloured folk thought the same in reverse. I agreed with both points of view! As usual in such cases the Mission had varying fortunes in different Parishes for one reason or another. It undoubtedly gave a challenge and in almost every case resulted in an increase in Communicants in the ensuing years and drew into the orbit of Church work and sense of responsibility several valuable people who had hitherto been rather on the circumference than at the centre of the Church's life. Our Missioners were besides the Bishop of Ontario, the Principal of Codrington College, Barbados, two delightful coloured Senior Students from Codrington, and the Rev. T. Dyson, the Rector of Warwick Parish, Bermuda, whose contribution was outstanding in many ways.

Later on another of my endeavours was the Revision of the Church Vestries Act, then nearly a century out of date. Here again, with much valuable help from the more knowledgeable members of our Church Synod we produced a new Measure, better suited to the needs and conditions of the mid-twentieth century. Sir John Cox and other Members of Parliament who were also members of Synod, were invaluable on this occasion, as was the careful and scholarly work put in by Archdeacon Cattell, who had succeeded Archdeacon Stow, now returned to England. Parliament accepted our Measure and it became law after a smooth passage.

One of my most consistent efforts was to attempt to make our beautiful Cathedral, in effect as well as in name, the Mother

Church of the Diocese. All sorts of activities were organised to this end and some success was achieved. It had to be remembered that until almost the beginning of this century the Diocese had had no Cathedral, and even when this large and handsome building was finally built, the Diocese was conscious that it had managed quite comfortably without any cathedral for almost three hundred years. Indeed many devotees of St. John's Church, Pembroke, rather tended to object to the intrusion of another important ecclesiastic centre in its Parish. When I had been at least three or four years in Bermuda I met a businessman, a prominent supporter of St. John's, Pembroke, and a life-long resident in our little capital city. I made some remark about the interior of the Cathedral. He replied—

"I really don't know. I have never been inside. I pass it every day going to my office; but, you see, I attend St. John's."

I tried to get people accustomed to attendance at the Cathedral for the principle national and special services and we had a good deal of success in this direction with the annual Festival of the Mothers Union and the various Guilds, also the opening and closing services of the Mission (with its Procession of Witness). We were also delighted to lend the Cathedral to the Americans in Bermuda for their annual Thanksgiving Day Services. In any case the Cathedral could hold up to twelve hundred people quite easily, whilst none of our other churches could take more than about four or five hundred.

At the Lambeth Conference in 1958 one Diocesan Bishop from the West Indies asked me with great feeling the poignant question:

"How do you get on with your Dean at your Cathedral?"

"Oh, I have known him all my life," was my cyptic reply.

"That must be a help indeed."

Not to mislead him further I went on to explain that in Bermuda the Bishop was also Dean. Archbishop Fisher thought that this was a good thing under existing conditions, and on the whole that was my opinion also after some experience.

On the average on Sundays I spent half my time at the Cathedral and the other half at the various Parish Churches and their respective Chapelries. I must have visited each Parish Church at least about three times a year including Confirmations. There were few large Parochial efforts at which my wife and I did not attend. This enabled me to get to know personally practically all the principle workers in each Parish as well as the actual officials (Church-wardens, etc.). Indeed this was one of the greatest joys which a small diocese could provide. I know that some people (including some Diocesan Bishops in England and elsewhere) think that Bishops should not be seen too frequently in their Parishes lest that Office be cheapened as it were. In a small diocese however I think that the cultivation of the family feeling is possible and that an accessible Bishop, need not be too interfering. In Bishop Brown's time (1925-49), before the introduction of the motor car, it was not physically possible for a Bishop to be at St. George's on a Sunday morning, at some afternoon function in Sandys or Southampton Parish, and to take a Confirmation in the evening, say at Bailey's Bay. To state that there were Sundays when I motored sixty or seventy miles does not sound much when one thinks of Canadian Bishops frequently motoring two or three hundred miles in their vast dioceses; but at least one could keep in close touch and show that there was no corner of our Islands which did not matter. We always received the most friendly and cordial welcome wherever we went and had friends in every Choir and Sunday School, as well as in the Rectories and the home of Church officials.

On the whole I think I enjoyed being Bishop more than being Dean of the Cathedral, although it was naturally easier to correlate the relationship of the Diocese and what should be the "Mother Church", if the Diocesan was also Dean. I have seen so many illustrations of Bishops and Deans pulling in opposite directions in England, and I have heard the complaints of more than one Colonial Bishop who had Deans at their See Churches who were the leaders of any opposition to their considered over-all policies. There may be a few obvious disadvantages in having one man holding both posts; but in a small Diocese there are some points in favour. It was probably a good thing to appoint a separate Dean of Truro; but I came to agree with the opinion of Archbishop Geoffrey Fisher that there were good reasons for combining the Deanery and Bishopric in Bermuda, where the Cathedral was a comparatively new institution.

A good deal was done to the Cathedral during my time in Bermuda. My first task was to get the proposed Memorial Chapel to Bishop Arthur Heber Brown completed before all the people interested had died. After Bishop Brown's death a Committee had been appointed to deal with this question and some hundreds of pounds had been contributed. Six years had passed and nothing more had happened. As soon as I arrived, with the help of Sir John Cox and one or two others, I raised the rest of the money required and an English Altar with angel-topped riddel posts and curtains was designed by and brought out from Messrs. Wippell and Company, Exeter. Three stained glass windows, the work of a gifted young Dutch artist, were put in to replace the plain glass of the three lights. They represented the Good Shepherd (behind the altar), St. Barnabas (the Saint on whose name day the good Bishop had been consecrated), and St. Michael (the Saint to whom his former Church in Paddington had been dedicated). The colouring especially of the St. Michael window, was particularly fine. Since then wrought iron gates have completed the Chapel.

Next I raised the Bishop's throne on two steps, adding some dignitary to a not very impressive piece of work. My friend Will Harrington, the leading artist resident in Bermuda, executed in gold and enamel on carved oak, a very beautiful mitre and coat of arms of the diocese, which was placed on the central panel and quite transformed the whole structure.

I then set out to collect money to put a reredos behind the High Altar where there was nothing except a rather dreary expanse of stone wall with poor cementing between the stones. A good design was produced by a local F.R.I.B.A., E. D. (Bob) Ede. The plan was to have a large central figure of the Risen Christ and in seven canopied niches either side slightly smaller figures of various Saints. These were to include those Saints to whom Churches in Bermuda were dedicated (e.g. St. John, Apostle and Evangelist, Pembroke, and St. Anne, Southampton), the other Evangelists, the Patron Saints of England, Ireland, Scotland and Wales, and the Irish Saint Brendan, who according to a tradition had sailed with some of his monastic companions to Bermuda in the sixth century.* A talented Canadian sculptress resident in Bermuda, by name Byllee Lang, undertook the work of producing these figures, and the central figure of the Christ and eight of the fourteen other figures are her work, leaving only three empty niches each side. These were filled later. This well balanced group looks good and the figures have great interest and character. A white marble tabernacle, originally made for a Roman Catholic Church in America, was removed from the high altar and re-erected on another altar in the east side of the south transept. Curiously enough the most vocal objector to this replacement was the most Protestant member of our congregation. Neither the artistic nor the doctrinal objections to a tabernacle of this sort on the High Altar of an Anglican Cathedral registered. It had been on the Altar as long as he could remember and that was enough!

*(Born early in the century, he did most of his travelling c. 545 A.D. Died at Clonfert c. 577 A.D.)

As I had also planned to build a Chapter House and more adequate Vestry accommodation beyond the North transept I originally appealed for twenty thousand pounds and when we left in the late summer of 1962 some nineteen thousand pounds had been received. The problem of the Vestries, etc. has since been met, and certain exterior parts of the windows and porches have been repaired. The stone used for these parts was a soft Caen stone, entirely unsuited for the moist salty winds and atmosphere of these islands.

The series of windows, illustrating New Testament events, on the north side of the nave was completed and two more windows by the Dutch artist, Ackërt, were added towards the western end of this north aisle. The interior of this fine building has certainly gained considerably in richness and dignity by all these additions.

From time to time the tourist trade, so to speak, provided problems for the Church. In Holy Week each year hordes of American students descended upon Bermuda and a week's programme of activities has always been arranged for them by the local authorities. We found that on Easter Day these fixtures began so early that many who wished to get to early Services found it almost impossible. So I and the President of the Free Church Council approached the right quarter and we got things altered so that those who wanted to get to Church could do so without missing their tournaments, competitions and outings. One had to keep an eye continually on problems of this sort. We did our best also to advertise Church Services in the hotels (as I had done whilst Rural Dean of Bournemouth), and we all did what we could to make visitors welcome. A great many non-Anglicans attended the Cathedral Services, partly because of its central and prominent position in the highest part of the little city, with its great tower dominating the harbour and the general landscape. One got the occasional odd comment. A whole pew full of white Americans from South Carolina turned up one Sunday morning in time for the 9.15 a.m. Sung Eucharist and I noticed that they stayed on for Matins as well. I spoke to them after the second service at the South porch as they left the Church. They said how much they had "enjoyed" everything, and then added rather unexpectedly:

"But, O my, aren't you 'High' in this Cathedral! "

I said that I imagined that they were referring to the Sung Eucharist at which we used vestments, but, no, that was not it at all! It was our Choral Matins.

"*Singing* those *Psalms* instead of *reading* them! "

That was the "highest" thing they had ever experienced in any church. No comment that I could think of seemed relevant, so I just smiled and we said a friendly farewell. Some people's reactions are quite unpredictable—especially those of American tourists from the "deep South" and the "Middle West", when they go abroad.

Moral problems in Bermuda were very plangent. To put it briefly, some of the white people were too keen on marriage and some of the coloured people not keen enough. In other words a high percentage of white Bermudians and American residents had had divorces, and a certain number of coloured people (though not as many as in the West Indies) had families without matrimony. Apart from these exceptions morality was, I suspect, neither higher nor lower than in Britain or the U.S.A.; but because Bermuda was small everything stood out more. Still the following Memorial Notice, culled from one of the local papers certainly struck me as somewhat unusual:

IN MEMORIAM
in loving memory of our dear Mother and Grandmother
Miss X - Y
who departed this life 6 years ago
January 2nd
May she rest in peace.
Sadly missed by the entire family.

White people might do well to remember that in the bad old days of slavery, the coloured people were frequently forbidden to marry. In the West Indies at any rate, there is a definite hangover from those times. It can be imagined that Bermuda was not the easiest place in which to run the Mothers Union on a large scale; but I must say that my wife did a good work in this direction as Diocesan President, M.U. Under her leadership the number of branches and the number of members doubled in six years. Our first Diocesan M.U. Festival in the Cathedral produced a congregation of about fifty members. In our last year the total was on to two hundred, white and coloured.

The general atmosphere of Bermuda was as genial and warm socially as it was in climate. The hospitality was wonderful. Every week there were on the average two luncheon parties, two dinners and a sherry party or some other social function to attend. I valued these principally as a means of getting to know more and more people. One could at times even meet people's deepest needs on such occasions. Once I spent half an hour at a Garden Party helping an American woman to find reasons for believing the Christian doctrine of the Resurrection: a faith which she had never been able to accept. Some weeks later I got a very happy and grateful letter from her written from her New England home. Often one was able to get people to come into the circle of regular worshippers or to hear of some trouble or sickness where one's help could be given. The wealthy Bermudians entertained us with great kindness and my artistic interests found many lovely homes and treasures to enjoy. It was a great pleasure also to be asked to many of the homes of the coloured people where the greatest kindness and courtesy was invariably accorded. The coloured people had a keen sense of humour and were very quick to see a joke. They had a real sensitivity.

The only kind of dinner that was ever a little dull was some formal occasion of protocol when one always sat next to the same people. I remember Sir John Woodall, our first Governor during our period, grumbling to me once in a rather amused way about such an occasion then imminent.

"Well, I suppose it will be the same people, the same conversations and the same food; and the same request from me for the mustard which will not be on the table, but will be brought looking rather lonely on a large plate after I have nearly finished my steak!"

Our first two days in Bermuda were spent at Government House. Then we moved into Bishops Lodge at 11.0 a.m. The kind ladies who had arranged the house and furniture gave us a cup of tea and then Mollie retired to bed with a sharp attack of influenza. Our suitcases remained in the hall, together with the packing cases containing my books and the other things (china, pictures, etc.) which we had brought with us. That afternoon between two and five o'clock no less than forty-seven people came to call! The following day only twenty-four called. I had to grapple single-handed on the first occasion. By the Saturday Mollie was up again and staggering around. On the Monday night I attended the Annual Parliamentary Dinner at the Castle Harbour Hotel on the kind invitation of The Speaker, Sir John Cox. At the responder to the Seventh Toast and so the fourteenth speaker of the occasion I rose to my feet to speak at about one o'clock in the morning! Ignoring nearly all that I originally prepared, I said that as I was the fourteenth speaker of the evening I intended for everyone's sake to be also the briefest. This produced the most hearty applause of the whole evening. The influenza had by this time begun to claim me and eventually I got home to bed at about 2.30 a.m. with a temperature and a raging headache. For the next two days Mollie entertained the streams of callers alone. We had landed on the Wednesday morning and on Thursday afternoon we had had the Enthronement Service, attended by about fourteen hundred people, all the clergy and most of the Free Church ministers. Dr. Barfoot, the Primate of Canada and Archbishop of Rupertsland also attended, a most friendly gesture which I greatly appreciated from this old friend of my uncle Canon Ion Murray. Every moment of those first few days remains vividly with me. They were certainly hectic and happy, as were the weeks and months that followed. The front door bell of the Bishop's Lodge rang all day long and so did the telephone. After two abortive attempts I succeeded in getting a charming secretary in (Mrs.) Martha Gentry, an American lady, whose husband was working in Bermuda. She did a very good piece of work with me. The only trouble was with our British Geography and spelling. Place names such as Worcester, Leicester, Gloucester were a continual problem to her. I tried to explain English "shires" and Irish "counties" to her, but we did not manage to avoid ultimately the following address, "Sunderland, Co. Durham, Southern Ireland". My other problem with her was that in my letters I now talked about "transportation", "gotten", "theater" and "color" and so on. Some British friends thought that my Americanisation was preceeding a-pace. After Mrs. Gentry had to give up the post at the end of six or seven months I was lucky enough to obtain the help of Mrs. (Sylvia) Pitt, born and married in Bermuda but educated at Winchester. She remained as my secretary until the end of our time in the Islands. Tactful, discreet and delightful, she became one of our best friends, and her intimate knowledge of Bermuda, its people and customs, saved me much trouble and no doubt many blunders.

The old Bishop's Lodge was not a bad nor an ugly house (inside); but its situation was impossible except for the stone deaf. It stood right on the street and on the corner of two of the noisiest busiest roads in the lively little town. Nearby were some of the less quiet hotels and night clubs. Behind the house was a hall let for many purposes until late at night. To dictate letters to one's secretary in the morning one almost needed a megaphone. Motors hooted and "revved" their engines from both roads, cheerful crowds screamed and shouted until the small hours of the night. After seven months we moved out of town about a mile and a half up on to the top of the hill at Camden North: two hundred feet up above the town, five degrees cooler and fresher in the humid heat of summer. Save for the calling of the red cardinal birds and the soporific croaking of the tree frogs, we enjoyed a country calm. Unlike the beautiful but shy and elusive blue birds the red cardinals were bold and amusing. Also they were very imitative. Mollie used often to call me from the verandha when I was reading, writing or working in the garden.

"Lewis, Lewis," she would cry.

"Lueece, Lueece," the birds would shriek.

To my calls for "Nickie or Pussy", they did not respond quite so well. "Neekie, Neekie" was not so bad; but "Puddie" was less convincing. Their uncanny way of caricaturing the tone of a voice exceeded their powers of pronunciation.

The house was less episcopal. It was a fair sized bungalow with three sitting rooms, three bedrooms (and three bathrooms) and nearly two acres of garden sloping down gently to the South with a fine view of many flowering shrubs and trees, Hungry Bay and the limitless ocean. It was absolute bliss. I could get to the Cathedral by car in seven minutes and had regular times for being available in the Vestry there. People who had no real reason for calling did not bother to come and I could get to every part of the Diocese, except Pembroke Parish, without going through all the ever increasing traffic of Hamilton. For perhaps a few weeks two or three of the old Cathedral ladies moaned that the Bishop was deserting the Cathedral. That was not so: also we were getting some sleep. We owed all this to the kindness and cleverness of our financial genius Mr. M. A. Gibbons, of the Church Society. He bought this charming country home for us at a bargain price (sixteen thousand pounds) and then proceeded to let the old Bishop's Lodge so advantageously (as a Children's Nursery School), that the money spent on the new house would soon be recouped. The old Lodge battered from without by noise by day and night could now retaliate from within with the shrill shouts and cries of the children in their classes and games.

My normal daily routine was much as follows. Canon Manning and I shared the daily early celebrations of the Holy Communion at the Cathedral each week. After breakfast I usually took a quick walk for twenty minutes to half an hour before the heat became too great. I devised several short jaunts through lanes ("Tribe" roads) and fields. I found that on the average I worked all morning from 9.30 a.m. until luncheon and from about 3.30 p.m. on until bedtime, with another half hour's break for a stroll round about 6.0 p.m. In summer time walking was practically unbearable between 10.0 a.m. and 6.0 p.m. At least three or four nights each week there were evenings engagements. We tried to take Fridays off and, when successful, took our lunch or tea (or both) with us, also our bathing things and my paints, to some quiet and beautiful spot. Altogether I painted about sixty sketches in six years. Of these I gave some twenty away to friends or so some Church Fête or Bazaar. I sold fifteen at the Art Exhibitions or through an art shop. My large sketches got twenty-five pounds. Once I got thirty pounds for a picture I wanted to keep and priced high enough (as I thought) to stop it selling. About fifteen of my Bermuda paintings have been brought back to England and I expect that people who have never been to those Islands think their colouring very bright.

Plays and concerts were very rare in Bermuda, although we did get two or three good pianists or violinists most years during the winter season. There was also the occasional amateur theatrical performance; sometimes remarkably well done. We hoped that when the new City Hall, with its beautifully appointed little theatre was built that Drama would begin to flourish more; but the cost of hiring was almost prohibitive. Accustomed to good theatre and music we felt the cultural dearth; and had to rely upon a record player, although it was none too easy to get up-to-date recordings and the stock to choose from was small; unless one wanted jazz or pop music (which we definitely did not). As we neither golfed nor yachted our recreations were walking, swimming, record-playing and above all reading and sketching. Here again we had to rely on getting most of our literature from England. We took The Times (which arrived intermittently by air from three to five days late), The Church Times and The Illustrated London News, and how we revelled in them. There was no really good book shop in Bermuda, but there was a very good Library in Hamilton. This, supplemented by getting books two or three times a year from Blackwell's in Oxford, kept me going. I also found some good bookshops in Montreal, Vancouver and Washington when travelling in North America. I had left about four thousand books in store in Bournemouth with our furniture, taking only about three hundred books with me, mostly theological and reference books and some of my favourite books on art and travel. We also had a few classical novels which one could read again—my favourite Dickens (*Bleak House* and *David Copperfield*)—the Barchester Trollopes and some drama and poetry and the Oxford History of England in many volumes. Most of my reading was done at night between ten o'clock and midnight. Not many people in Bermuda seemed to read much, although of course there were the brilliant exceptions.

The Bishop was expected to do a good deal of entertaining and my wife and I were happy to do our best in this direction. Every week we had people to lunch, tea, dinner or to sherry parties. We had parties for all Church workers at the Cathedral round Christmas each year. We made a special point of entertaining the clergy and invited all Incumbents plus wife (if any) annually to luncheon, apart for other occasions when they were asked with other people. I well remember one winter when after a busy two weeks my wife and I counted up and found that in the first of these two weeks we had fed and entertained seventy-four people and in the second forty-seven. Social entertainment is of course almost bound to be the main activity of a small community in a small and rather isolated country; but we have nothing but pleasant recollections of these occasions, and the hard work entailed both before and after was more than compensated for by the happy contacts made. One can do so much more, for and with people, if one can get a real and friendly social intimacy as a basis upon which to begin.

Much as we loved Bermuda as a place and enjoyed exploring every nook and cranny of it, we used to find that after ten or twelve months a sort of claustrophobia began to envelope us. We wanted more space and a change of scene. I wanted to jump into a car and just drive and drive hundreds of miles. I remember one very intelligent old lady whom I used to visit sometimes who had a car and a chauffeur-gardener. I asked her on one occasion why she never went out for a drive. I shall never forget her answer.

"What point would there be in it? I *know it all* without ever leaving my house and garden. I have only just to shut my eyes."

Bermuda is very varied and pretty for its size: but after a year I always began to feel that its size was very limited.

We came back to England in 1958 (Lambeth Conference) and also in 1960 and 1961. We visited Canada (Quebec Province only) in 1957. In 1957 we also spent a short holiday in Washington, Virginia and Maryland. In 1959 we went right across Canada to Vancouver and Victoria, visiting Montreal again and also Ottawa, Kingston (Ontario) and Winnipeg, where we were the guests of the Archbishop of Rupertsland (Dr. Barfoot). I have preached in Quebec, Montreal and Winnipeg Cathedrals, also in another Winnipeg Church and taken a Confirmation in a third. After this trip to Canada we visited the States again and I preached in

Trinity Church, New York, and at Mount Calvary Church, Baltimore. We spent four days in Boston which, with Richmond (Virginia), we found the most interesting historically of American cities. We also liked Philadelphia, but not, I am afraid, New York. If I had to live in the North American continent I should prefer it to be one of the following places and in the following order of preference—Vancouver, Victoria, Montreal, Ottawa or Washington, D.C. I should put Washington, a lovely city, higher on my list if it had a nicer climate. I have stayed there in March, June and early October and I do not know which was climatically the most unpleasant. March, when it sleeted and blew nearly all the time, or the summer when one nearly boiled every time one went out of doors. Richmond, with a dry temperature of one hundred and four, was less unbearable than Washington at ninety-six (and a saturation point humidity). Everywhere we went we received the most wonderful kindness and hospitality. We loved our visit to the eighteenth century home of my cousin Sally Blackwood, a great niece of Mr. Pierpoint Morgan, near Centreville, Maryland, and the marvellous hospitality in Ottawa, Winnipeg and Victoria and indeed in New York City. During one visit to Washington, in one day I breakfasted with Vice-President Nixon, lunched at the British Embassy with Sir Harold and Lady Caccia and the same afternoon had tea at the Deanery with Dean and Mrs. Sayre. The Anglican Cathedral in Washington, though smaller than that of St. John the Divine in New York, seemed to us to be the finest ecclesiastical building that we visited in the New World. Apart from the still unfinished Cathedral in Victoria, none of the Anglican Cathedrals in Canada appeared to be equal to our own Cathedral in Bermuda.

Except in Virginia and Maryland life in the States struck us as being too "high-pressure". People seemed to be un-relaxed both in business and in social activities. In Canada it was not quite so tense. Montreal seemed to be a city where folk knew how to enjoy themselves—rather in the French manner. It was the only big city except New York, where people appeared to walk abroad in the streets in the evenings for pleasure, air and exercise. Nearly all the other large cities in the New World which we visited, apart from the rushing taxis, seemed to be deserted after seven or seven thirty in the evenings. Pedestrians were conspicuous by their absence. To walk in the empty streets in Toronto after eight o'clock in the evening gave one quite an eerie feeling, although Toronto is no doubt a most model and respectable place as large cities go. I always smile at the story of the Montreal man who when asked if he had ever been to Toronto, replied:

"Why yes, I once spent a week there on a Sunday." There are however some very good hotels and stores in this city and a very nice and large park. Evening amusements are not particularly outstanding apart from a few cinemas. We could not find a theatre or a concert. Washington also curiously enough, in spite of all its beauty and importance, is weak in this direction when compared with the more important European capitals—Dublin has much more culture to offer, especially in the evenings.

No other great city that I have ever visited has a site to compare with that of Vancouver; but then I have not visited San Francisco nor Rio. Venice and Stockholm are set so differently that they do not invite comparison with Vancouver and its surrounding snowy mountains.

One of our greatest joys in Bermuda was the companionship of our Bournemouth domestic pets: my orange cat Nicholas, then six years old and in his prime, and our two dachshunds, Gretel (Hansel's widow) and her son Jerry (Jeremy Humperdinck in the Pedigree). Later we found a little orange kitten dying of thirst and starvation on one of the beaches and gave him a home. Horace grew up into the family, never quite such a rich deep orange as Nicholas; but a fine cat, not apparently handicapped by one blind eye, the result of an early argument with Jerry. Nicholas was the most intelligent and affectionate cat I have ever known. We could not leave him behind when we left England for Bermuda, so he travelled out first class in our cabin on the Reina del Pacifico. He had a very pleasant journey.

A life long bachelor he concentrated his affections on me. Every morning we enacted the same pantomime. He "called me"; but I feigned sleep. I was patted on the face and meawed at. Finally my left ear (always the left one) was gently bitten. Then I awakened and we had our morning pleasantries and he had his saucer of milk. When I was out in the day time he used to wait in the bushes in the garden until the car with the right engine noises climbed up the hill and I was ceremoniously welcomed back home. Sometimes if I had been out rather too long I was scolded. He must have spent hours, either on my shoulder or sitting beside me on my desk or the back of my armchair. He was also devoted to Gretel who had mothered and washed him when he was a kitten and Jerry and his sisters were puppies. Actually he was much fonder of her than was Jerry her real son. One day fame came to Nicholas and his portrait graced the local paper *The Mid Ocean News* under the headline "Bishop's Cat Proves Valiant Warrior" The following is a quotation from the account of a stirring event:

"Self possessed immaculate and aware of his dignity as the senior cat of the Lord Bishop of Bermuda, Nicholas of the generous proportions and deep orange fur has recently proved himself a valiant warrior on the side of law and order and a defender of his friends. As is his custom Nicholas accompanied his master the other day on a peregrination of the circular road on North Camden near the new Bishop's Lodge. Also in this daily procession are the two dachshunds Gretel and Jerry. But a villain in the form of a much larger dog sprang from the bushes and beset Jerry pinning him by the throat to the ground. Nicholas with split-second timing, charged the enemy head first, a blazing ball of orange fury. The interloper, with bleeding face, retreated yelping in complete route to the shelter of his own garden, hotly pursued by a triumphant Nicholas. Jerry finding that he was not murdered after all, collected his composure, and Nicholas returned and resumed his stately walk, tail in air."

Along side of this exciting announcement was a notice of the engagement of Canon W. J. Manning to Miss Erica Pepler of Victoria, British Columbia; but the photograph of the Canon was only half the size of the imposing portrait of Nicholas!

We had these delightful companions for almost the whole of our time in Bermuda and all of them undoubtedly preferred the house and garden at Camden to the former noisy town residence. Nicholas had always rather enjoyed superintending the endless traffic from the vantage point of the first floor balcony of the old Bishop's Lodge; but the dogs at times literally showed terror and nervous strain when the noises in the street outside became too violent. I shall never forget the occasion at our first Christmas time in Hamilton when the coloured "Gombey Dancers" (complete with feathers and drums) processed past our house accompanied by a shrieking and admiring crowd. The dogs who were out in the garden took one look at this sudden invasion of their privacy, decided that the end of the world was at hand and jumped clean through the closed wire screen of the French windows into our dining room. Although uninjured they then proceeded to have hysterics. Gretel used also to be absolutely terrified by the frequent violent thunder storms, until in old age she went stone deaf. The cats never appeared to mind noise in the least. Gretel died in 1960. Nicholas died in April 1962, and Jerry was put to sleep in July 1962 the day before we left

Bermuda. Nicholas had developed heart and liver trouble in the last few weeks of his life of nearly twelve years and slowly faded away. He spent his last days sitting in the garden he loved so much and died quietly in his sleep in his own bed one night. He and Jerry were buried side by side in the garden. Jerry had taken his mother's death very philosophically; but Nicholas had fretted quite obviously, searching house and garden for his foster mother for several days. The only survivor was our little Bermuda waif, Horace. We gave him to the Davis-Jones at Southampton Rectory where he spent two happy years. After that he went up in the social scale taking up residence with the Earl and Countess of Essex at Little Cassiobury on their neighbouring hill top. Algy Essex (who first wife was a cousin of Molly's) and his present charming wife, Christine, like us, were great lovers of animals and Horace (now called "Bish-cat") did well for himself. If Nicholas and Jerry had been younger and in good health, we might have tried bringing them back to England with us; but there would still have been that dreadful six months quarantine.

At the risk of giving too much space in this chapter to animal friends who made our house more like home to a couple who were greatly missing their own family, I append one more anecdote.

We had another friend who could hardly be described as "a domestic pet", he was an emerald green chameleon lizard who lived in a tree near our favourite bathing place at Castle Harbour overhanging a calm and secluded rocky pool.

I suppose that we bathed here about twice a week for nine months each year during the last three or four years of our time. We undressed and dressed on a smooth rock plateau and dived into about six or seven feet of clear water. Afterwards we unpacked a picnic tea. A whole bevy of black pink-faced rock lizards used to watch us from afar. Occasionally they would rush forward and seize the crumbs we scattered for them. Any sudden movement on our part and they disappeared like a flash into their corners and crevices. They never became any more tame. "Christopher", as we called him, was a completely different case. He always appeared on a branch of his little tree as soon as we arrived and there he sat watching us affably and blowing out his handsome little orange frill under his chin. Never another movement until we began to unpack the picnic basket—then with confident deliberation he would come down to within six inches of us and accept our hospitality. The only thing he did not like was ginger bread. For three years our intimacy ripened and

Christopher became quite fearless. One is tempted to imagine that he must have had some curious intimation of our impending departure, for the very last time we went to bathe at Castle Harbour he let us into his great secret, he was married and had a family! On this sad occasion of our last meeting he suddenly disappeared for a few minutes from his tree branch returning proudly later with a plump emerald green wife about two-thirds of his own size. Mother was duly followed by a diminutive little green fellow, a perfect miniature of his parents. When Christopher came out at the psychological moment for his farewell meal with us, the family quietly withdrew. We were fortunately permitted to take a colour transparency of our small friend on this last occasion as he glided towards us through a yellow flowered cactus. Now his likeness is often cast upon our projector screen to remind us of this attractive little personage.

When I was offered the Bermuda Bishopric we called on my predecessor Bishop John Jagoe at Schull Rectory in S.W. County Cork. One of the things he told me was that the anonymous letter was rather a feature of public life in Bermuda. He had accumulated about three drawersful during his six years in the Islands! I only received two during my episcopate and Mollie got one; but at the time that I was moving the Roman Catholic Tabernacle from the Cathedral High Altar and inserting the Stone Reredos and the figures in it, there were, all told, about ten or twelve anonymous letters in the Mid Ocean News, expatiating upon the enormities of my crime. The main arguments were—the beauty of the Tabernacle (more like something in a milk bar in my opinion)—and what right had a stranger to come and interfere with *their* Cathedral? No-one wanted the Reredos anyway. (Why then did I receive nearly twenty thousand pounds in donations?) The most amusing of these effusions was one which was headed "Sacrilege at the Cathedral", and then went on poignantly to describe the way in which the Tabernacle was smashed to powder and the rubble remains thrown ignominiously out of the Cathedral. This letter I answered in detail. In fact the Tabernacle had been most carefully taken to pieces by a professional stone mason, under the personal supervision of our Architect. All the different parts had been carefully numbered and the whole packed into wooden boxes ready to be duly re-erected in its new position over the South Transept Altar (where it now is)! Actually I knew who the writers of these highly imaginative letters were: a little group of aged persons who wrote under different indignant pseudonyms in turn.

Perhaps there were four or five of them. After the Reredos was completed and some of the figures inserted, one of "the opposition" met me in the Cathedral one day and a delightful little episode took place. This anonymous person stopped me and said—

"Bishop, I have been one of the naughty ones! I hated any idea of change in the High Altar and its surroundings; but now I can see the effect of the new work, I am completely converted; I think that it is beautiful. Will you accept this for your fund? Of course on condition that my gift remains completely anonymous! " I was handed a plain envelope which contained ten five-pound notes.

Naturally I was delighted with this donation, but even more so by the quite charming and honest manner in which a change of mind and heart was expressed. As it seems to me there are two possible attitudes to anonymous leters. One (which is mine) is that if anybody has anything worth saying one should not be afraid or ashamed of putting one's genuine signature to it. To me there is something mean and cowardly in the anonymous letter—like the stab in the back, the shot from behind the hedge. I know however that some excellent people (not only in Bermuda) take the opposite view. Bermuda was a small place, everyone met everyone else at close quarters continuously. A name to a critical letter might accentuate disagreements and make them into personal feuds. Well, they are entitled to their own views, and I to mine; but I still think that "honesty is the best policy".

Apart from this one little disagreement with an infinitesimally small elderly group at the Cathedral I do not remember any noteworthy break in the general harmony of my time in Bermuda —certainly not in the performance of my duties as Bishop; and that is why I look back with so much happiness to those six years. By and large we received nothing but warm hospitality and ready friendliness from all classes and types in a very cosmopolitan community: from the fine old established Bermudian families in their beautiful homes; from the local Americans and Canadians; from the coloured, wealthy and highly educated, and simple and unpretensious; from the resident Azorean Portuguese, from the business people of Hamilton and the more countryfied folk in St. David's Island and in the Parishes of the western parts of the Mainland and Somerset.

When we left we were loaded with gifts—cheques to the value of some nine hundred pounds, beautiful china, cedarwork furniture, embroidered house linen, and many books on Bermuda's life and history, some autographed by the authors themselves: all evidence of the greatest generosity and kindliness of heart.

When I went to Bermuda in 1956 at the age of sixty-four I hoped to stay seven years if my health held up. Actually I left one year short of this when I was seventy years old. I had several reasons for this. The hot damp climate did not suit me too well (I have never much liked hot weather) and it suited Mollie even less. During our last year there her rheumatism increased to such an alarming degree that for some months she was walking with a stick, and feeling quite crippled the first thing in the morning. Also I have always disliked the idea of being a limpet in a job which is in danger of becoming too much for one's health and strength. The Church has suffered too much from old men who think that they are indispensable or "as good as ever they had been" and who stay on and on so that they become too old to face up to the effort of resignation and change. Then there was the impending Toronto Conference, planned for 1963. If I stayed for this, then I should stay, at the very least, for another year after this Conference to see its projects implemented in the Diocese. If I was not prepared to stay another two years, then I ought to get out in 1962 to give my successor a year to prepare for all these projects. Altogether the summer of 1962 appeared to be the right point in time. The Toronto Conference seemed to me to be likely to mark the beginning of a new era in Church life and work. Others will know better than I how far this has proved to be the case. I think that I could probably have carried on without any harm to the Diocese for another couple of years if there had been no Toronto Conference in the offing; but I certainly did not think that I should be justified in staying on until after the next Lambeth Conference in 1968. So 1962 it was. At least with an improvement in health we would both be retiring at a time when we would still be young enough to develop a new rhythm of life and interest in retirement; and we have found this to be so, although it was not an easy decision at the time.

We felt leaving Bermuda very much, and indeed the last year or two of our time there brought us several new opportunities and interests in the work, and new friends in addition to those whom we made when we first arrived. I had succeeded in bringing several good new men into the work of the Church. The clergy and their wives were personal friends and it is still a great joy to keep in touch and to see most of them from time to time. On the other hand we looked forward to seeing more of our children and grandchildren. We had bought a charming Georgian house at Woodstock in our favourite Oxford and Cotswold area of England, with three of our four children and their families quite close to us. The Bishop of Oxford wrote me a very kind letter of welcome and both he and my son-in-law the Vicar of Wendover told me that I could have as much work as I wanted. Nor have I been disappointed.

A chapter on my work and impressions as a Colonial Bishop would not be complete without two final comments: one quite brief and the other rather longer.

First of all, I had felt from the very time of my consecration the inestimable advantages which I had had through my close and unforgetable connection with Bishops T. B. Strong and Arthur Burroughs as Domestic Chaplain and personal secretary, in the Ripon Diocese. Again and again I felt the benefit of a sort of vicarious experience of problems and people. I think also that the twenty-five years spent as Incumbent of two very large and important Parishes had taught me a great deal, as had twenty years as Rural Dean, first of a mainly Rural Deanery and later in an Urban one. I had observed the invariable tact and wisdom of Tommy Strong and the conscientious and pastoral affection of Arthur Burroughs in positions of official authority.

The other footnote to Bermuda concerned the other part, if one may so describe it, of that Diocese.

The Diocese was really to be thought of as the Bishopric of Bermuda *and the Azores*. In this respect it was a diocese unique, as being partly in the New World of the American continent and partly in the old world of Europe. What other Diocese touches two continents? The only trouble was that these two so different groups of Islands were about two thousand miles apart, and even air travel between them was becoming more and more difficult. Bishop Browne never got to the Azores. Bishop Jagoe hoped to do so, but never arrived. On my appointment I was the recipient of several pressing invitations to remember this part of the Diocese. I promised to go, and we achieved this twice. The first time was in the early summer of 1958 when we were en route for the Lambeth Conference. The second time was a little later in the season in the summer of 1960.

It would be hard to find two groups of Islands which differ more than the Azores and the Bermudas, although both lie slantwise in the vastness of the Atlantic Ocean, and both have problems owing to the density of their population.

None the less these island groups are utterly different. Probably Bermuda is more beautifully girt by the sea. The pinkish white sands submerge into generally reasonably calm waters within their protecting reefs. Owing to its white sands Bermuda's sea is, in-shore, a translucent green, glinting from emerald to aquamarine. Beyond is the bluest of oceans streaked with purple. In contrast, owing to the dark grey sands of volcanic origin the in-shore waters of the Azores are at first sight a little grim and menacing, although further out is the deep blue ocean.

Bermuda has no mountains; its highest "hills" are under 300 ft. The Azores can boast magnificent mountain scenery, especially at the western end of Santa Maria, all over San Miguel and San Jorge, whilst supreme above all the great mountain of Pico rises nearly 8,000 ft. from the centre of the island to which it gives its name. This is a peak which is snow-capped for about seven to eight months of the year and is a landmark to mariners for miles out to sea. The Azores have therefore greater scenic variety.

In size of course the Azores also excel, stretching for some 400 miles from Santa Maria in a north westerly slant to Flores and Corvo. The utmost length of Bermuda is only twenty-eight miles. In population Bermuda has perhaps some sixty thousand people—white Bermudians, coloured Bermudians, Azoreans, British, Americans, Canadians. It also has well over a dozen religions, although the Anglican Community predominates. The Azores have on to four hundred thousand people, all Portuguese and all Roman Catholics, except for the merest handful. Some of the population of the Island of Fayal is said to have a Flemish and Breton origin, but except for its windmills and a certain air of sturdy independence the people of this delightful island seem to be in language and culture similar to their neighbours in the other islands.

Another difference between Bermuda and the Azores is the economic one. The Azoreans are a poor but industrious agricultural people. The Bermudians are urbanised and wealthy. Bermuda lives handsomely off the tourist trade. Tourism is almost nothing in the Azores. There are perhaps a hundred good hotels and guest houses which cater for the two hundred thousand tourists who swarm over Bermuda each year. In the Azores there were perhaps a dozen all told.

Bermuda has its own colonial Government. The Azores are an integral part of metropolitan Portugal and return members to the Lisbon parliament. For this purpose these latter islands are grouped into three constituencies: San Miguel and Santa Maria (population about 200,00); Terceira, San Jorge and

Graciosa (c. 100,000): the remaining more north-westerly islands, Pico, Fayal, Flores and Corvo (c. 60,000) constitute the third constituency. It is said that the two N.W. groups like to know election results from San Miguel and Santa Maria before they vote, so that if one party wins there they can assert their independence by electing people of different opinions for their own smaller groups. If the Azoreans are a simple and unsophisticated people they are not lacking in humour and intelligence.

Everything in the Azores for the visitor starts at Santa Maria. This is the international Airport for those who come by air. It is also the first Azorean port of call for those coming from Lisbon or Madeira by sea. Actually there is no "port" or harbour to speak of. One gets off one's ship into a rowing boat with one's luggage—quite an adventure if the sea is at all rough. It is also an adventure getting off the rowing boat on to the jetty. We did all his in the dark. This island is flat at the eastern end, hence the Airport. The runways are just about long enough. They end in an awe-inspiring cliff with a two hundred foot drop into a rocky sea bed. At the other end of the island lies a mass of blue mountains. Between these two contrasting areas is the fascinating little old town of Vilo do Porto, with its black and white church. This church is much older than it looks outside. It is said to have been visited by Columbus on his return from "discovering America" in 1493.

From Santa Maria the boat from Lisbon goes on to the largest island, San Miguel, with its capital city of Ponta Delgada and so on to the other islands to the N. West. One can also go by plane to San Miguel and even on to Terceira. This is the local Air Line and it is very informal to say the least. The plane holds a pilot and about five or six passengers. I recollect two amusing incidents connected with our first flight to Ponta Delgada. Our pilot had a little English and was very talkative, looking over his shoulder with carefree abandon he told us many things, whilst the tiny plane sped on its half hour journey. "This very dangerous Air Port. Very small runway: plenty currents of airs, much mists." To reassure us further he continued "First time plane fly to Ponta Delgada—only pilot and three passengers: one old man and a bride and bridegroom. She have the beautiful bouquet. All their friends they seem them off. No one ever see them again! The plane, it never arrive at Ponta Delgada! " He smiled brightly at us and then, I suppose, remembered that he was flying his plane and devoted a few minutes to that task.

As we drew nearer we saw the mountainous silhouette of

San Miguel. Soon we were over this green and fertile big island. Now we could see the runway as we began to come down. They were evidently almost ready for our arrival: two people were hastily driving some cows off the undulating surface.

When we landed my wife and I were greeted by almost the whole English population of Ponta Delgada. Eight or nine people had most kindly come to meet us, including the Vice Consul and his wife, Mr. and Mrs. Parkin, and the Portuguese Evangelical Minister and his wife Senhor and Senhora Coelho. My wife was given a bouquet. The other passengers in the plane were going on to Terceira except for one man who walked quietly off and got into a taxi. The next morning I read in the local paper of the arrival of the prevous day's plane from Santa Maria and was surprised to be informed that the only passenger from Santa Maria was Senhor X, a hairdresser from Madeira. We commented on this to our host and hostess and Mr. Parkin laughingly explained. The Roman Catholic Bishop was said to have ordered the newspapers to omit any reference to an Anglican Bishop! Actually when we came again two years later we got a **full page** headline and a long column, but this second time the local Bishop was away in Rome! All this of course was before good Pope John and no doubt things might be different now.

On Sunday we had two services at the beautiful little Regency period Anglican church of the Holy Trinity. At 8.30 a.m. we had Holy Communion with a one hundred per cent attendance of confirmed Anglicans and at 11.00 a.m. we had a combined Service with the Evangelical Portuguese Church members, about two hundred being present. Their minister, Senhor Coelho, read the prayers in Portuguese. Mr. Parkin read a lesson. We sang three hymns including the Trinity hymn "Holy, Holy, Holy"; only it was "Santo, Santo, Santo" but to the well known tune. I preached a short sermon of seven minutes and then the good Minister rendered a Portuguese version of what I had said. (I had sent a copy in advance and George Hayes who spoke both languages perfectly had done the translation.) Senhor Coelho gave a fine rendering and I realised what an eloquent preacher I could become when translated into that fascinating language. Such well rounded periods. I do not know how far people generally know that Anglican (and all Protestant) Churches are subject to certain curious legal restrictions in Spain and Portugal. Their churches must not be noticeable from the road. Therefore they must have no spire nor tower nor bell. Also they must be surrounded by a high wall. However the next day the photographers' shops in Ponta Delgada were full of pictures of a goodly crowd of worshippers streaming out of the gates of our little churchyard. By Tuesday however no more were to be seen. The news had reached the Roman Catholic authorities and all the photographs, still unsold, were withdrawn. I suppose the theory was that Protestantism was not supposed to exist. When I visited Madeira I was to hear from the Evangelical Minister in Funchal something of the persecutions which Evangelicals had had to endure there, even into the nineteenth century. I saw in their Church in a glass case the precious Bible which in earlier days they had had to keep hidden under the floorboards in the room which they had used for their proscribed and therefore secret services. It is now of course their greatest treasure, proudly exhibited.

Incidentally I had, with the fullest approval of the Archbishop of Canterbury (Dr. Fisher) made a twenty-one year agreement with the members of the Evangelical Church in Ponta Delgada for them to have the use of our little church of the Holy Trinity. The arrangement was for this period and then to be subject to a fresh review. They were to have the building free of charge on condition that it was kept in good order. If the Bishop or any other authorised Anglican wanted the building for services then the Anglican Church had first claim. During my time as Bishop this arrangement worked splendidly. The fabric of the Church was thoroughly overhauled by the Evangelicals and the interior redecorated, the fine oak work being carefully treated and handsome chandeliers hung from the roof. Incidentally these fixtures became our property. The appreciation of the Evangelicals was quite touching. Their community numbered over two hundred in Ponta Delgada, devout and progressive folk. For years they had sought in vain for some large room or hall in which to hold their united worship. Many times they seemed to be on the verge of getting just what they wanted, only to be told at the last minute by the people with whom they were negotiating that they were very sorry but they had been informed that the matter must be dropped. Everybody knew what that meant. Knowledge of my action in solving this problem for an increasing body of non-Roman Christians apparently was not limited to Ponta Delgada, or even to the Azores, and both in Madeira and in Lisbon I was met at the boat or the Airport by grateful Evangelicals who put themselves and their cars at our disposal, providing transport for us and our luggage, and in some cases giving up a whole day to take us for lovely sight-seeing drives. In this way when our ship stopped at Funchal on the way from the Azores to Lisbon, we were driven all round the hills and beauty spots of Madeira by the local Evangelical Minister.

I made a careful examination of our charming little Church at Ponta Delgada and of our registers and plate. The Church had been built during the Napoleonic Wars when there were many British ships to and fro and quite a number of British naval and commercial people resident, many with their families. In those days there had been a resident Chaplain. Gradually however the number of British residents had dwindled. Occasionally American consular officials and others came who were members of the Protestant Episcopal Church, or Presbyterians; but recently the English speaking population rarely exceeded a dozen. The largest English speaking community in the Azores is now at Horta in the Island of Fayal where there are the British and American Cable Stations. In my time there must have been between forty and fifty all told in Fayal; but there we have no church and services have to be held, when there is anyone to take them, in the hospitable home of the head of "Cable and Wireless". For a few years there I had the co-operation of an excellent man whom I appointed as a Lay Reader. It was impracticable to try and have a resident priest for the Azores. The two communities of respectively twelve and forty-five, two days' journey by boat apart, could not even have been served the same Sunday. The expense of travel would also have been considerable and in the winter time would no doubt have seen any priest storm stayed in either San Miguel or Fayal for weeks on end. The good weather in the Azores lasts from May until the end of August. The storms of the Autumn, winter and spring round those mid-Atlantic islands have to be seen to be believed. The only good natural harbour was that at Horta (as Sir Walter Raleigh found out four hundred years ago). Even the large town of Angra in the populous island of Terceira has no harbour at all. Terceira has now of course got a large U.S.A. Air Station, comparable to that in St. David's Island, Bermuda; and there now also a few times a week, comes the little aeroplane from Santa Maria, via Ponta Delgada in San Miguel some eighty miles away.

Twice we stayed with the British Vice-Consul and Mrs. Parkin in their charming home on the outskirts of Ponta Delgada and saw something of that lovely island. Their kindness was wonderful. On the second occasion we also stayed at Furnas at the Terra Nostra Hotel. This luxuriant and sheltered volcanic valley of Furnas surrounded by rugged mountains, seemed to have everything—exotic flowers, ferns, shrubs, trees and lakes: also a thermal establishment and several geysers, noisy and boiling. At one spot two little rivers meet, one warm and sulphur-yellow, the other cold and of a curious greeny-blue tint. This veritable little Garden of Eden has now of course been discovered by the Americans at the Air Station in the neighbouring island of Terceira and at the weekends, especially, the Americans come with wives and children from Lajes to enjoy the comforts of a really good hotel and scenery only to be equalled, I imagine, by the more exotic parts of the North Island of New Zealand. We also visited the curious mountainous district at the west end of the island of San Miguel which is called Sette Citades (Seven Cities) with its two adjacent lakes, one always bright blue and the other an equally vivid green.

We soon got acquainted with all the extremely friendly and hospitable British people in Ponta Delgada. I also called at Government House. The Governor of the Azores was away; but I was most kindly received by his deputy and we had an amusing conversation conducted partly in English, partly in Portuguese, but mostly in French.

There is much to see in San Miguel. Its mountainous beauty is slightly reminiscent of Glendalough and the Wicklow Mountains in Ireland. There are several interesting churches in the Island, and Ponta Delgada has many other fine buildings, practically all of them being externally white with black stone facings on the corners and round the windows. Remarkable also is the elaborate stone paving of the long sea front promenade, with its mosaic designs in black and white stones depicting local flowers and foliage.

We visited five of the nine islands during our two visits to these attractive islands. Santa Maria has its comfortable Air Port Hotel, called like that at Furnas on San Miguel, the "Terra Nostra". San Miguel, the largest and richest is also one of the most beautiful. Terceira is interesting but less exciting scenically. It has in Angra the ecclesiastical capital of the islands, a quaint little town. This island during the sixty years Spanish occupation of Portugal (1581-1640) was the centre of nationalist resistance and for a time the exiled Court and many of the nobility resided here. Impressive carved stone coats-of-arms are still to be seen over doorways in the little city and over some of the old stone farm houses in the rural areas. Since World War II the Americans have had their Air Base at Lajes. This is the only island in the Azores where the children beg. Perhaps the two facts are not unconnected. I well remember one persistant young monkey of about twelve years old who followed us for about half a mile chanting "Vinte (20) escudi!" He refused "cinco" (5) with injured dignity, and in the end we told him as emphatically as possible to take himself off. The Cathedral in Angra is not an attractive building, built in a heavy style of debased Portuguese Baroque it has an interior which is rather reminiscent of a tasteless and overcrowded Victorian drawing room.

The small island of Graciosa we saw only from the sea, a little island of low hills and a few white villages.

The next island north-west in this wonderfully varied chain is San Jorge. This island is quite romantic and exciting, for it consists of a line of jagged mountains sloping steeply down to the Ocean on either side. It is about thirty miles long and perhaps about three miles wide. Its little capital, Velas on the western side, is charming and quaint. We wondered how often the little bandstand in its tiny square was used. We took a taxi drive on the main road which runs along the middle of the island and gives dizzy views of slopes and cliffs. Amongst other things there is a grim reminder of the volcanic activities from which this beautiful and strange island has suffered. In one sloping field a church spire sticks up out of the grass; all that is left of a once considerable village, overwhelmed by a sudden eruption of lava some two hundred years ago. Since our visits in 1958 and 1960 this island has again suffered severely from earthquakes and Velas lost many houses.

The greatest thing in the island of San Jorge however is the superb view of the island of Pico some ten or twelve miles to the West. There, rising out of the second largest and least spoilt of all the Azores the mightly volcanic mountain of Pico raises its sharp pyramid to the height of almost eight thousand feet. It is said to be the highest mountain in a direct line beween the Urals in Russia and the Rockies in Canada and the U.S.A. At all seasons this mountain is a thing of almost unearthly beauty. For the colder months its proud head is dazzling white in snow. In the summer it shimmers, in every shade of orange, green, blue and purple. Often it has a curious white necklace of cloud or mist above which rises its triumphant summit. On our second visit (1960) we were taken an unforgettable drive all round the island on the magnificent eighty-seven mile coast road which now encircles it. From almost everywhere the great mountain in the centre was visible, subtly changing in aspect from the innumerable viewpoints. Whereas in the other islands the roads are flanked by hedges of hydrangeas (mostly azure blue) the roads of Pico are hedged by masses of red and pink rambler roses. To see that mountain behind such a colourful background was an unique experience. There is talk of an airstrip and runway in Pico, which would bring this undisturbed paradise within three hours of Lisbon; but in 1960 the three ancient little white towns slept in the sun and the country lanes were still at peace. Pico has about 25,000 inhabitants, mettlesome, independent and friendly. Industrious agriculture scratches a living out of a soil as rocky as that of Connemara. Actually they grow an excellent wine there and in the days of Imperial Russia, the Tsars used to buy the whole crop of "Pico" annually. Now presumably the natives enjoy it themselves. The only other industries are provided by fishing and the whale oil factories.

Barely four miles north of Pico lies the island of Fayal with its capital of Horta. Again Pico can be enjoyed as a superb view, this time with blue hydrangeas and windmills as a foreground. Slighly smaller in population than Angra, Horta, with its fine harbour is a well laid out town with some good churches and public buildings. Here are the three great cable companies: the British "Cable and Wireless" and the American "Commercial" and "Western". In and around Horta live some forty or fifty English speaking folk.

Here during a short weekend was on the occasion of my two visits the main scene of my religious activities. I had a celebration of Holy Communion at which all the confirmed Anglicans (except those on duty) attended, and a morning service and sermon. The previous afternoon there was a Garden Party at "Waldorf" and that night I had a Confirmation. In 1960 I also had a Baptism—only just. Our second visit was of rather limited duration, as our ship from Lisbon was late arriving with us: Sunday afternoon instead of early morning. Mrs. X was due to have a baby and the plan was that I should baptise it; but much to everyone's chagrin she arrived bright and smiling at the Garden Party on the Sunday afternoon, looking very pretty in a china blue frock. However she was a clever woman. From 3.30 to 5.30 p.m. she enjoyed the Garden Party. At midnight she was taken to the Nuns' Hospital and at 5.00 a.m. she was the mother of a fine son. Our ship was due to arrive at 11.00 a.m. and to sail within half an hour. I planned to baptise the little fellow at 10.00 o'clock en route for the boat. There was only one particle of grit in the well oiled wheels. At the breakfast table our host was called to the telephone. The Mother Superior was off duty and the second-in-command at the hospital had just announced that no heretic Bishop would baptise any baby in the hospital whilst she was in charge! Incidentally our English host was a Roman Catholic; but a very reasonable and sensible one. He rejoined us at the table in an explosive condition shouting "We'll have no nonsense of that sort! " First of all he rang the hospital board chairman, who backed him completely. Then he rang the militant Sister-in-Charge and told her fairly emphatically that I would be at the hospital at 10.00 and that everything was to be ready for the service. I arrived in my purple cassock and capella rather wondering about my reception; but all went more than well. The Mother Superior herself met me in the entrance hall, took my hand and gave me a profound and graceful curtsey and then with many charming smiles conducted me and Mr. X to the little private ward where the ceremony duly and happily took place.

The first time we visited Fayal the island was enjoying (?) the excitements of a fourteen months' period of earthquakes and volcanic eruptions. Fortunately the scene of activity was not the great volcano of Caldeiro, which was supposed to be extinct and stood only five miles away overhanging Horta. The new volcano was about twelve miles away in the sea nearly a mile to the N.W. of the western most point of the island. Starting out at sea the eruptions gradualy formed a new island which in time joined up with the mainland and completely changed the adjacent geography. When we returned to Fayal in 1960 what we had remembered as a bay lying at the base of sheer cliffs had become a sandy beach. The tall lighthouse which had been visible for miles out to sea, was now several hundred yards inland with a new hill between it and the waters over which it had previously presided. Several houses had been buried in the molten lava and dark red volcanic dust, and the general level of the fields (now changed from green to red) had been raised anything from ten to thirty feet. The ground was still hot, but we were told that in time it should make fertile farm lands. Over a thousand people lost their homes and livelihoods and many emigrated to Brazil or the U.S.A. All that Horta knew of all this, after the first false alarm that the Caldeira was erupting and about to overwhelm the town, was the constant tremors from the earthquakes convulsing the western tip of their island, and the fine powdery dark red dust which penetrated everywhere, even where windows were shut and curtained.

We were very thrilled to be taken to see the island volcano in action, although no one was allowed within a mile of it all. We saw torrents of smoke, molten lava and red hot fragments of rock flying hundreds of yards up into the air. I got an impression of showers of red hot pebbles shooting into the sky; but was told that these "pebbles" were some of them the size of a small house and the lesser ones comparable to the size of a grand piano. I began to realise then why we were not allowed to approach any nearer to such a display. Even twelve miles away in Horta the noise from the volcano was an almost continuous dull roar; rather like what Dover and Folkestone heard from across the Channel during certain periods of World War I.

We made a great many friends in Fayal and again received each time a wonderful welcome. Both times we were there our stay was limited by the length of time the Lisbon steamer took to go on to Flores, the most North-Westerly of the Islands, and then return, calling in at Horta on its leisurely way back to Portugal via the rest of the Islands and Madeira.

Our visits to the Azores were amongst the high-lights of my time as Bishop of Bermuda. My only regret was that two thousand miles of Ocean lay between our two groups of Islands; and that the journey was becoming progressively more difficult. When we first went to Bermuda three Air Lines called occasionally at Santa Maria; but before we left in 1962 both the Dutch Line (K.L.M.) and the Venezuelan Service (S.A.S.) had given up this route to and from Europe. I should dearly have liked to do more for these truly responsive British and American friends; but the distances, even when one got to the Azores themselves, and the smallness of Anglican numbers, made the whole thing impracticable. I can only hope that my successors will find it possible to visit these delectable islands from time to time and to minister to the two small groups in San Miguel and Fayal; also to make contact with the U.S.A. Air Base personnel in Terceira, which I had found impossible to fit into our timetable on either of my visits.

There was one very pleasant aftermath to our first visit to the Azores. Our ship arrived back in Lisbon nearly a day late, and we reached our hotel at about 9.30 a.m. on the Sunday instead of about mid-day on the Saturday. Again a kind Evangelical Minister had met us at the docks and conveyed us rapidly with our luggage to the Hotel Eduardo Settimo. There was a note awaiting me there from the British Embassy Chaplain, marked "urgent". Written on the Saturday morning "to await arrival", it asked me to preach on the Sunday morning at the Embassy

Church. I telephoned to explain that we had only just arrived but would do our best to get there by eleven o'clock. The collection was to be given to the earthquake victims in Fayal who had lost their homes and livelihood. Fresh from it all I certainly preached from the heart to a large congregation of the British Colony in Lisbon. I was delighted to hear afterwards that the collection for this good purpose actually exceeded that taken for the same cause at the Roman Catholic Cathedral. Like the little Church in Ponta Delgada the Lisbon Embassy Church was completely hidden from sight. A high stone wall entirely surrounded the Churchyard and the Church itself must have been quite a hundred yards from the entrance gate.

My one regret on this our first visit to Lisbon where we were marvellously entertained by many of the leading British people in the Lisbon area, was that I was unable, owing to the opening of the Lambeth Conference to which we were bound, to accept an invitation to join with two other Anglican Bishops in the Consecration of the first Bishop of the Lusitanian Church. This branch of the Catholic (but non-Roman) Church, is in Communion with the Anglican Church. It now has two Churches in Lisbon as well as one or two elsewhere in Portugal and has a growing number of enthusiastic adherents.

Amongst those we met in Lisbon and later in Estoril during visits to Portugal were several charming English speaking members of the Portuguese aristocracy. In the U.S.A. one found that most people of this calibre liked to speak of ancestors who had "come over in the Mayflower". In Portugal one is "de Lancastre", i.e. descended from John of Gaunt. We know indeed from history that John of Gaunt's daughter, Philippa of Lancaster, became one of the most remarkable Queens of Portugal, and provided amongst her five sons, two kings, a saint, and, greatest of all, the famous Infante de Sagres, Prince Henry the Navigator. Not least of her later achievements has however apparently been becoming the ancestress of almost everybody who is somebody in that delightful and historic little country. Incidentally she is also credited with the introduction of table cutlery and pocket handkerchiefs, to replace the more primitive use of fingers. Her husband was inconsolable when she died. In the royal mausoleum in the church at Batalha they now lie side by side, their stone effigies clasping hands through the centuries. This political marriage evidently became a real love match.

*   *   *   *

One remark made to me shortly after my retirement gave me

considerable amusement if also a little irritation.

At a dinner I found myself seated next to the Incumbent of a pleasant Thameside parish. We had just been introduced, and as he sat down he gave me a searching look and said:

"Ah, I suppose that you are one of those poor old broken-down retired Colonial Bishops, come home to die on a completely inadequate pension! "

Swallowing down my surprise at this unasked for and quite unnecessary expression of inordinate compassion from a complete stranger, I replied brightly—

"Well, I suppose that you *could* put it that way; atlhough I am not contemplating an immediate decease, nor do I consider myself either poor or an object of pity! "

He then began to express his low opinion of the English Episcopate in no measured terms. I evinced a considerable lack of interest; but completely failed to discourage him.

Curiously enough when I got up to depart at the end of the proceedings he shook me most cordially by the hand, remarking what a pleasure it had been to meet me!

How stupid can some people be!

Now we are happily settled in our charming little Georgian house in Woodstock, one minute from Blenheim Park. We have all our own "things" around us again and best of all our children and grandchildren.

We have picked up the threads once more with old friends in Banbury, Oxford, Cheltenham and so on and made some good new friends in this area and in Oxford, including the University.

The Bishop of Oxford has been very kind and I take several confirmations and other Services (Youth Services, M.U. Festivals) and preach for my clerical neighbours and friends. Best of all has been helping regularly on Sunday mornings in my son-in-law's parish at Wendover. We have also made many friends in that parish. When I "resigned" there in November 1965 the Parochial Church Council asked me still to come, say, one Sunday a month; and I was happy to promise this. I am now again in a position to help three Sundays a month there at the Eucharist and look forward to this, more or less indefinitely. This leaves one Sunday a month for getting further afield if one wants to. We enjoy the beauty of Christ Church Cathedral from time to time and the good music there. It has been a privilege also to preach in such places as far apart as Worcester and Gloucester Cathedrals, All Saints, Margaret Street, London, Exeter College Chapel, Oxford, Harrogate, Methley and Leeds in Yorkshire;

Banbury and Bournemouth (in my own old Parishes). In Switzerland during the vacancy of the Bishopric of Fulham in 1966 on behalf of the Bishop of London, I took five or six confirmations and made many friends.

To keep up one's painting and one's reading is also a joy. Meantime we have a succession of visitors which, apart from our own family, Milroys, Flemings, Williams and from further away the Nimmos (Brighton). Scores of old friends and many Bermudians visiting England, including both clergy and laity continue to look us up.

In the past years we have had holidays in Portugal (1962), Ireland (four or five times, North and South): and Sweden and Denmark (1965), Switzerland (twice) and France. If we are spared for a few more years we hope to visit Austria, Spain (a Cathedral tour?) and we would also like to see Southern Italy. We would also enjoy revisiting France and Sweden if time permits; but then we are not immortal, as, alas, the deaths of so many friends keep on reminding us:

We do feel how good God has been to us, allowing us still to enjoy so many things in this wonderful world, and the friendship of so many friends both old and new. To find retirement almost as busy and interesting as a full time job has been an additional happiness.

This year I am eighty years old. Now we are looking forward to our Golden Wedding and to the weddings of three of our grandsons: altogether, for us, an Annus Mirabilis.

MARCH 1972